Making Young Voters

In 2016, 90 percent of young Americans showed an interest in politics and 80 percent intended to vote. Yet, only 43 percent of people between the ages of 18 and 29 ended up actually casting a ballot. *Making Young Voters* investigates what lies at the core of this gap.

The authors' in-depth, interdisciplinary approach reveals that political apathy is not the reason for low levels of youth turnout. Rather, young people too often fail to follow through on their political interests and intentions. Those with "noncognitive" skills related to self-regulation are more likely to overcome internal and external barriers to participation. This book combines theory from psychology, economics, child development, and more to explore possible solutions rooted in civic education and electoral reform.

This potentially paradigm-shifting contribution to the literature of American politics serves to influence not only our understanding of voter turnout, but also the fundamental connections between the education system, electoral institutions, and individual civic behavior in a democracy. How young people vote affects not only each individual future, but that of the United States, and of us all.

John B. Holbein is Assistant Professor of Public Policy at the University of Virginia.

D. Sunshine Hillygus is Professor of Political Science and Public Policy at Duke University.

Making Young Voters

Converting Civic Attitudes into Civic Action

JOHN B. HOLBEIN
University of Virginia

D. SUNSHINE HILLYGUS
Duke University

CAMBRIDGE
UNIVERSITY PRESS

University Printing House, Cambridge CB2 8BS, United Kingdom

One Liberty Plaza, 20th Floor, New York, NY 10006, USA

477 Williamstown Road, Port Melbourne, VIC 3207, Australia

314–321, 3rd Floor, Plot 3, Splendor Forum, Jasola District Centre,
New Delhi – 110025, India

79 Anson Road, #06–04/06, Singapore 079906

Cambridge University Press is part of the University of Cambridge.

It furthers the University's mission by disseminating knowledge in the pursuit of education, learning, and research at the highest international levels of excellence.

www.cambridge.org
Information on this title: www.cambridge.org/9781108488426
DOI: 10.1017/9781108770446

First published 2020

A catalogue record for this publication is available from the British Library.

ISBN 978-1-108-48842-6 Hardback
ISBN 978-1-108-72633-7 Paperback

Contents

Figures

Tables

Acknowledgments

We have many people to thank for help with this project – perhaps none more so than Republican Senator Tom Coburn (R-OK). Senator Coburn does not like political science. For more than a decade, Coburn has criticized the field for being irrelevant, even calling for the defunding of the political science program of the National Science Foundation. In 2013, Coburn proposed an amendment to the government funding bill that would have blocked federal funding of political science research. While many offered a vocal defense of the profession and the broader value and relevance of our scholarship, the criticisms also helped to spark conversations between Sunshine and John, then a PhD student in public policy at Duke, about research topics that clearly married scholarly interest, methodological rigor, and broad policy relevance.

As we brainstormed ideas, the North Carolina legislature passed a repeal of preregistration for sixteen- and seventeen-year-olds: a law that had been passed with large bipartisan support just four years earlier. We realized that for all of the media coverage and controversy about the legislation, no empirical research existed evaluating whether or not preregistration laws were actually effective. That first inquiry sparked a journal publication, engagement in a federal lawsuit, and a broader research agenda focused on understanding youth civic engagement–a topic we believe has both intellectual importance and public relevance.

We are relieved that Sen. Tom Coburn was not successful in killing National Science Foundation (NSF) funding of political science research as we subsequently became grateful recipients of two NSF grants to study the topic of youth turnout (NSF SES-141681, NSF SES-1657821). We are deeply grateful to Dr. Brian Humes, Political Science Program Director, for his enthusiastic and continued support of our research, including plucking one of our proposals from the reject bin of another program. The NSF's financial support has funded a fruitful collaboration with the Wake County Public School System, which has been central to this project. We thank Matthew Lenard, Dr. Darryl Hill, and Dr. Sonya Stephens for making that partnership possible. For providing access to the Fast Track Data, we thank Karen Bierman, John Coie, Kenneth Dodge, Mark Greenberg, John Lochman, Robert McMahon, Ellen Pinderhughes, Jennifer Goodwin, and Jeff Quinn. We thank Jim Moody for coordinating access to the restricted-use Add Health data and Inger Bergrom, Peter Levine, and Nancy Thomas for providing access to the NSLVE data.

At Duke, we want to recognize the Social Science Research Institute (SSRI) and its director, Tom Nechyba, for numerous invaluable contributions to this project. At SSRI, Dr. Alexandra Cooper identified grant opportunities and always helped with the mad dash to pull together grant applications. Our qualitative interviews of civics teachers were conducted by SSRI post-docs, Dr. Noelle Roth and Dr. Jack Zhou. Dr. Steven Snell and Dr. Kyle Endres, post-docs with the Duke Initiative on Survey Methodology (DISM) at SSRI, did the heavy lifting on our original survey data collections. SSRI also helped to fund Duke's modules on the 2014 CCES and provided secure data storage for the restricted-use data from WCPSS, Add Health, and Catalist. Finally, the project received funding through the Education and Human Development Bass Connections Program at SSRI. A big thanks to our Bass Connections teams and undergraduate research assistants: Emily Ahlers, Sarah Ali, Hannah Bartlebaugh, Lindsay Campbell, Eddy Cook, Christian Covington, Noah Eckberg, Ryan Geitner, Carlee Goldberg, Ketan Gupta, Donghun Lee, Matthew Mizota, Sakiko Nishida, Anshul Shah, Kyle Shofi, James Wang, and Eli Weed.

At BYU, we thank the directors of the Center for the Study of Elections and Democracy (CSED) – Chris Karpowitz and Jeremy Pope – for providing financial support, computing resources, and student research assistants. We are especially grateful to all the CSED faculty fellows and CSED student research fellows who helped on this project: Brittany Bair, Drew Brown, Matthew Baldwin, and Matthew Easton. Without the support of faculty at CSED and BYU, this project would not have come to its full fruition. Our colleagues at BYU provide some of the best feedback in the discipline.

At the University of Virginia, we thank Jen Lawless, Christine Mahoney, Jay Shimshack, Ian Solomon, Allan Stam, and Craig Volden for their generous support of this project. We are grateful to the entire Batten School faculty for their in-depth feedback on an earlier version of our manuscript. The Batten community has been incredibly supportive in helping to see this book to completion

The book benefited tremendously from a manuscript conference at BYU in July 2018. We extend a heartfelt thank you to the discussants who provided thoughtful feedback and useful advice: Andrés Blais, Barry Burden, David Campbell, Cindy Kam, Chris Karpowitz, Jan Leighley, David Magleby, and Laura Stoker. The chapter-by-chapter feedback resulted in a major reorganization of the book's structure and too many improvements to list. Thank you to Sven Wilson and Ben Ogles for funding the conference, Carina Alleman who organized it, Matthew Baldwin who took notes, and the following colleagues (not previously listed) who offered feedback at the conference: Lisa Argyle, Michael Barber, Adam Brown, and Adam Dynes. We are also indebted to Kyle Endres, Susanne Haastert, Amy Cummings, and Nancy Heiss for reading and copy-editing the manuscript in its entirety; we apologize for sharing the too-early manuscript in such rough form.

For valuable conversations and advice along the way, we would like to thank Marisa Abrajano, John Aldrich, Elizabeth Ananat, Elizabeth Bennion, Adam Berinsky, Nick Carnes, Eddy Cook, Michael X. Delli Carpini, Kyle Endres, Bernard Fraga, Anna Gassman-Pines, Brian Guay, Edie Goldberg, Hahrie Han, Hans Hassell, Andrew Heiss, Eitan Hersh, Shanto Iyengar, Chris Johnston, Bradley Jones, Sunny Ladd, Peter Loewen, Jesse Lopez, Tali Mendelberg, Gabe Madson, Quin Monson, David Nickerson, Markus Prior, Marcos Rangel, Jason Roberts, Joshua Robinson, Brad Spahn, Lucy Sorensen, Steven Sexton, Sarah Treul, Nick Valentino, Jake Vigdor, Marty West, Ariel White, Ismail White, and Chris Wlezien. We are especially grateful to Steven Snell, Christina Gibson-Davis, and Matthew Tyler for early contributions to this project. Our discussions and debates with all of these people have helped to sharpen our arguments and improve our analyses. We have received helpful suggestions and feedback from participants at various workshops and presentations at Boston University, Columbia, Indiana University, Massachusetts Institute of Technology, Princeton, Reed College, Tufts, University of Chicago, University of North Carolina–Chapel Hill, University of Texas, Fordham University, University of Virginia, and the University of Tennessee. We are especially grateful for the Center for the Study of Democratic Politics (CSDP) at Princeton University for providing John with a fellowship to work on this and other projects. We also would like to thank the anonymous reviewers who rejected work from this project so many times that we felt compelled to write a book in order to answer all of their criticisms and questions. It has also been a great pleasure working with Robert Dreesen, senior editor at Cambridge University Press; he has helped to make the publication process the very easiest part of writing a book.

Last but not least, we want to thank our friends and family for helping to keep us sane during the process of writing a book. Sunshine is grateful to the brilliant and fun L.i.P.S. team, Tasha Philpot, Maggie Penn, and Jessica Trounstine, Marco Polos with Suzanne Turner and Stephanie Gergard, her Chez Nous family, the Forehead Flyers, and especially Jodi Koviach, Katy Bartlett, and Amy Cummings for providing much-needed friendship and distraction. John would like to thank Mr. Scholl for being the kind of civics teacher that every student in America deserves, as well as his parents (Gordon and Geraldine), siblings (Julia, Jane, and William), and extended family members (especially Kate Rademacher, Chris Holbein, and Lynn Holbein) for their unwavering love and support.

We are most grateful to our spouses, Joel Hillygus and Brittney Holbein. We dedicate this book to them and to our children: Jake Hillygus, Carter Holbein, and Emma Holbein.

1

The Puzzle of Low Youth Turnout

Young citizens' track record of participation in American elections is dismal. Although young people comprise the largest block of voting eligible citizens, they turn out at significantly lower rates than older Americans – often *half* the rate of those 60 years and older in midterm congressional elections. The 2018 congressional elections raised hopes of a surge in youth participation. Outspoken young activists amassed millions of social media followers, organized political rallies, and dominated the news during the campaign. Headlines predicted a "youth wave" that would fundamentally shape the election outcome.

Estimates indeed showed a historic increase in voter turnout rate among eighteen to twenty-nine year olds – jumping from 21 percent in 2014 to 31 percent in 2018. Although a laudable increase from the previous midterm election, far more young citizens (almost seven in ten) sat out the election than cast a ballot. Moreover, a lingering question is whether this increase will be sustained in future elections or will become a temporary spike in youth participation. Unfortunately, history would suggest the latter. We've seen this pattern before. For instance, the 2008 presidential election saw an impressive increase in youth participation – the highest in three decades – but turnout levels sank again by the next election.[1] For all of the media attention to young voters in 2018, tepid levels of youth voting have long been, and remain, an intractable problem in the United States. Why is youth turnout so low? And what can be done about it?

[1] Less than half of young citizens voted in the 2012 and 2016 presidential elections and only one in five voted in the 2010 and 2014 midterms. See, "New census data confirm increase in youth voter turnout in 2008 election," *CIRCLE Report*, April 28, 2009.

Although there is widespread recognition of the enduring problem of low youth turnout, still too little is known about the basic reasons so few young people vote or, more importantly, possible policy solutions to promote higher levels of youth engagement. Most voting research is focused on identifying the correlates of participation among adults. Political surveys tend to include only those already old enough to vote, making it difficult to trace the development of civic attitudes and behaviors through adolescence. Without a better understanding of the factors that shape the development of civic engagement, we are left with an inadequate foundation for finding policy solutions. While there is almost certainly no silver bullet, the first step toward increasing political participation among young people is a clear understanding of the personal and contextual factors that contribute to youth turnout.

In this book, we develop a more complete theory of voter turnout that recognizes the action of voting requires both an initial civic orientation that creates a desire to participate *and* the ability to follow through on that participatory intention in the face of obstacles and distractions. The act of voting can take considerable time, effort, and planning. Citizens not only have to deal with the institutional hurdles – such as voter registration and voter identification – they have to do so while managing life's many other demands and distractions. These voting obstacles are magnified for those participating in the electoral process for the first time. As a result, there are a great many citizens – young people, especially – who fail to vote *even though they want and intend to do so*. The simple fact is that civic attitudes do not directly translate into civic action.

We propose that voting might not be so different from achieving nonpolitical goals, like exercising, healthy eating, or performing well on an exam. Those who are best able to follow through on their goals and intentions, political or otherwise, are those with strong *noncognitive skills* – competencies related to self-regulation, effortfulness, and interpersonal interactions. These noncognitive skills enable individuals to persevere in the face of anticipated and unanticipated obstacles. Whereas cognitive abilities – especially political knowledge and verbal capabilities – have traditionally been considered the cornerstone of theories of voter turnout and civic education policies, we argue that noncognitive skills are a missing piece of the turnout puzzle.

1.1 THE PROBLEM: LOW YOUTH TURNOUT

Young Americans have been underrepresented at the polls ever since eighteen-year-olds earned the right to vote with the passage of the

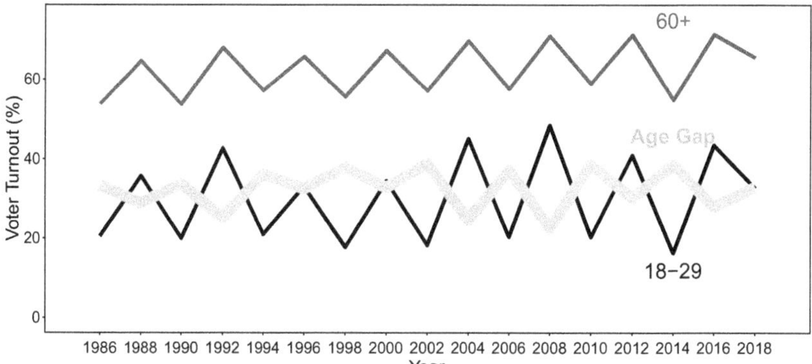

FIGURE 1.1 Age gap in voter turnout in the United States

Voter turnout by age. Source: Current Population Survey (CPS) November Supplement (via the United States Elections Project). The dark gray line plots turnout among citizens 18–29; the medium gray line is for those 60+; the thick light gray line plots the gap between these groups

twenty-sixth amendment in 1971. Although eighteen to twenty-nine year olds account for nearly 22 percent of the voting age population, they made up just 13 percent of the voting electorate in 2018, for example. Age gaps in turnout are especially stark. Figure 1.1 shows this visually, plotting voter turnout rates by age over the last three decades. For example, 65.5 percent of those 60+ voted in 2018 compared to 32.6 percent of those 18–29 years old. The age gap is stubbornly persistent – averaging 33 percentage points across all elections, 28 percentage points in presidential elections, and 37 percentage points in midterms. The age difference in turnout is even more dramatic in local elections, where the gap in turnout between old and young voters can be as high as 50 percentage points (see Hajnal and Trounstine 2016, figure 1). Our longitudinal analysis (see Figure A.2 in the book appendix) further finds that the gap has widened across generations, suggesting that young people today are less likely to becomes voters as they age.

The age gap in voter turnout in the United States is one of the worst among advanced democracies. Figure 1.2 compares the United States to other countries using self-reported turnout data from the Comparative Study of Electoral Systems – a highly respected source on cross-national voting behavior. In virtually all countries, young people report voting at a lower rate than older citizens, but the United States stands out.[2] In the

[2] Brazil and Greece – the two countries with higher rates of voting among younger than older voters – are exceptional in many ways, including an institutional context of compulsory voting.

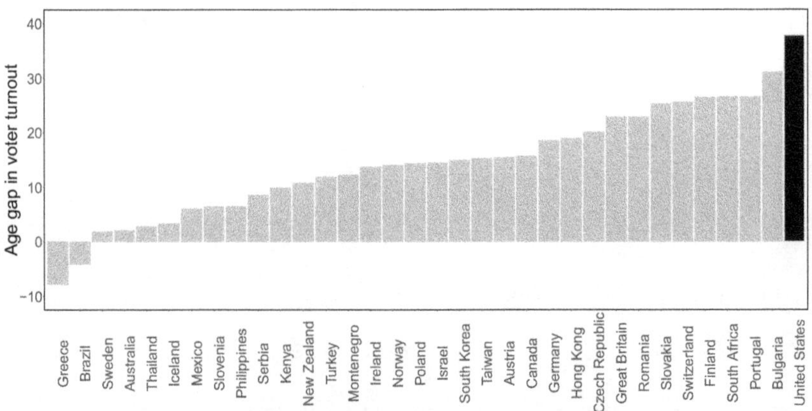

FIGURE 1.2 The age gap in voter turnout by country

The age gap in voter turnout across all of the thirty-four available countries in the CSES. Source: Comparative Study of Electoral Systems (Module 4; 2011–2016). Bars indicate the turnout rate in the Lower House of the most recent election for those 60+ minus those 18–29 in each country, with the United States highlighted

United States, the age gap is more than twice as large as in other advanced democracies like Germany and Canada. The United States has the dubious honor of having one of the (if not the) very worst age-based participatory inequalities. This large age gap helps make the overall voter turnout rate in the United States among the lowest in the world (see Figure A.1 in the Appendix). If young people had voted at the same rate as older Americans in the last presidential election, the United States would jump from twenty-sixth to twelfth out of the thirty-two developed countries in the Organisation for Economic Co-operation and Development (OECD).[3] While there are surely a multitude of reasons for cross-national differences in turnout, scholars view the voter registration system in the United States as a key hurdle (Wolfinger and Rosenstone 1980) – a fact our analyses will confirm is especially true among young people.

1.2 WHY LOW YOUTH TURNOUT MATTERS

Before presenting our theoretical perspective and analytic approach, we first outline the reasons low youth turnout is so important to study. Beyond the normative perspective that civic engagement is critical to

[3] This despite the fact that six of the countries ranked ahead of the United States have compulsory voting. www.pewresearch.org/fact-tank/2018/05/21/u-s-voter-turnout-trails-most-developed-countries/.

notions of citizenship and the general health of democracy, targeting young people should be the most effective path to increasing overall voter turnout rates in the United States. Research suggests that voting is habitual and persistent. For experienced voters, voting is less challenging and going to the polls becomes routine through behavioral repetition. Individuals who participate when they are young are more likely to continue voting throughout their lives, while those who don't are often locked-in as perpetual nonvoters (Coppock and Green 2016; Fujiwara, Meng, and Vogl 2016; Gerber, Green, and Shachar 2003; Meredith 2009). The Center for Information & Research on Civic Learning and Engagement (CIRCLE) – the leading nonprofit organization focused on youth voting – puts it this way: "Voting is like any other habit: it must be taught, facilitated, and nurtured .... Like most habits, the earlier one develops it, the easier it is to keep at it later in life."[4] Political scientist Mark Franklin similarly concludes, "Older people are, on the whole, too set in their ways to be responsible for social or political change ... [b]ecause young people hold the key to the future, any reform that primarily affects young people can have large effects on voting behavior" (Franklin 2004, 216). Franklin's analysis of voter turnout across established democracies finds that aggregate changes in turnout are primarily attributable to the way new cohorts experience their first election. All of this research suggests that the easiest way to increase overall turnout in American elections may be to focus on young people.[5] Thus, setting young people on a path toward civic engagement is critical to current and future turnout rates in American democracy.

Low and unequal turnout levels also matter because of distortional impacts on representative government. It is well-documented that the policy preferences of voters and nonvoters differ markedly (Leighley and Nagler 2013). Extensive research has shown that turnout inequalities shape not only who gets elected but also what policies get implemented (Anzia 2013; Berry and Gersen 2011; Bertocchi et al. 2017; Fowler 2013; Lee, Moretti, and Butler 2004; Madestam et al. 2013). This means that age-based gaps in voter turnout act to bias public policy toward the preferences of older citizens.[6] It is perhaps no wonder that Social

4 "Teens and elections," Center for Information & Research on Civic Learning and Engagement (CIRCLE), January 23, 2018.

5 Some have also found evidence of household spillover effects (Dahlgaard 2018; Nickerson 2008), suggesting that increasing turnout among young people could potentially mobilize older household members as well.

6 It is often assumed that young people will overwhelmingly vote Democratic, but research shows their preferences are less predictable and more complex than often assumed, with

Security is considered the "third rail" of American politics, even as public education spending takes deep cuts (Campbell 2003). If young people fail to show up at the polls, elected officials have little incentive to pay attention to their concerns.[7] As political philosopher William Galston puts it, "[Youth] disengagement increases the already powerful political tilt toward the concerns of the elderly" (Galston 2004, 263). More colorfully, former Congressman Barney Frank (D-MA) once quipped, "Elected officials pay as much attention to those who are not registered to vote as butchers do to the food preferences of vegetarians."[8]

Understanding youth turnout is also worthwhile because voting may be a proxy for or may influence other desirable social attitudes and behaviors. Voting has long been used as a marker of social cohesion and social capital (e.g. Putnam 2000). Places with low voter turnout – the logic goes – are also likely to have lower levels of social connections between individuals, making transactions more difficult and depleting society from the inherent value of interconnectedness. Scholars speculate that there is a reciprocal relationship between various civic attitudes and behaviors, so that voting is both fostered by and reinforces attitudes like social trust, tolerance, and humanitarianism, and promotes other civic behaviors like volunteering, belonging, and donating (e.g. Lijphart 1997). While the empirical literature on this topic is rather sparse, the general theoretical underpinning is straightforward. Increasing youth turnout may serve to broadly improve the communities in which young people live.[9]

Finally, focusing on young people can help shine light on other disparities in voter turnout. Age is not the only dimension by which voter turnout is vastly unequal – indeed, we know from previous research that massive gaps by race and socioeconomic status exist (Fraga 2018). These gaps are already present when young people come of voting age (see Figure A.3 in the Appendix). Even in their first voting experience, those who are poorer,

many self-identifying as independents and having policy attitudes that buck traditional two-party categorizations (see "The generation gap in American politics," *Pew Research Center*, March 1, 2018).

[7] For evidence of the nuances of how youth public opinion differs from other adults, see for instance "The generation gap in American politics," *Pew Research Center*, March 1, 2018.

[8] See, "Barney Frank: Here's how to not waste your time pressuring lawmakers," *Mic.com*, February 7, 2017.

[9] For empirical work that explores the effects of voting experiences on broader social attitudes and behaviors, see Shineman (2018); Braconnier, Dormagen, and Pons (2017); Loewen, Milner, and Hicks (2008); and Holbein and Rangel (Forthcoming).

less educated, and nonwhite are much less likely to vote than their more advantaged counterparts. This suggests that stubborn inequalities in voter participation have their roots in the experiences that predate adulthood. Studying what causes these disparities requires examining citizens before they become eligible to vote.

1.3 THE PUZZLE: IT'S NOT FOR LACK OF POLITICAL MOTIVATION

Apathetic, disengaged, narcissistic, selfish, entitled, shallow, lazy, impulsive, confused, lost, impatient, and pampered: all of these words are frequently used to describe young people. These descriptions have not been restricted to the youth of the current generation; for hundreds of years, young people have faced the contempt of their elders. At least as far back as ancient Greece, youth have been described as hellions detached from society:

> The children now love luxury; they have bad manners, contempt for authority; they show disrespect for elders and love chatter in place of exercise. Children are now tyrants, not the servants of their households. They no longer rise when elders enter the room. They contradict their parents, chatter before company, gobble up dainties at the table, cross their legs, and tyrannize their teachers.
>
> —Socrates[10]

This hypercritical view of young people has spanned the decades – from concern over the rebellions of baby boomers, to worries that Generation X would fail to be as engaged as the great generations that proceeded, to apprehension over the disconnected nature of millennials.

These descriptions also hint at a common explanation for low levels of youth voter turnout: Young people just aren't politically motivated. The conventional wisdom is that young people lack an interest in politics, a sense of civic obligation, or the other attitudes that create a desire to vote. As one journalist bluntly put it, "Young people don't care about voting."[11] This narrative of a disinterested youth is also apparent in scholarly work (e.g. White, Bruce, and Ritchie 2000). Political scientist Stephen Bennett laments that "today's young Americans on and off campus have a visceral dislike of politics" and they show a palpable "indifference to public

[10] Attributed to Socrates by Plato, according to William L. Patty and Louise S. Johnson, *Personality and Adjustment*, p. 277 (1953).

[11] "Young people don't care about voting," *Bloomberg*, October 31, 2014.

affairs" (Bennett 1998).[12] Philosopher Marshall McLuhan observed that "American youth attribute much more importance to arriving at driver's license age than at voting age" (1994, 194).

It is a truism that those who don't want to participate in politics usually don't. Abundant research has shown that markers of political motivation – most commonly, self-reported political interest or a sense of civic duty – are strong predictors of voting, volunteering, and belonging.[13] Political interest is a motivation that "nourish[es] the willingness to go to the polls" (Blais 2007, 632), while a lack of interest poses an "obstacle to a widely informed … and participating electorate" (Prior 2005, 578). Whether measured as a desire to fulfill one's civic duty (Blais and Achen 2018; Campbell 2006b), a general interest in politics (Prior 2010, 2018), an orientation toward politics that is driven by hobbyism (Hersh 2017) or one's shared social interests (Stoker 1992), political motivation plays a foundational role in existing theories of political behavior.

Certainly, it might not be surprising if young people were turned off by the rampant political polarization and animus in the country today. It's easy to imagine that cynicism about the current state of American politics could depress general interest in and enthusiasm about politics. In a recent report, the Institute of Politics (IOP) at Harvard University argued that "the hyperpartisanship and gridlock that has befallen Washington, D.C. is having a traumatic effect not just on our nation's status at home and abroad, but on the political health of tens of millions of once (and hopefully future) idealistic young people."[14] Perhaps the nature of politics today is leading young people to avoid politics altogether. Though this explanation seems plausible on its face, other scholars counter that "cynicism and negative attitudes toward politics and politicians" are unlikely to account for the discrepancy in turnout between the young and old because cynicism affects all citizens in the same way (Rubenson et al. 2004, 407).

[12] For recent popular examples, see: "Why young people don't vote," *The Economist*, October 29, 2014; or "Apathy or antipathy? Why so few young people vote," *The Guardian*, April 19, 2015.

[13] Prominent examples of such work includes Blais (2000); Blais and Achen (2018); Blais and St-Vincent (2011); Blais and Young (1999); Rubenson et al. (2004); Söderlund, Wass and Blais (2011); Theiss-Morse and Hibbing (2005); Verba, Schlozman, and Brady (1995).

[14] As reported in "For 'Millennials,' a tide of cynicism and a partisan gap," *New York Times*, April 29, 2013.

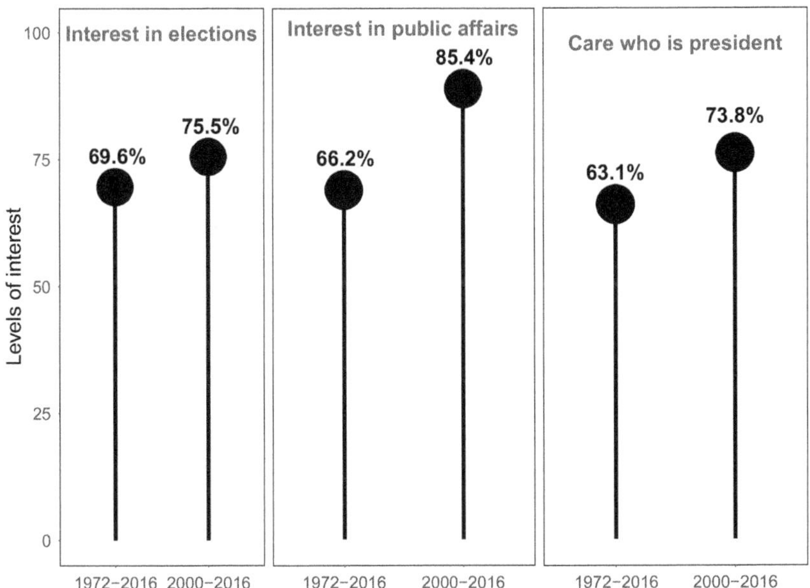

FIGURE 1.3 Political interest among young people

Levels of political interest among young people, ANES cumulative file (1972–2016). Young people defined as those aged 18–29

A more fundamental problem with the narrative of disinterested young citizens is that it simply is not empirically true. By multiple metrics, most young people *are* politically interested and motivated. And, despite the increased rancor in American politics, some measures find young people to be even more interested in politics in recent years than in the past. Figure 1.3 displays young people's levels of political interest from the American National Election Study (ANES) – one of the longest running and most respected political surveys of the American electorate. The figure graphs three different measures of political interest – expressed interest in elections, caring about who is president, and interest in public affairs – shown separately for the entire time series and for elections since the turn of the century, when political polarization has been most pronounced.[15]

[15] Each of these measures is available in only some of the ANES waves. Interest in elections was not asked in 1974. Caring who is president was only asked in Presidential election years. Interest in public affairs was asked in all years. The ANES has only measured civic duty sporadically over time – last doing so in 1992 – so we do not include it in our visualization.

As can be seen, despite having low levels of voter turnout, young people do have a civic orientation. Across these various measures, a dominant majority of young people show signs of political motivation.[16] In recent years, the number of young people who express an interest in elections (76 percent), care who is president (74 percent), have interest in public affairs (85 percent), and intend to vote (83 percent) is especially high.[17] We see no evidence in the aggregate that today's polarized political environment has depressed the attitudinal precursors to political participation. Moreover, when compared to older citizens, we find a much smaller gap in political interest by age compared to what we saw in voter turnout: We see a 10 percentage point age gap in political interest, compared to the 30 to 50 percentage point age gap in voter turnout.[18]

These patterns are also apparent in other data collections, including the General Social Survey (GSS)[19] and UCLA's annual survey of first-year college students in the United States, which found in 2015 that political interest had "reached the highest levels since the study began fifty years ago."[20] By some measures of political interest, young people are virtually indistinguishable from their older counterparts. According to an analysis by the nonpartisan Pew Research Center, measures of election interest show that Millennials are tied with Gen Xers, and only 2 percentage points behind Boomers. And when directly asked why they don't participate in politics, only a small fraction (20 percent) of young people attribute their lack of engagement to "there not [being] any issues they care about."[21] It seems clear that young people are not turned off by politics – they are politically motivated and interested – and yet they are not voting in US elections.

[16] Those who are above the median value are coded as interested. In practice, this means those who say "somewhat" or "some of the time" are coded as interested. Theoretically, we take the position that individuals need at least a minimal level of motivation. Empirically, this group also looks more like the highest category ("very much interested" and "most of the time," respectively) than the lowest categories in terms of their validated voter turnout.

[17] Over the entire time series a majority of young people express an interest in the election (70 percent), care who is president (63 percent), have interest in public affairs (66 percent), or intend to vote (74 percent).

[18] See "The generation gap in American politics," *Pew Research Center*, March 1, 2018.

[19] See Russell Dalton, "Why don't millennials vote?" *Washington Post* (Monkey Cage), March 22, 2016.

[20] See CIRP Freshman Survey; "College students' commitment to activism, political and civic engagement reach all-time highs," *UCLA Newsroom*, February 10, 2016.

[21] See "Diversity, division, discrimination: The state of young America," *MTV/PRRI Report*, January 10, 2018.

One possible explanation for this puzzle might be that young people have simply redefined what it means to be a good citizen. Rather than voting, they are channeling their political interest into other forms of civicengagement: protests, online activism, or volunteering. In *A New Engagement?*, Cliff Zukin and his colleagues conclude that the United States is experiencing "a subtle but important remixing of the ways in which U.S. citizens participate in public life," with young people taking the lead in forms of political engagement beyond voting. They suggest that "young people who eschew voting were nevertheless involved in an impressive variety of activities that speak in a different voice" (Zukin et al. 2006, 7). Russell Dalton similarly contends that young nonvoters are still "involved – sometimes more so – as civic volunteers, by contacting politicians, and in other ways ... millennials display about the same level of political interest as the youngest generation did in 1987, and millennials contact local government and work with others in the community at essentially the same rates as did youth in the earlier surveys. And today's youth are likely to get involved in protests or other political confrontations."[22]

While it is true that young people may be more voluntaristic than older generations, other forms of civic engagement do not substitute for voter turnout in an electoral democracy, and young people do not appear to view volunteering and voting as substitutes. Rather, our scrutiny of the survey data finds that young people say they intend to vote; they just often fail to actually do so. We see a persistent gap between turnout intentions and turnout behavior. Looking across election years in the ANES, the difference between turnout intentions and actual turnout averages around 20–30 percentage points, depending on whether we use self-reported or validated voting.[23]

This gap between intention and behavior is also *much* larger for young citizens than older citizens (Quintelier and Blais 2015). Figure 1.4 shows the intention-behavior gap – that is, the difference between turnout intentions and turnout behavior – for younger (i.e. 18–29) and older (i.e. 60+) citizens. We see that young people are consistently worse at acting on their participatory intentions. Indeed, older citizens are more than *twice* as

[22] See Russell Dalton, "Why don't millennials vote?" *Washington Post* (Monkey Cage), March 22, 2016.

[23] The ANES cumulative file contains validated voting for the years 1964, 1976, 1978, 1980, 1984, 1986, 1988, and 1990. The 20 percentage point estimate comes from an average over these years. Vote validation is available also in the 2016 Time Series.

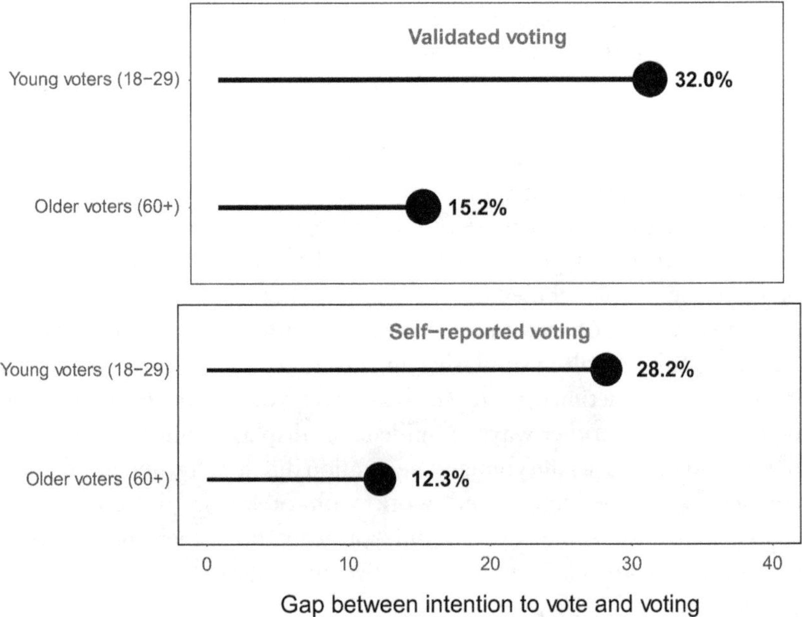

FIGURE 1.4 The difference between turnout intentions and actual turnout by age
Figure 1.4 plots the average gap between turnout intentions and turnout. The top panel uses validated voting; the bottom uses self-reported voting. Data drawn from the ANES cumulative file (1972–2016)

likely to follow through on their turnout intentions as young people and this difference has grown in recent decades. Even if political motivation is a precondition for participatory behavior, there remains a critical missing piece of the puzzle.

The gap between turnout intention and turnout behavior is one that has long vexed election pollsters (Hill 2018; Rogers and Aida 2011) and has often been attributed to survey measurement error. Although a somewhat technical point, we want to briefly consider the possibility that the observed gap between turnout intention and self-reported voting might be an artifact of people lying about their turnout intentions to present themselves more favorably to interviewers – a so-called social desirability bias. After all, it is well-documented that self-reported voting behavior in surveys far exceeds actual turnout, and research has shown that some of that is attributable to overreporting. For example, one recent study comparing survey responses to voter files found that 6 percent of respondents to the ANES said they had voted when administrative records indicated that they had not (Spahn and Jackman 2018).[24] However, over-reporting of self-reported voting would widen the gaps we have documented, whereas over-reporting of vote intentions would make these gaps smaller. Moreover, over-prediction is conceptually different from over-reporting – the former is the internalization of a social norm that leads to making optimistic projections about the future, whereas the latter represents an intentionally dishonest survey response. The very presence of such an optimistic norm is arguably suggestive of a civic orientation that some have assumed young people lack (Achen and Blais 2015).

We are able to conduct a cursory test of potential social desirability bias on self-reported turnout intentions using the 2016 ANES survey. To do so, we leverage the unique data collection structure of the study – in this year, parallel surveys were run, one conducted face-to-face with an interviewer and the other self-completed online by the respondent. Survey methodology research has shown that the presence of an interviewer increases social desirability pressures compared to answering a questionnaire without an interviewer (Holbrook and Krosnick 2009). We can thus compare the reported turnout intentions across samples to get an estimate of the extent to which social desirability is biasing self-reported turnout intentions. The comparison finds that 90.7 percent of eighteen to twenty-nine year olds in the face-to-face sample said they intended to vote compared to 90.2 percent of those in the online sample – a small and insignificant difference ($p = 0.861$).[25] We see similar trivial differences in estimates of political interest, campaign interest, and the gap between turnout intention and self-reported voter turnout. On the latter, 19.6 percent of those intending to vote reported not doing so in the face-to-face sample, whereas the percentage was 20.4 percent in the web sample – again, an insignificant difference. In sum, this analysis offers little evidence that individuals are deliberately lying about their intention to vote. Rather, it simply appears young citizens intend to vote, but too often fail to follow through on their civic attitudes and intentions.

To be clear, we are not arguing that political motivation does not matter. We believe it is a worthy topic to try to understand the roots of people's

[24] Overall, there was a 13 percentage-point overestimate of voter turnout in the study; the other sources of the overestimate are nonresponse bias and the mobilizing effects of participation in the study. See also Belli, Traugott, and Rosenstone (1994) and Abelson, Loftus, and Greenwald (1992).

[25] Estimates exclude those who had reported already having voted by the date of interview in the pre-election survey.

desire to participate and to identify approaches for nurturing those civic attitudes. Rather, we argue that political motivation is a necessary, but not sufficient, condition for political action. Our focus is on the puzzle introduced in Figures 1.3 and 1.4: Why do so many politically motivated young people fail to participate? That is, what accounts for the persistent gap between turnout intentions and actual turnout? This intention-behavior gap has been largely overlooked by scholars, policymakers, and grassroots organizations, but understanding it might offer the most promising path for increasing youth turnout.

To help illustrate the value of refocusing scholarly attention, we compare the asymmetries in validated turnout rates among those who are politically motivated versus those who are not. Among those young people who said that they did not intend to vote in the 2016 election, only 8.8 percent actually did so; among those who said they did intend to vote before the election, less than half of those same individuals ultimately cast a vote.[26] Clearly, the differences in predictive error between those motivated compared to those unmotivated suggests it might be a more difficult task to mobilize the unmotivated than to help the motivated follow through on their behavioral intentions. The comparison also highlights that increasing turnout is not as simple as just increasing levels of interest given the large number of those with the top level of self-reported interest who still fail to vote.

1.4 CONSIDERING FOLLOW-THROUGH THE ROLE OF NONCOGNITIVE SKILLS

We argue that many people fail to vote *not* because they lack political interest or a sense of civic duty, but rather because they lack the skills and strategies that would help them follow through on their behavioral intentions.

Our perspective starts from the well-established premise that the costs of voting are high, and especially so for young people. In order to vote, citizens not only have to deal with institutional hurdles – they have to register to vote, often many days before the election, gather the procedural items requisite to vote, locate and travel to polling locations, navigate long lines – while simultaneously managing life's many other demands

[26] By another comparison, among those young people who said they were "very" interested in politics in 2016, 38.4 percent failed to vote; whereas among those who said they were "not at all" interested, 80.4 percent failed to do so.

and diversions. In the United States, the costs of participation are incurred repeatedly, given the large number of elections held and the need to update one's registration with any changes in home address – making this an especially acute hurdle for young people, who are more geographically mobile (Ansolabehere, Hersh, and Shepsle 2012). On top of these contextual barriers, voting occurs amid daily life, with all the stresses, demands, and tensions that constrain day-to-day behaviors. Young citizens are especially sensitive to these barriers as they have to navigate the voting process "at a time when their lives are filled with the problems of establishing themselves in adult relationships and circumstances ... young adults are only starting to establish the social networks that will ultimately serve to guide their political choice and motivate their vote" (Franklin 2004, 64). Because of these – and other – obstacles, many young people never make it to the polls, despite the best of intentions.

We propose that an overlooked part of the puzzle relates to *follow-through*. That is, while many young citizens have an orientation or intention to participate in politics (i.e. political motivation), they often lack the skills to follow through on their intentions in the face of obstacles or distractions. Those best equipped to overcome the personal and contextual costs to voting are those with strong noncognitive skills – capabilities related to self-regulation, effortfulness, and interpersonal interactions.

Although we (and others) use the label "noncognitive" to contrast with measures of cognitive skills, including reasoning, reading, and mathematics, we should be clear that this does not mean that these attributes do not require thinking or other processes within the human brain – they too involve executive functioning and top-down processing (Farrington et al. 2012). Within the educational system, these noncognitive attributes are sometimes called psychosocial skills, soft skills, character skills, or emotional intelligence – they all refer to self-regulatory skills not captured by cognitive aptitude tests. Recently, these skills have received a great deal of attention in economics, education, and child development research – with scholars in these fields showing that noncognitive skills are predictive of school and career success, are independent of cognitive aptitude, and are malleable (e.g., Farrington et al. 2012; Heckman 2000; Heckman and Kautz 2013; Shechtman et al. 2013). Some research has focused on individual noncognitive skills like grit, locus of control, or delayed gratification, but we follow the approach of recent scholars in conceptualizing noncognitive skills as a broad umbrella term that captures a constellation of capacities related to self-regulation. We contend that those with better control of their thoughts, emotions, and behaviors are also able to better fulfill their behavioral intentions in the realm of politics. While political motivation might be a necessary trait for an individual to set a political goal, those best equipped to follow through on their goals – including in the political domain – are those with well-developed noncognitive skills.

Noncognitive skills have been well-documented regarding their effects on educational performance (e.g. Cunha and Heckman 2007; Jackson 2018; West et al. 2016) and earnings (e.g. Heckman and Rubinstein 2001), but have not been previously evaluated for possible impacts on civic behaviors. In our view, voting might not be so different from achieving nonpolitical goals, like getting to the gym after a long day at work. Just as with these desirable non-political behaviors, people often lack the skills and strategies to see them through. In examining the role of noncognitive skills, we also build on an emerging field of research in political science that examines the relationship between various non-political attributes and political participation (e.g. Carmines 1978; Condon and Holleque 2013; Denny and Doyle 2008; Fowler and Kam 2006; Hill 2018; Sigel and Hoskin 1981; Sniderman 1975).

Bridging the fields of political science, education, and human development, this book offers a thorough examination of the nature and influence of noncognitive skills for voter turnout. To be sure, this is not an easy empirical task. Definitional and measurement concerns loom large – noncognitive skills are varied, multifaceted, and interrelated. Available data constrain the possible tests of the theory. And, of course, voter turnout is a well-trod topic in political science. Despite these inherent challenges, there are strong theoretical reasons to expect that noncognitive skills have been overlooked as resources that help individuals overcome the obstacles to electoral participation.

In the chapters that follow, we give thorough consideration to the conceptual issues involved in examining the relationship between noncognitive skills and voter turnout. We carefully test our expectations against alternative perspectives using multiple operationalizations of the concept of interest. Across various datasets, measures, and analytic techniques, we consistently show that noncognitive skills contribute to making active voters.

1.5 THEORETICAL AND POLICY IMPLICATIONS

Understanding the civic effects of noncognitive skills has implications both for scholarly theories of voting and the potential policies that might promote civic engagement. While much of our analysis is focused on young Americans, we offer a general theoretical framework for understanding voter participation. Our focus on young people reflects both the fact that youth face more barriers and obstacles to participation – thus greater need for noncognitive skills – but also because they are more susceptive to policy interventions to increase voter turnout.

Again, we argue that citizens, especially those voting for the first time, often need persistence and fortitude to act on their voting intentions. Many have an orientation to participate but lack the skills to overcome the obstacles and distractions that get in the way of voting. Our perspective challenges the assumptions and findings of previous models of voting behavior in important ways. First, we argue – and have shown with evidence in this chapter – that political motivation is not enough to ensure voter turnout. Second, our results reveal the limitations of existing models of participation, which emphasize the importance of education, political knowledge, and cognitive aptitude. This perspective assumes that political knowledge and cognitive skills are the key personal attributes related to participation – as evidenced by the strong relationship between education and voter turnout (e.g. Verba, Schlozman, and Brady 1995) – and this view has dominated the structure and content of civic education in the United States. In contrast, we build on work showing the cognitive requirements for voting are lower than and different from what is often assumed by classic theories of voting (Lupia 2016). And we show that noncognitive skills are an overlooked resource that play an integral role in getting people to follow through on their participatory intentions.

In considering the implications of the observed relationship between noncognitive skills and voter turnout, we want to emphasize that our take-home message is *not* that young people simply need to pull themselves up by their metaphorical bootstraps to engage in the foundational act of democracy. Just as it would be inappropriate to conclude that the lesson from research showing income predicts turnout is that poor people just need to (magically) get better paying jobs, we are not proposing that young people simply need to increase their noncognitive skills. In making sense of our findings, we must consider the institutional structures that constrain and incentivize individual-level behaviors. Voting does not exist in a vacuum; policymakers can influence citizens' voting habits by shaping how, where, and when individuals can cast their ballot. Obstacles and barriers to participation in this country are not evenly distributed across the population. The very fact that it can take a great deal of determination, perseverance, and fortitude to vote suggests there is a need to scrutinize the institutions that are relevant to getting young voters to the polls.

Thus, in the second half of the book we look specifically at the role of education and electoral institutions in making young voters. We first consider lessons from our findings for the educational system, which since our country's founding has been tasked with promoting active citizenship. Civic education currently tends to focus on teaching facts about government and politics: an approach consistent with the dominant theories of voting that have emphasized cognitive ability and political knowledge as the key determinants of voter turnout. Using various datasets and methods, we demonstrate that this approach to civic education has not been effective at promoting youth participation. Teaching young people facts about government and politics is not enough to make young voters. Our analyses highlight the need for schools to help young people develop the skills required to follow through on their orientation toward participating in politics. Instead of requiring rote memorization of Supreme Court justices, civics educators need to teach students what to do if they arrive at a polling location and their name isn't on the voter rolls. More broadly, schools need to transform into labs of democracy that give young people the applied knowledge and practical skills they need to follow through on political participation. Our findings also offer further justification for the emerging line of research by policy scholars evaluating ways the education system can better develop and promote noncognitive skills (e.g. Farrington et al. 2012; Heckman 2000; Heckman and Kautz 2013; Shechtman et al. 2013).

We next turn to evaluating the role of electoral reforms. By showing that individuals require well-developed noncognitive abilities to participate in politics, our analysis draws attention to the voting obstacles themselves. After all, if it takes a great deal of determination and effort to vote, making voting easier should increase turnout for those with lower levels of noncognitive skills. While this logic seems clear, the empirical evidence regarding various electoral reforms is mixed and has rarely considered the impacts for young people specifically. We thus examine which electoral reforms are most effective at increasing turnout among young people. The analysis speaks to how we should structure the electoral rules that determine how, when, and where young people can vote. We explain why these institutional reforms might be especially important to youth turnout and show that the conclusions drawn from research focused on adults generally do not always hold for young people, who appear to be especially affected by the electoral barriers that they face.

We find the most effective electoral reforms to increase youth turnout are those that lower the obstacles for new voters, minimizing the need for voters to activate or develop noncognitive abilities. For example, same-day registration – which allows individuals to register whenever they show up at the polls (be it on Election Day or during an early voting period) – enables voting among those who procrastinated in registering to vote. Preregistration laws, which allow young people as young as sixteen to complete their registration form, expand the window of time in which young people can remove the registration barrier. This means, for example, that high school registration drives can target nearly all juniors and seniors, so that a wider pool of young people are able to register with the support and instruction of the education system. These findings confirm the conclusions of recent research about the distinction between voting reforms "that bring in new voters and therefore increase turnout from those reforms that simply provide alternative opportunities for voters who would cast a ballot under almost any set of rules" (Burden et al. 2014, 97). The electoral reforms we find to be effective at increasing youth turnout are ones that bring in new voters by reducing the need for noncognitive skills.

To summarize, we make three key arguments in this book. First, political motivation is a necessary, but not sufficient, condition for participation. Thus, a key puzzle is why so many who intend to vote don't follow through on those behavioral intentions. Second, we propose that noncognitive skills help to predict who will follow through on their turnout intentions in the face of voting obstacles. Finally, we contend that focusing on follow-through has implications for identifying institutional reforms in schools and the electoral system that should be effective at increasing youth turnout.

1.6 OVERVIEW OF THE BOOK

We cover a lot of ground in this book. We offer a thorough examination of the experiences, attributes, and external forces that shape the participation of young people. We also consider the implications of this revised model of voter turnout for potential policy reforms. That is, while our primary focus is to speak to the broader theoretical question: "What makes young people vote?" we do so with an eye toward the policy question: "What can be done to increase youth turnout?" We build on theoretical work from many different fields including economics, education, psychology, and child development. And we evaluate our expectations using a variety of different methodological approaches – surveys, experiments, natural experiments, administrative records, and qualitative interviews. With this multi-method approach and our broad theoretical perspective, we hope to provide a better understanding of why people vote and how we might best promote higher levels of voter turnout.

The book proceeds with two parts. The first articulates and tests our framework that noncognitive skills matter. The second applies these insights to test the effect of public policies on youth turnout. This reflects our dual goals to speak to both theory and public policy.

In Part I, Chapter 2 we outline our theoretical framework. It expands on our understanding of what drives people to vote by providing a more thorough overview of the voting costs, obstacles or barriers that voters face and by incorporating noncognitive skills into a broader theory of voting. We compare our expectations to the conventional academic and popular wisdom about youth participation. Building on the evidence presented in this chapter that political motivation is not enough to bring voters to the polls, we then explain why cognitive resources are also insufficient to explain who does and does not vote. Briefly, the cognitive requirements of voting are less than typically assumed (Lupia 2016), and, as such, noncognitive resources that enable following through on turnout intentions are just as important (if not more-so) than a raw accumulation of knowledge and facts about politics.

We then turn our attention to evidence testing this perspective. To do so, in Chapter 3, we first delve into the conceptual and practical issues related to studying noncognitive skills. We discuss definition, measurement, and data, as well as provide a descriptive overview of where the concept of noncognitive abilities originated and how these attributes relate to other constructs known to predict voter turnout. In Chapter 4 we provide the empirical results that connect noncognitive abilities and voter turnout, showing that noncognitive skills are strong predictors of political participation and that this relationship cannot be explained by many common individual and contextual observed and unobserved characteristics. We also report on the available experimental evidence that links noncognitive skills and voting.

In Chapter 5, we consider the implications for the education system. This is a key area for institutional reform given the strong connection between the education system and noncognitive skill development. In making the case that civic education needs to be reconsidered in light of our findings, we start by evaluating the effectiveness of civic education today. Although civic education has been shown to increase cognitive capacities, particularly those related to the knowledge citizens possess about government and politics (Campbell and Niemi 2016; Green et al.

2011) – a worthy goal in its own right – we show that exposure to traditional civic education has no effect on turnout. These findings illustrate the fundamental failing of the current civic education system and have implications for how we view cognitive capacities as an input in the decision to vote. We then review possible paths forward for reforming civic education.

In Chapter 6, we consider the implications for electoral reforms. We provide evidence of the effects of multiple electoral reforms over time, considering them both individually and together. We find that young people are especially sensitive to the external costs of voter registration. This chapter helps to identify electoral rules most conducive to higher youth turnout. It shines light on the importance of easing voting barriers, thus making it easier for citizens to follow through on political goals.

In our final chapter of the book, Chapter 7, we conclude with our broader thoughts for theory, policy, and practice. We focus on the future research agenda that is needed to help turn this initial work into effective policy change.

Together, these chapters serve as a thorough overview of the factors – personal and environmental – that matter for youth voting. In short, they help us understand what makes young voters.

PART I

NONCOGNITIVE SKILLS AND YOUTH TURNOUT

2

Rethinking What Makes Voters

Aerosmith, Madonna, Miley Cyrus, Leonardo DiCaprio, Robert Downey Jr., Janet Jackson, P. Diddy, and Justin Timberlake all want young people to vote! Over the past twenty-five years, the youth mobilization organization Rock the Vote has traipsed out these (and many other) celebrities to encourage young citizens to participate. Rock the Vote "engages youth in the political process by incorporating the entertainment community and youth culture into its activities. From actors to musicians, comedians to athletes, [it] harnesses cutting-edge trends and pop culture to make political participation cool."[1] Through slickly produced commercials, coordinated voter contact initiatives, and savvy social media outreach, Rock the Vote has been one of the leading nonprofits seeking to engage young people. On such mobilization activities alone, the nonprofit has spent more than $20 million in the last five election cycles and more than $50 million since its creation.[2] A common assumption of many youth advocacy groups (such as Rock the Vote) seems to be that low levels of youth turnout can be increased by making voting "cool" – that is, by increasing political motivation or interest.

Unfortunately, research largely concludes that this approach doesn't work (Hoover and Orr 2007; Vavreck and Green 2004). Journalist Jeff Softley writes that "the ugly truth" is that Rock the Vote "has failed miserably in its mission ... yet the self-aggrandizing, self-important awards

[1] Quoted from the Rock the Vote website cited in "MTV's rock the vote: Beyond useless," *The Raw Story*.

[2] Source: ProPublica and Guidestar.

presentations go on ... an orgy of celebrity and media back-slapping."[3] Rock the Vote is not alone. A review of various youth turnout initiatives is mostly a disappointing parade of failures. Research has found that mobilization efforts made by Votes for Students – an organization that undertook an email get-out-the-vote (GOTV) campaign targeted to college students in multiple states in 2002 – and Youth Vote – which made similar efforts in 2003 – had no effect on youth turnout (Nickerson 2007). Depressingly, one randomized Rock the Vote experiment was found to have actually *reduced* voter registration rates compared to a control group (Bennion and Nickerson 2011). Overall, rigorous analyses of youth mobilization efforts consistently find null or very small effects (Bennion 2009a; Collins, Kalla, and Keane 2018; Kalla 2018a,b,c; Michelson 2006; Miller, Reynolds, and Singer 2017; Nickerson 2007; Nickerson, Friedrichs, and King 2006).[4]

Why do mobilization efforts that focus on drumming up youth political interest fail to work? We have argued – and empirically demonstrated in Chapter 1 – that civic attitudes and intentions are not enough to get young people to the finish line. Many young citizens fail to vote even though they are politically motivated to do so. In 2016, the American National Election Study found that 79 percent of young citizens reported they were interested in the presidential campaign. Indeed, 75 percent reported they intended to vote in the election. A check of state administrative records, however, found that only 38 percent of young adults in the sample actually voted, including less than half of those who reported that they intended to vote. So, while it is a worthy task to understand the roots of political motivation and to identify approaches for nurturing it, we focus on a different puzzle: Why do so many young people not follow through on their behavioral intentions to engage in politics? Our analysis is primarily focused on young people, but we start by outlining a broader theoretical framework for understanding voter participation. Briefly, we argue that individuals need political motivation – the desire to participate – *and* they need a set of nonpolitical skills that enable them to follow through

[3] Quoted from the Rock the Vote website cited in "MTV's rock the vote: Beyond useless," *The Raw Story*.

[4] According to a recent meta-analysis of GOTV experiments, only small effects on overall voter turnout are found. Mailers average a 0.16 percentage point increase, canvassing (the type of GOTV intervention often thought to have the largest effects, given its use of personalized face-to-face contact) averages a 2.5 percentage point increase, and phone calls average an increase in turnout by a mere 0.16 percentage points (Green, McGrath, and Aronow 2013).

on their behavioral intentions in the face of obstacles and distractions. We argue that noncognitive skills – capabilities related to self-regulation, effortfulness, and interpersonal interactions – are an overlooked factor helping to explain who ultimately casts a ballot and who does not.

2.1 CLASSIC THEORIES OF VOTER TURNOUT

Almost all theories of voter turnout start from the fundamental assumption that the act of voting is costly. Previous research has empirically documented that these costs include registering with the state (Corvalan and Cox 2018); navigating complex electoral rules that govern how and when one can vote (Leighley and Nagler 2013); finding and traveling to polling place locations (Brady and McNulty 2011), dealing with potential inclement weather on Election Day (Fujiwara, Meng, and Vogl 2016; Gomez, Hansford, and Krause 2007; Henderson and Brooks 2016), waiting through long lines at the ballot box (Pettigrew 2016), and (one would hope) becoming informed about the candidates and the issues for which one is voting (Wolfinger and Rosenstone 1980). More broadly, voting takes time and effort that could be used for other valuable things, whether working for pay, socializing with friends, or playing video games. For those who are habitual and experienced voters, the costs of voting – especially when voting for the first time – can be easy to forget, but they are foundational to scholarly explanations for why some people vote and others do not.

The most prominent theory of voter turnout, the rational choice model, posits that these costs will almost always exceed the benefit of voting because the chance of casting the pivotal vote (i.e. in an otherwise tied election) is so minuscule.[5] This calculus of voting is modeled as $pB - C$, in which B represents the benefits of having one party (versus the other) in office, multiplied by p, the probability of casting the deciding vote, and subtracting out the costs of voting (C). In his classic 1957 work, *An Economic Theory of Democracy*, economist Anthony Downs explains how utility-maximizing citizens make the turnout decision: "If the returns outweigh the costs, he votes; if not, he abstains" (260). From this view, the puzzle is not why turnout is so low, but rather why anyone votes at all. In fact, the basic empirical fact that many citizens *do* vote despite the theoretical expectations of the rational choice theory, is often called

[5] For a review of rational choice theories of voter turnout and the voting paradox, see Blais (2000).

"the paradox of voting." Political scientist Morris Fiorina once quipped that "turnout is the paradox that ate rational choice theory" (Fiorina 1990, 334).

The solution to this paradox scholars have proposed is to incorporate the expressive (noninstrumental) benefits of voting. That is, for individuals who receive some benefit not linked to the probability of influencing the outcome, the benefits of voting can outweigh the costs. Formally, Riker and Ordeshook (1968) modified the calculus of voting to add a *D*-term, representing a sense of civic duty. Other scholars have called this expressive benefit the *I* term, for political interest, or even the *M* term, capturing political motivation, whatever the particular source (Blais 2000; Ferejohn and Fiorina 1974; Grofman 2018). Expressive benefits simply represent political motivation, thereby mirroring popular wisdom about how to increase youth turnout.

Decades of empirical research has indeed found a strong statistical relationship between measures of political motivation and voter turnout. However operationalized, measures of political motivation strongly correlate with the turnout decision. Not surprisingly, those who report an interest in politics are more likely to vote.[6] In a recent treatise on political interest, Markus Prior (2018, 9) summarizes the extensive body of scholarship on the topic as follows:

> Political interest is typically the most powerful predictor of political behaviors that make democracy work. More politically interested citizens know more about politics, think more systematically about their political decisions, vote at higher rates, and participate more in the political process in other ways.

According to this perspective, those who are politically motivated will put in the time and effort to become politically informed and involved. And in today's high-choice media environment, those who are interested can easily feed that interest, while those who are not can avoid politics entirely (Prior 2005). As one journalist explained,

> It's easy for those that are passionate about and interested in politics to read around it. But for those who are put off by its tedious, dry reputation, those who are talked over in heated discussion, those who are too embarrassed to ask the basic questions, it is harder to get involved. Large amounts of the non-voting

[6] Political scientist Markus Prior writes that "political interest is not the only intrinsic motivation that leads to political involvement, and other motivations may sometimes compensate for its scarcity. But the consistency, scope, and magnitude of its effects on political behavior easily justify this study's focus on a single variable that stands out so clearly" (Prior 2018, 15).

population feel they cannot dip their toe in the political pool for fear of being sucked in by a complicated and competitive world beyond their comprehension – so they avoid any involvement at all.[7]

Although political motivation might help to solve formal theory's paradox of voting, this perspective is not very practically satisfying. For one, it simply shifts the question of "why do people vote?" a small step upstream to "why do people become interested in politics?" The observation that those who have a taste for voting are more likely to vote has been critiqued as trivializing the rational choice perspective (Green and Shapiro 1994). Fiorina (1976, p. 393) asks, "why bother with decision theoretic models, symbols, rational choice terminology and other trappings which add little?" Other scholars call it a tautology to say that those who are more interested in politics are more likely to behave politically. Measures of political motivation are "perilously close to activity itself. This makes them robust predictors of political participation but trivial (and possibly spurious) explanations for participation" (Brady, Verba, and Schlozman 1995, 271). The authors of the classic empirical political participation text, *Voice and Equality*, put it this way: "Asking whether someone feels able to participate in politics or is interested in politics is sufficiently proximate to that which is to be explained, activity, that any relationship becomes less interesting theoretically" (Verba, Schlozman, and Brady 1995, 279). It seems likely that political interest and voter turnout are jointly determined – as one study explains, much like "an individual's demand for gin is very highly correlated with their demand for tonic" (Denny and Doyle 2008, 292).

More fundamentally, the rational choice theory is focused on intention, rather than behavior. According to this perspective, citizens weigh the (known) costs and benefits in their *decision* to vote. The calculus of voting is silent about what happens after making that decision – when unanticipated obstacles and distractions can interfere with the implementation of that decision.

2.2 THE RESOURCE MODEL

Another prominent theory of voter turnout, the resource model, grew out of survey research of voting and the stylized fact that education is the most consistent and strongest empirical predictor of voter turnout

[7] See "Why don't young people vote? Because school teaches us nothing about politics," *The Guardian*, June 8, 2017.

(Verba, Schlozman, and Brady 1995). The resource model of voting also starts from the premise that voting is costly, but emphasizes that individual-level resources such as money, time, and cognitive skills determine one's ability to overcome these costs.[8] Different resources matter more for different types of political participation – money is a resource that is especially important for political donating, for instance. For the act of voting, this theory considers cognitive abilities – especially verbal skills and political knowledge – as the critical resource and typically assumes that education is what imparts these cognitive abilities.[9] As this perspective was recently summarized, "education is considered to increase turnout by developing the voters' cognitive skills which in turn enables them to process complex information about the political system" (Denny and Doyle 2008, 291). Similarly, Nie, Junn, and Stehlik-Barry (1996, 64) contend that "formal education influences the characteristics of democratic enlightenment *almost exclusively* through verbal cognitive proficiency."

A wide and diverse literature has documented the relationship between education and voting across different contexts and datasets (e.g. Burden 2009; Campbell 2006a; Nie, Junn, and Stehlik-Barry 1996; Verba, Schlozman, and Brady 1995; Wolfinger and Rosenstone 1980), including recent research that finds exogenous increases in educational attainment increase voting (Dee 2004; Henderson 2018; Milligan, Moretti, and Oreopoulos 2004; Sondheimer and Green 2010). According to the resource theory, education develops the verbal abilities necessary to write or speak persuasively and the political knowledge necessary to understand and engage in politics. As explained in the classic book *Who Votes?*:

> [Education] increases cognitive skills, which facilitates learning about politics. Schooling increases one's capacity for understanding and working with complex, abstract, and intangible subjects such as politics. This heightens one's ability to pay attention to politics, to understand politics, and to gather the information necessary for making political choices. Thus education is a resource that reduces the costs of voting by giving people the skills necessary for processing political information and making political decisions (Wolfinger and Rosenstone 1980, 35).

8 A related literature focuses on the way that the costs can be externally subsidized, either through mobilization efforts on the part of parties, candidates, and groups (Rosenstone and Hansen 1993) or electoral reforms that make voting more convenient (Traugott and Katosh 1982).

9 For more on this perspective, see Denny and Doyle (2008) and Verba, Schlozman, and Brady (1995).

Education is thought to "increase one's capacity to deal with complex and abstract matters such as those found in the political world" (Jacobson 1983, 115); cognitive capacities help individuals learn what is required of them to vote, where they are supposed to vote, who is running, and what are the predominant issues of the day. Language skills developed in school, in particular, assist citizens in understanding, communicating about, and ultimately engaging in politics (Verba, Schlozman, and Brady 1995).

To be sure, there are active debates about the mechanisms explaining the enduring empirical relationship between education and turnout. Some argue that the observed relationship is spurious, with the acquisition of political knowledge and skills happening through alternative pathways, such as parental socialization, social networks, or the media.[10] For example, organizational membership might provide a "counterbalance" to formal education by providing opportunities for the development of verbal skills to those who would otherwise be resource-poor (Verba, Schlozman, and Brady 1995). Most provocatively, some have argued that educational attainment reflects, rather than develops, the cognitive abilities that enable individuals to make sense of politics. Political scientist Robert Luskin concludes that "education's effect may really be intelligence's" (Luskin 1990, 253). In their controversial book, *The Bell Curve*, Hernstein and Murray (1994, 349) conclude that "education predicts political involvement in America because it is *primarily a proxy* for cognitive ability."

Across these different perspectives, the underlying assumption seems to be the same: Cognitive abilities promote political participation. These skills facilitate the acquisition of the political knowledge and sophistication needed for civic participation. Given the presumed link between cognitive ability and political knowledge, many political scientists lump them together in their empirical measures (Carpini and Keeter 1996; Zaller 1992).[11] In other words, cognitive ability is thought to reduce the informational costs of voting. In the classic book, *What Americans Know about Politics and Why It Matters*, Michael Dell-Carpini and Scott Keeter explain,

10 Some research also emphasizes that education instills a sense of civic duty (Campbell 2006a,b) and promotes political interest (Converse 1972; Prior 2018), thereby increasing political motivation.

11 In contrast, economists more often focus on cognitive ability rather than context-specific knowledge, given the close theoretical, empirical, and practical connection between the two.

> [K]nowledge is a keystone to other civic requisites.... A well-informed citizen is more likely to be attentive to politics, engaged in various forms of political participation, committed to democratic principles, opinionated, and to feel efficacious. No other single characteristic of an individual affords so reliable a predictor of good citizenship, broadly conceived, as their level of knowledge (1996, 5–7).

In contrast, our view is that mastery of a standard political knowledge quiz is neither necessary nor sufficient for voting or voting competently. The informational requirements for voting are quite distinct from general political knowledge measures – in order to vote, citizens do not need to possess expansive facts about historical figures or dates in American political development (Boudreau 2009; Cramer and Toff 2017; Lupia 2016). A long line of scholars have lamented low levels of political knowledge in the American public, but an equally long line of research has countered with ways that citizens are nonetheless able to behave as responsible voters (e.g. Popkin 1994). Citizens are not asked to select the ideal candidate from all eligible individuals in the United States. In most contests, they simply have to decide whether a Democrat or a Republican will best represent their interests and values.

While some minimum level of political knowledge might be needed to know when, where, and how to vote, this information is less than and different from what is typically taught in a standard civic curriculum. We would go so far as to say that the current emphasis on political facts and knowledge has not only distracted scholars and policymakers from potentially more relevant information and skills but it may have also created counterproductive expectations about what citizens *should* know to be qualified to vote. For example, recent polling found that many young people (48 percent) agree that "not knowing enough about the issues is a reason they do not get involved."[12] And young people hold themselves to a higher knowledge standard than older citizens. When asked the question "Do you feel that all eligible American citizens should vote, or should people only vote if they are well-informed about the elections?" 64 percent of those age 65+ said all eligible American citizens should vote compared to only 40 percent of those 18–29.[13]

In many ways, this debate parallels those being had in economics, psychology, and education policy about the limits of cognitive ability for

[12] See "Diversity, division, discrimination: The state of young America," *MTV/PRRI Report*, January 10, 2018.

[13] See: the HuffPost Polling poll from October 9–11, 2018 of 1,000 US adults, https://big.assets.huffingtonpost.com/athena/files/2018/10/18/5bc909f7e4b0a8f17eeaaa37.pdf.

various measures of well-being – the very dispute that helped to spawn the study of noncognitive abilities (Heckman, Stixrud, and Urzua 2006). Whereas previous turnout research has emphasized the importance of cognitive skills for political participation, we propose that noncognitive skills may be a critical resource (primarily) because these skills enable individuals to follow through on participatory intentions.

2.3 REVISING THE CLASSIC THEORIES

As demonstrated in Chapter 1, there are a great many young people who are interested in politics – and intend to participate – but do not ultimately follow through on their behavioral intentions. We propose that the act of voting requires some minimal cognitive abilities and a desire to participate but it can also require persistence, fortitude, energy, and patience to actually make it to the ballot box.

2.3.1 Revisiting the Costs of Voting

The first way we diverge from the most prominent theories of voter turnout is that we have a more comprehensive take on the costs of voting. Rational choice models assume that costs can be fully anticipated and factored into the turnout decision. In contrast, we expect that there may be unanticipated costs that interfere with carrying out the turnout intention. Moreover, we recognize that anticipated and unanticipated costs tend to be higher for young people.

For new voters, the registration requirement, in particular, is recognized as especially burdensome – it typically must be completed by a certain deadline, it must be updated with every change in address, and the content and language of the registration form varies across states. This complicated system has particularly striking consequences for young people. A handful of empirical analyses find that registration requirements depress turnout among young people (Ansolabehere, Hersh, and Shepsle 2012; Brady and McNulty 2011; Leighley and Nagler 2013). One recent study found that the *majority* of young people made errors in completing voter registration forms – often major ones such as failing to include their signature or social security number that could result in the form being rejected by the registrar (Gershtenson et al. 2013). In Chapter 6, we examine the ways in which various registration and voting rules can make it harder or easier for young people to participate.

For college students, specifically, there is the added complexity of navigating the rules and requirements about voting at their college address versus their parents' address. For most citizens there is no ambiguity: They register and vote in the voting district in which they live, which means the location of their one and only residence. For students who move away from home to go to college – and move multiple times during their time there – there is substantial ambiguity as to how federal and state laws apply. States have established varying standards and tests for determining a person's intent with respect to voting residence. In New York, for example, the standard is whether the place is the "center of the individual's life now, the locus of primary concern." In Hawaii, "a resident must ... intend to make Hawaii their permanent residence." Other states have address matching requirements that disproportionately burden students. Until 2019, Michigan had a law that required, the voter registration address to match the address listed on the voter identification and required first-time voters to vote in person, rather than by absentee ballot–both constraints impacting students away at college.

More states than ever now require voter identification at the polls, but there is variation in whether student IDs are considered a valid form of identification. A 2016 Brennan Center report found that nine states never accept a student ID, some accept student IDs if the ID includes criteria such as an address or expiration date, and some accept them only if they are government-issued – which qualifies those attending a state school, but not those attending a private university.[14] Further compounding confusion, college campuses can be divided across counties or voting districts – indeed, campuses are often times deliberately gerrymandered to dilute student influence in local elections. For example, Bowdoin College in Maine was split into four different voting districts, creating confusion about polling locations and the candidates on the ballot.[15] At Prairie View A&M University, a historically black university, students are not given individual mailing addresses, so county and university officials instructed them to use the campus book store address, which turned out to be in a different voting district than the on-campus polling location.[16]

The costs of voting are not only higher for new voters; they are also more complex than often recognized. Political scientist Eric Plutzer explains,

[14] See "Policy brief on student Voting," *Brennan Center for Justice*, March 8, 2006, www.brennancenter.org/analysis/policy-brief-student-voting.

[15] See "Students could face confusion at polls," *The Bowdoin Orient*, October 22, 2004, http://bowdoinorient.com/bonus/article/432.

[16] See "Confusion for Prairie View A&M students on the last day for voter registration," *Houston Chronicle*, October 10, 2018, www.chron.com/politics/election/state/article/Confusion-for-Prairie-View-A-M-students-on-the-13294007.php.

"As young citizens confront their first election, all of the costs of voting are magnified: they have never gone through the process of registration, may not know the location of their polling place, and may not have yet developed an understanding of party differences and key issues. Moreover, their peer group consists almost entirely of other non-voters: their friends cannot assure them that voting has been easy, enjoyable, or satisfying"

—(2002, 42).

Casting a ballot must also fit in among the stresses, demands, and uncertainties of daily life, and daily life tends to be less stable for young people. Young adults are less likely to have the predictable schedule that comes from working a 9–5 job and having kids in school. For those with less-consistent daily schedules, the opportunity costs of voting can be difficult to predict in advance, and there can emerge immediate competing demands that impinge on the time and energy needed to vote. Many young people today also lack experience in managing the responsibilities of daily life. Research finds the transition to adulthood is occurring later and later in the United States, with young people still dependent their parents for everything from financial security to the scheduling of dentist appointments well into their college years.[17]

To gain a better sense of the perceived barriers to participation facing young people, we conducted qualitative interviews with young citizens and high school civics teachers.[18] These consisted of structured interviews with fourteen North Carolina Civics teachers in the Spring of 2017 and with eighteen young citizens in the Fall and Winter of 2018.

When asked about their personal experiences, young people frequently admitted to initial confusion about the mechanical aspects of registering and voting – and the embarrassment that came from not quite understanding exactly how it works. One twenty-one-year-old college student who voted by absentee ballot explained, "Requesting an absentee ballot, since I'm not in my home state, was a little bit confusing. You know, there's sites that try to make it easier. Personally, I was a little bit confused. I had to ask my dad." In walking through the process she went through to register to vote, another twenty-year-old acknowledged, "It intimidated

[17] It is now widely recognized that adulthood no longer begins when adolescence ends; researchers use the term "early adulthood" to describe eighteen- to twenty-nine-year-olds. As individuals are later to complete their education, they are also delaying employment, marriage, and childbearing – often considered the markers of adulthood. See "Young adulthood in America: Children are grown, but parenting doesn't stop," *New York Times*, March 13, 2019.

[18] Additional details, including the structured interview guide for these qualitative interviews, can be found in the Appendix to this chapter.

me at first. I didn't even know what kind of process was involved or if I need to go get a bunch of personal documents and when I found out it's going to take maybe two minutes it was a big relief." Another college student explained the inconvenience of needing to update her registration after moving to a different dorm on campus: "It just gets confusing, you know? At least I had friends who are like, 'Okay. You moved, you can't go on actual election day unless you go and change your address.' So I had people who explained that to me but it just gets confusing, you know?" One nineteen-year-old explained why he did not vote, despite intending to do so: "I tried to vote. I went online and read about it . . . if you hadn't been in the state within 20 days, you were not supposed to vote. And so I read through that and then decided I better not vote."

The role of follow-through was also evident from our interviews. One college student explained that she had planned to vote, but never ended up doing it: "I had the wrong address. I couldn't vote on actual voting day because I didn't reregister my new address because that's technically voter fraud supposedly or what I heard through the rumors." Others mentioned daily distractions that got in the way. In giving a list of excuses about why she didn't vote, one twenty-one-year-old college student said, "These are all stupid reasons, but it just all piled up and I just didn't. . . . [I] got caught up [with] friends visiting and just never made it." Another student explained her appreciation for being able to vote early on campus, "Classes would be very difficult to miss just to go to the polls . . . voting day is actually on a day that I have, like, my busiest schedule . . . I don't know if I'd be able to find the time to go to the polls on the actual voting day. There's always club events going on and it makes it really difficult to get off campus sometimes." When asked why she thought young people didn't vote, another person explained that "younger people like to do things that are captured immediately, such as . . . Amazon Prime. . . . They just don't have the patience. So if they're going to have to go out of their way to do something, they might not be as inclined to do it."

These interviews also revealed a tension between the factors that teachers saw as hurdles to youth participation and those that the young people themselves articulated. The civic teachers consistently reported on their role in making good citizens, but also repeatedly emphasized the importance of teaching students knowledge and facts about government and history. One teacher explained that, "if [students] can understand how to read a complex document in history, then it will maybe help them be able to . . . understand . . . political platform[s]," thus making them more likely to participate in politics. A third-year civics teacher emphasized that her role was to help students "understand how [to] become a citizen, what a budget is, what credit cards are ... what your rights are, how your rights happen, [and] what that looks like." When asked what stopped students from voting, one seventh-year civics teacher curtly responded that "they can barely read."

Many of the young people interviewed thought also they *should* know more. Despite the fact that a long line of research has shown that citizens are able to behave as responsible voters even in the absence of encyclopedic knowledge of politics (Lupia 1994; Popkin 1994), the young people we interviewed seemed to assume that most other voters researched the candidates and issues extensively, and they should not cast a ballot unless they had put in similar effort. One nineteen-year-old explained her sister's rationale for not voting: "She didn't vote in the midterm elections because she's too busy being an athlete. And obviously, she is very busy, but she was like, 'I didn't want to vote without knowing, without doing research'." A twenty-year-old explained why she didn't vote: "It's super-dumb, but I didn't vote, you know? There's no reason I didn't. Well, okay, the reason that I didn't [vote] is I feel like you shouldn't vote if you're not educated on who you're voting for. I'm very against voting down party lines. I think that's idiotic. I don't know. So I don't want to be an uneducated voter." Another student explained, "I struggle with [party voting] ... there are definitely times where I've walked into the voting booth and have not known people on the ballot, so I'll vote straight ticket ... but I don't feel totally comfortable doing it because it's like I don't, in some cases, know who these people are and what [I'm] voting for. I think that one should, in a perfect world, know exactly who's running and what the issues are and how the candidates stand on them instead of voting straight ticket."

Our qualitative interviews (and previous research) suggest that the costs of voting may be more nuanced than previously recognized by the rational choice and resource models of voting. Young people coming into the electorate for the first time show signs of being especially burdened by the basic processes governing how, where, and when they can vote. Many young people fear that the costs of voting are higher than they really are. Moreover, the costs that young people face go beyond the institutional hurdles to voting and registration. Young people face a variety of day-to-day obstacles and distractions that get in their way. They often lack the practical knowledge and skills needed to follow through on their desire and intention to participate in politics.

2.4 NONCOGNITIVE SKILLS AND VOTING: PROMOTING FOLLOW-THROUGH

Given the potential unanticipated obstacles and distractions that might interfere with following through on a desire to vote, we contend that voter turnout is more likely among those with strong noncognitive skills – a constellation of capacities related to self-regulation, effortfulness, and interpersonal interactions. These skills are often called "noncognitive" to signal their distinctness from measures of cognitive ability that capture logic, reasoning, and memory, but that is *not* meant to imply that they do not require executive functioning or brain processing (Farrington et al. 2012). Beyond raw cognitive capacity, however, the general ability to work through the mental process of anticipating, planning for, and working through obstacles or distractions should better equip individuals to overcome the barriers to voting. That is, those with noncognitive skills should be better able to follow through on their political goals.

Building on recent research in economics, psychology, and education policy, we argue that these attributes enable follow-through on a goal in the face of obstacles (Shechtman et al. 2013). To be sure, operationalizing this broad concept brings measurement challenges. However, as we more explicitly review in Chapter 3, noncognitive skills are conceptually and empirically distinct from cognitive ability, personality, and other attributes thought to be relevant for political behavior. Before discussing the operational and measurement challenges of noncognitive skills, we start by outlining why noncognitive skills might be expected to shape voter turnout.

Although we outline indirect paths, we primarily focus on our hypothesized direct path between noncognitive skills and voter turnout – promoting follow-through on behavioral intentions and attitudes. Despite the best of intentions, individuals can be derailed from their desire to vote by unexpected work, family, or social responsibilities on Election Day or in the lead up to a registration deadline. Noncognitive skills should help citizens follow through on an intention to participate in politics.

In that way, voting is not so different from many other life behaviors. Voting takes time, energy, motivation, and effort. For most people, voting occurs amid a normal daily schedule, with all the demands and distractions of day-to-day life. On Election Day people get side-tracked, tired, or indolent – they might fail to follow through even though they had intended to participate. Indeed, recent empirical work finds that being tired reduces the likelihood of voting among those who want to participate (Schafer and Holbein Forthcoming; Holbein, Schafer, and Dickinson 2019). Just like exercise, healthy eating, academic achievement, and other desirable behaviors, people often fail to follow through on what they set out to do. Those with strong noncognitive skills are better equipped to do the planning, systematic thinking, and hard work to achieve their goals in the face of obstacles. As electoral forecaster (and neuroscientist) Sam Wang explained,

> Registering before an election may not sound difficult in theory, but psychology suggests otherwise. Our brains are good at seeing the cost of acting now – but not so good at weighing a benefit that is months or years away. And in states where advance registration is required, voting relies on being able to imagine what one might want to do on the first Tuesday of November, as far as two years off. Such advance planning requires executive function, the brain's ability to plan and execute.[19]

This quote summarizes our broad perspective that in order to vote, citizens need more than just political interest and political knowledge about government and politics, or the verbal skills to express themselves politically. They need the noncognitive abilities that help them see through their political goals. Whether the car breaks down, a deadline is looming, the to-do list is long, or one simply feels worn out, those who have developed self-regulatory skills should be more likely to follow through.

Beyond the hypothesized direct link, we do want to acknowledge possible indirect paths by which noncognitive skills might influence voter turnout. Broadly, noncognitive abilities might increase voting through the enhancement of political motivation, social networks, and resource development. It seems possible that noncognitive abilities may orient individuals toward participating in politics in the first place. It could be the case, for instance, that those who generally strive for success in other aspects of life are also high-achieving and goal-oriented in the civic domain. Social skills could also help to establish the social networks and connections that promote political involvement. Finally, noncognitive skills might simply contribute to the resource development identified in previous models of turnout, especially the acquisition of money and education (Akee et al. 2018b). Those with higher levels of noncognitive skills have greater academic achievement, educational attainment, and career success (e.g. Heller et al. 2017). These outcomes have long been ascribed to cognitive ability, perhaps explaining why researchers have

[19] See "How behavioral science could get more Americans to vote," *Washington Post*, June 15, 2016.

held fast to their ideas that cognitive ability predicts turnout. Likewise, noncognitive skills may also help individuals avoid negative life events that get in the way of voting. Randomized-control trials have shown that helping individuals develop noncognitive skills reduces their participation in crime (Blattman, Jamison, and Sheridan 2017; Heller et al. 2017; Sorensen and Dodge 2016). A similar logic may be used for indirect connections through channels such as teenage pregnancy (Pacheco and Plutzer 2007), individual health problems (Burden et al. 2017), and school dropout (Dee 2004; Henderson 2018; Milligan, Moretti, and Oreopoulos 2004; Sondheimer and Green 2010), for instance. In an effort to account for these indirect paths, our analysis will attempt to sort out the mechanisms behind the observed relationships.

Given the well-recognized relationship between education and turnout, it is especially important to consider how noncognitive skills fit in. Noncognitive skills may promote voting by increasing the time young people spend in school and by enhancing the experiences they have while they are in school. At the same time, we should consider the possibility that schooling might help to develop the capacities that transfer across life domains, including politics. If so, education might matter for different reasons than the cognitive-based explanations that have dominated the literature; rather than simply bestowing knowledge and facts, it might help to teach children how to work within preset deadlines, to be where they are supposed to be when they are supposed to be there, and to work well with other people. In other words, noncognitive skills may very well help to explain the strong and enduring relationship between education and turnout.

2.5 BUILDING ON PREVIOUS LITERATURE

Our theory builds on several different literatures. First, there is a growing body of research in education policy, childhood development, and economics that has linked noncognitive abilities to success in school and beyond (e.g. Dee and West 2011; Heckman and Kautz 2013; Heckman, Stixrud, and Urzua 2006). In recent years, education scholars and policymakers have increasingly paid attention to these noncognitive skills as a means of reforming school curricula (Farrington et al. 2012; Heckman and Kautz 2013; Shechtman et al. 2013) given findings regarding their impact on academic performance (e.g. Cunha and Heckman 2007; Duckworth et al. 2007; Meyers, Pignault, and Houssemand 2013), earnings (e.g. Blanden, Gregg, and Macmillan 2007; Heckman and Rubinstein 2001), and other measures of well-being (Heckman and Kautz 2013).

The concept of *grit* has especially captured the national spotlight in recent years with Angela Duckworth's "genius grant," viral TED talk,[20] and bestselling book (Duckworth 2016). Across fields, scholars have found that grittier individuals tend to stay in school longer (Meyers, Pignault, and Houssemand 2013), perform better while in school (Strayhorn 2014), have healthier habits (Reed, Pritschet, and Cutton 2013), and score higher on measures of subjective well-being (Kleiman et al. 2013). While some might reasonably argue that the soaring popular rhetoric about grit has outpaced the empirical evidence currently available (e.g. Rimfeld et al. 2016), the more fundamental idea that success depends not only on aptitude but also self-control has strong theoretical and empirical backing outside of political science. Our analysis thus marries the literature on education and political participation with this interdisciplinary literature on noncognitive skills.

Within political science, we build on an emerging literature that examines the role of nonpolitical correlates of participation. A handful of studies have previously hinted at the importance of noncognitive attributes in political participation. In *The Paradox of Mass Politics*, W. Russell Neuman observes that it takes "a great deal of initiative, energy, [and] perseverance ... to be heard" (Neuman 1986, 2). A study of inner-city African American mothers speculates that "perseverance could conceivably account for why some ... overcome the start up costs of registration," thus making it easier for them to actually vote (Plutzer and Wiefek 2006, 674).

Other political science work has shown an empirical relationship between participation and various individual constructs related to noncognitive abilities. For example, using an online panel from California and a behavioral measure of delayed gratification, one recent study found that individuals who are more patient are 23 percentage points more likely to vote than less patient individuals (Fowler and Kam 2006). Two papers using alternate measures of delayed gratification found the same – those who have this ability are much more likely to vote than those that do not (Hill 2018; Schafer 2016). Researchers have also shown a correlation between general self-efficacy – a belief about causal agency across all tasks and domains of action – and turnout. Using data from the

[20] see "Grit: The power of passion and perseverance," *TED Talks Education*, April 2013.

2006 Children of the National Longitudinal Survey of Youth (CNLSY) and a self-reported turnout measure, one study found that general self-efficacy predicts an increase of 12 percentage points in self-reported voting, conditional on individual demographics (Condon and Holleque 2013).[21] Measures of sociability also show a relationship with political participation and find it to be twice as large for individuals of low socioeconomic status (e.g. Fowler and Kam 2007; Uhlaner 1989). Teacher assessments of an adolescent as being hard-working and even-tempered have also been found to be predictive of future political participation (Denny and Doyle 2008). Relatedly, a classic literature in political science argues that self-esteem and feelings of personal competence are relevant to political behavior (Sigel and Hoskin 1981; Sniderman 1975).[22]

While political science is starting to accumulate empirical findings showing the relationship between turnout and nonpolitical, noncognitive attributes, these attributes tend to be examined in isolation of one another.[23] Moreover, personal characteristics are often interpreted as personality traits – enduring psychological tendencies rooted in biology – rather than malleable skills that can be developed and reinforced. For example, Fowler and Kam (2007) conceptualize delayed gratification or patience as "a more or less stable individual difference that influences how a person responds to situations that arise" (115). Likewise, Condon and Holleque (2013) conceptualize self-efficacy as a "psychological trait as opposed to a more conditional and fluctuating state" (169). We directly assess the distinction between noncognitive skills and personality traits in Chapter 3, but simply emphasize here that this conceptual distinction is critical to considering the policy implications of our findings.[24] Most notably, previously studies have explored the individual components of

[21] This was an idea that dates back to Lane (1959), but the field has tended to focus instead on *political* efficacy.

[22] Sigel and Hoskin (1981, 178) write that "competent-feeling people tend to have the energy, zest, confidence, curiosity, and skill to be concerned with what goes on around them and to involve themselves in it, while people who lack such feelings of self-confidence are so exhausted by inner conflicts that they have no psychic energy left for public affairs."

[23] A notable exception is a new analysis by economist James Heckman and colleagues that shows that a composite measure of noncognitive abilities is associated with a variety of non-market outcomes including voter participation (Heckman, Humphries, and Veramendi 2018).

[24] Recent empirical research concludes that noncognitive attributes are generally stable but "not set in stone at birth" and thus susceptible to activation, learning, and reinforcement – especially during childhood (Heckman and Kautz 2013, 4).

noncognitive ability separately, obscuring the conceptual and empirical link between these various measures. Missing is a broad theoretical framework, leaving fundamental questions unanswered about the nature and importance of noncognitive abilities for political participation.

Most of the existing studies have also relied on observational cross-sectional data and analyses that only condition on observable characteristics like race, age, gender, and socioeconomic status. Rarely have noncognitive skills been evaluated along with cognitive ability and personality traits.[25] Studies have not leveraged intrafamilial comparisons, individual panels, or randomized control experiments (as we do) to explore the relationship between noncognitive ability and political behavior. In short, previous work has only scratched the surface as to the role of noncognitive attributes for voter turnout. We build on this nascent research, helping to construct a theoretical framework that connects different analyses.

Finally, we should note that given our focus on the link between intentions and behavior, our theoretical perspective deserves explicit comparison to the psychology research based on the Theory of Reasoned Action (TRA) and Theory of Planned Behavior (TPB). In proposing the Theory of Reason Action, Fishbein et al. (1980) initially assumed that intentions were the single most important predictor of human behavior. The initial theory proposed a precise causal pathway between attitudes and behaviors whereby "a single behavior is determined by the intention to perform the behavior in question. A person's intention is in turn a function of his attitude toward performing the behavior and his subjective norm" (Ajzen and Fishbein 1977, 888). Indeed, this research used voting as an example (Bowman and Fishbein 1978; Netemeyer and Burton 1990; Singh et al. 1995). Ajzen proposed the Theory of Planned Behavior as an extension of the TRA in recognition of the fact that factors outside the control of individuals might be relevant to predicting behavior.[26] The TPB incorporates perceived behavioral control – one's perception of the amount of control one has over engaging in the behavior or the ease with which they can perform the behavior – into their theoretical model. With respect to voting, this has most often been operationalized as

[25] A notable exception, Denny and Doyle (2008) controls for test scores.

[26] In recognizing the disconnect between intentions and behaviors, he also points out there the link is weaker when there is a longer time interval between the measurement of the intention and behavior.

political efficacy. Ajzen argues that perceived behavioral control gets taken into account in the formation of behavior intentions, a perspective consistent with recent work in political science (Condon and Holleque 2013).[27]

In contrast to this perspective, our starting point is the disconnect between intentions and behavior. We don't dispute that the initial desire to vote – the turnout intention – reflects a variety of beliefs and attitudes, including perceptions of behavioral control. The fundamental distinction is that we focus on what happens between intention and behavior. What matters is not just initial perceptions about the ease of voting but also the actual ease of getting to the polls. Noncognitive skills should help in overcoming *unanticipated* obstacles and distractions. If someone shows up at the polling location to find a long line, for example, those with more developed noncognitive skills should be more likely to persist; or those who arrive at the polling location to find their name not on the list should have necessary problem-solving skills and strategies.

Further limiting the TRA and TPB theories are the strong causal assumptions that can be impossible to sort out empirically. Indeed, some have argued that the theory of planned behavior has "outlived its usefulness" (Conner 2015). Much like the weakness of theorizing political interest causes voter behavior, critics of the theory of planned behavior argue that "findings under *ceteris paribus* conditions suggesting that individuals are more likely to engage in behaviours that they enjoy less, feel incapable of doing or do not intend to do seems implausible and would cast doubt on the data more than on the underlying theory" (Sniehotta, Presseau, and Araújo-Soares 2014, 2).

In sum, our theoretical expectations are distinct from, but rooted in, a rich and diverse body of existing research that crosses disciplinary boundaries. Given this previous literature, we are especially careful in attempting to address some of the limitations of previous research while building on their important theoretical contributions. In doing so, we hope to provide new insights about why young voters do not vote and how we might identify possible policy remedies.

27 As psychologist Ajzen succinctly put it: "Briefly, according to the theory, human behavior is guided by three kinds of considerations: beliefs about the likely consequences or other attributes of the behavior (behavioral beliefs), beliefs about the normative expectations of other people (normative beliefs), and beliefs about the presence of factors that may further or hinder performance of the behavior (control beliefs)" (Ajzen 2002, 665).

2.6 THE CHALLENGE OF EVALUATING THE ROLE OF NONCOGNITIVE SKILLS

Although the logic underlying our expectations is quite straightforward, we should acknowledge the empirical challenge in evaluating our theoretical expectations. To make a compelling case that noncognitive skills are worthy of attention in political science, we need to demonstrate that they are not simply a proxy for factors already known to influence turnout – factors like political interest, cognitive skills, family background, and individual resources. We face inherent definitional and measurement issues – that we discuss more thoroughly in the next chapter – and we must of course be concerned about selection and endogeneity. We are introducing a concept that is not well-known within political science, for which there is considerable debate regarding its operationalization and measurement, and for which compelling causal research designs are scarce (and often not feasible). Given the constraints of the available data, our empirical analysis is not ideal for testing our theory.

Because of these challenges, we approach the task from many different methodological angles. As we describe in greater detail in Chapter 4, when analyzing observational data, we rely on longitudinal data, and sibling and twin samples where possible. Given concerns about self-reported measurement of noncognitive skills, we look for behavioral measures or teacher reports. We also leverage a randomized controlled experiment and a survey experiment. The seemingly ideal design might randomize a cohort of young children to receive significant interventions designed to increase noncognitive skills with follow up in adulthood to observe if they are more civically engaged. Indeed, we report the results of available randomized control experiments, but we also recognize that even this "gold standard" design offers an incomplete picture as it cannot fully address questions about causal mechanisms.

In sum, although our empirical approach is not perfect, we believe a combination of various approaches helps to build a compelling test of the role of noncognitive skills for civic attitudes and behaviors.

3

What Are Noncognitive Skills?

What explains if young citizens vote or stay home? As we have shown, political motivation isn't enough – many young people are highly interested in politics and intend to vote, yet fail to actually show up. Although political science theories of voter turnout have focused on the predictive power of cognitive skills – political knowledge and verbal abilities – we contend that the citizens best able to follow through on their civic attitudes and intentions are those with stronger noncognitive skills.

But, what exactly are these noncognitive skills? How does one measure them? Can we disentangle them, conceptually and empirically, from other factors known to be important for political participation? This chapter will provide an overview of what these attributes are, how they are measured, and how they relate to other constructs already known to contribute to political engagement. We tackle these questions and introduce the data we will use in testing their effects in the political domain.

3.1 DEFINING NONCOGNITIVE SKILLS

As previewed in the previous chapters, we follow the lead of scholars in other fields and define noncognitive skills as *competencies related to self-regulation, effortfulness, and interpersonal interactions.*[1] These capabilities have been shown in other contexts to equip individuals to follow through on their behavioral intentions in the face of distractions or

[1] To be clear, "noncognitive" is a label used to contrast with standard measures of cognitive skills, including reasoning, reading, and mathematics, but these noncognitive skills still involve executive functioning and intellectual effort (Farrington et al. 2012).

obstacles. Although we argue that noncognitive skills are an important and overlooked predictor of political participation, we must start by acknowledging the challenge of conceptualizing and measuring these abilities. A growing body of research across many different academic disciplines has lauded the role of noncognitive abilities, but there is a lingering need to clarify terminology and measurement. Here we attempt to provide a clear characterization of the way we define and measure noncognitive skills, but we acknowledge, in advance, that we do not perfectly demarcate the conceptual boundaries of noncognitive skills nor propose an ideal operationalization that meets all the needs of theory, practice, and policy implementation. That being said, for all the concerns about measurement, existing research clearly finds that there is some "there" there. Our goal is not to be the last word on the nature and role of noncognitive skills, but rather to shed light on the potential of these attributes to explain political participation.

The first mention of noncognitive skills in the literature is often attributed to psychologist David Wechsler, best known for his development of widely-used intelligence tests (e.g. the Wechsler Intelligence Scale for Children, or WISC for short). Even while creating measurement scales of intelligence, he emphasized the relevance of other factors in predicting human behavior: "In addition to intellective there are also definite *non-intellective factors*.... We cannot expect to measure total intelligence until our tests also include some measures of the non-intellective factors" (Wechsler 1943, 103). Today, these non-intellective factors are often called "noncognitive" to signal their distinctness from measures of cognitive ability measured on standardized tests of academic achievement or intelligence, but they have also been variously referred to as socio-emotional skills, soft skills, character skills, emotional intelligence, social cognitive skills, and metacognitive learning skills (Farrington et al. 2012). Consistent with much of the recent literature and our own research, we consider noncognitive skills to be an umbrella term that captures a family of overlapping constructs that should enable someone to follow through in the face of adversity, obstacles, and distractions (Shechtman et al. 2013).

In the diverse literature in education, economics, and human development, conceptualizations of noncognitive skills are broad, multifaceted, and interrelated. Some scholars define noncognitive skills as having two sub-components: those involving *intra*personal skills – i.e. those that involve one's ability to regulate one's own emotions, thoughts, and behaviors – and those involving *inter*personal skills – i.e. those that involve how well one interacts with others. While research (and our evidence in this chapter) confirms that noncognitive skills are distinct from cognitive ability, the exact boundaries between interpersonal and intrapersonal skills are not particularly well-defined by previous research. It is not always theoretically or empirically evident which individual skills belong in which dimension. One body of work on childhood development groups together individual constructs like problem solving, intention detection, coping, emotion recognition, and emotion regulation as intrapersonal skills (labeling these "self-regulation capabilities"), and those like prosocial behavior and authority acceptance as interpersonal skills (labeling these "social capabilities") (Sorensen and Dodge 2016). In contrast, some psychologists categorize as interpersonal skills such characteristics as an ability to keep one's temper in check, to remain calm even when criticized to demonstrate respect for the feelings of others, to allow others to speak without interruption, to find solutions during conflict, and to recognize and show appreciation toward others, but categorize as intrpersonal skills characteristics such as the ability to prepare for the task at hand, to finish what one begins, to avoid procrastination, to remember and follow directions, to pay attention and resist distraction, and to work hard despite experiencing failure (Park et al. 2017).

In summarizing the literature on this topic, a comprehensive 2018 US Department of Education report, *Promoting Grit, Tenacity, and Perseverance: Critical Factors for Success in the 21st Century*, categorized perseverance, grit, forethought, initiative, and self-direction as intrapersonal skills and communication, collaboration, teamwork, cooperation, empathy/perspective taking, conflict resolution, and leadership as interpersonal skills (Shechtman et al. 2013). Thus, despite agreement on the broad contours of noncognitive skills, it appears there is little consensus as to (1) which individual constructs should be included in the long list of noncognitive abilities and (2) which individual constructs belong in which dimension – be it intra- or interpersonal skills. Not surprisingly, these two dimensions are highly correlated; indeed, for this reason, many scholars treat them as a single latent construct (e.g. Kautz et al. 2014).[2]

Unfortunately, the way the field has developed has not lent itself to clear measurement because studies tend to define and measure noncognitive

[2] Kautz et al. (2014) lump together measures of perseverance/grit, self-control, attentiveness, self-esteem and self-efficacy, resilience to adversity, empathy and the ability to work productively.

skills in disparate ways and typically assess individual constructs in isolation of one another. As Richard V. Reeves and Joanna Venator note, "A particular attribute may be labeled a 'skill' by an economist, a 'personality trait' by a psychologist, a certain kind of 'learning' by an educationalist, or a 'character' dimension by a moral philosopher. Each may have the same concept in mind, but miss each other's work or meaning because of the confusion of terms."[3] For example, across the various datasets we analyze in this book, there are (at least) 106 different items measuring constructs like delayed gratification, grit, emotional regulation, tenacity, self-control, and others. As we will show, these constructs often overlap theoretically and empirically.

Like many psychological constructs, noncognitive measures too often suffer from the so-called jingle-jangle fallacy – the erroneous assumption that two different things are the same because they bear the same name (jingle fallacy) or that two identical or almost identical things are different because they are given different labels (jangle fallacy) (Kelley 1927). We recognize that the individual constructs considered to be noncognitive skills are often interlinked in their measurement, development, and effects. For example, the concept of grit overlaps with constructs like academic tenacity, perseverance, persistence, engagement, autonomy, self-discipline, self-control, delayed gratification, self-regulation, goal-directedness, positive mindset, and so on. The 2018 Department of Education report makes an explicit call for more research to "1) tease apart conceptual distinctions that are critical to practice and 2) construct and work within consolidated frameworks that unify concepts and findings" (Shechtman et al. 2013, 88). We agree this is a worthy goal in its own right even though our first-order goal is to see whether noncognitive abilities, as a whole, influence civic participation.

We thus follow the lead of Nobel-prize winning economist James Heckman and others in examining noncognitive abilities broadly rather than focusing on any one individual sub-construct (Cunha and Heckman 2007; Cunha, Heckman, and Schennach 2010; Heckman 2000; Heckman, Humphries, and Veramendi 2018; Heckman and Kautz 2013; Heckman and Rubinstein 2001; Heckman, Stixrud, and Urzua 2006; Jackson 2018). That is, we conceptualize and operationalize noncognitive skills as a constellation of interrelated abilities, attitudes, and strategies.

[3] See "Jingle-Jangle Fallacies for Non-Cognitive Factors" *Brookings Institution Social Mobility Memos*, December 19, 2014, www.brookings.edu/blog/social-mobility-memos/2014/12/19/jingle-jangle-fallacies-for-noncognitive-factors/.

As we show, single measures and scales of various noncognitive measures often hang together remarkably well – suggesting that these all belong to a single family of attributes. Indeed, much of the research in psychology, economics, child development, and neuroscience explicitly operationalize noncognitive abilities as a single latent factor.[4]

3.1.1 The Malleability of Noncognitive Skills

Generally speaking, noncognitive skills are thought to be relatively stable at the individual level, but also malleable, perhaps more so than personality and cognitive ability. Theoretically, scholars have argued that noncognitive abilities can be "shaped by families, schools, and social environments" (Heckman, Pinto, and Savelyev 2013, 1). Given the relative nascency of the study of noncognitive abilities, few longitudinal datasets exist that compare the inter-temporal stability of noncognitive attributes over the life cycle. Still, there are several ways to see noncognitive skills' malleability, which are, arguably, more convincing than examinations of raw variation over time. For example, there is some evidence from family samples – research on siblings and twins that finds grit is correlated within families, but does not appear to be entirely heritable (Holbein et al. Forthcoming; Tucker-Drob et al. 2016). In student data we collected and analyzed from the Wake County Public School System (WCPSS), we can compare measures of noncognitive ability across twins and individuals measured repeatedly across years. If noncognitive ability were a rigid construct – like genes or personality traits – we would expect to see a high degree of correlation across twins and within individuals over time. In practice, this is not what we observe. The intra-cluster correlation (a covariance measure that looks at relationships among clusters, in this case twin pairs and individuals themselves) among twins is 0.3 and among individuals themselves is 0.6. This is lower than that for cognitive ability among twins ($ICC = 0.6$) and individuals ($ICC = 0.7$) in the same sample. It is not altogether uncommon to see noncognitive abilities vary

4 For examples of studies that explicitly operationalize noncognitive abilities as a single latent factor, see Borghans et al. (2008); Caprara, Alessandri, and Eisenberg (2012); Cunha and Heckman (2007); Cunha, Heckman, and Schennach (2010); Farrington et al. (2012); Heckman (2000); Heckman and Rubinstein (2001); Heckman, Stixrud, and Urzua (2006); Heckman et al. (2007); Heckman, Pinto, and Savelyev (2013); Heckman, Humphries, and Veramendi (2018); Jacob (2002); Jackson (2018); Kautz et al. (2014); Luders et al. (2009); Park et al. (2017); Sorensen and Dodge (2016); Vazsonyi et al. (2019).

across twins and within individuals over time. Again, this is not conclusive proof that noncognitive abilities can be taught, but this is descriptively consistent with the notion that these attributes can, indeed, be learned – they are not set in stone at birth.

Empirical research also shows that school experiences and social programs can affect noncognitive skills. For example, using nationally representative survey data and various panel techniques, one study found that class size reductions influence students' noncognitive abilities (Dee and West 2011). The Tennessee STAR program, in which children were randomly assigned to a smaller kindergarten class and a higher quality kindergarten teacher, resulted in higher levels of self-regulation later in life and higher earnings in adulthood (Chetty et al. 2011). Further follow-up work from the STAR intervention found increases in children's levels of grit (Gross, Balestra, and Backes-Gellner 2017). Using large-scale, longitudinal administrative data from North Carolina, another study found that teachers affect students' noncognitive ability, and this in turn influences long-run educational attainment, arrests, and earnings (Jackson 2018). Using a unique randomized control trial in six school districts,[5] Kraft (2019) shows something similar: High quality teachers improve students' growth mindset, grit, and effortfulness in class. A natural experiment in the United Kingdom found that children exogenously exposed to more education in childhood have more developed noncognitive abilities (Cornelissen and Dustmann 2019). The influential Perry Preschool program, which provided a randomly assigned treatment group with access to quality preschools, was shown to increase students' noncognitive abilities, including reducing externalizing behaviors and increasing academic motivation (Heckman, Pinto, and Savelyev 2013). In a novel study on the effects of unconditional cash transfers, researchers found that exogenous income supplements helped children develop noncognitive abilities involving behavioral control and sociability, likely as a result of increased educational investments (Akee et al. 2018a). Similar results were found by Fryer Jr, Levitt, and List (2015) in a randomized control trial evaluation of a conditional cash transfer program in Chicago Heights, Illinois, that measured noncognitive skills using the Willoughby Measures of Executive Function and the Preschool Self-Regulation Assessment (Willoughby et al. 2012).

5 Charlotte-Mecklenburg, Dallas, Denver, Hillsborough County, Memphis, and New York City.

More directly, there is a growing body of work showing that noncognitive attributes can be moved in response to programs specifically designed to teach these skills. For example, experimental evidence from a program providing Liberian young adults with eight weeks of cognitive behavioral therapy – "a therapeutic approach that … tries to make people aware of and challenge harmful, automatic patterns of thinking or behavior … by having people practice new skills and behaviors" – and cash transfers had lasting effects on levels of self-regulation, delayed gratification, and, ultimately, criminal behaviors (Blattman, Jamison, and Sheridan 2017). This finding is especially notable because it focused on individuals ages eighteen to thirty-five years old. Another study, using a similar treatment in Chicago (IL) schools, found in three separate experiments that cognitive behavior therapy increased middle and high schoolers' ability to slow down and reflect on whether "their automatic thoughts and behaviors are well suited to the situation they are in" (Heller et al. 2017). This increase in self-regulation had the downstream consequence of decreasing crime and increasing school graduation rates. These two studies also suggest that these noncognitive abilities can be developed in late adolescence, and beyond.

Likewise, a multipronged randomized-control intervention that taught students about the plasticity of the human brain, the role of effort in enhancing skills and achieving goals, the importance of goal setting and of constructive interpretation of failures had a significant and lasting effect on students' grittiness and, consequently, improved their performance on standardized tests (Alan, Boneva, and Ertac 2019). Another study showed that a multifaceted childhood curricula that used targeted case studies, stories, and in-class games was able to significantly shift students' ability to delay gratification, that these gains lasted for over three years, and that they had the downstream effect of increasing students' performance in the classroom (Alan and Ertac 2016). A targeted program (EPIS) that aimed to improve the noncognitive abilities of students in Portugal was found to have a noticeable impact on measures of noncognitive abilities as well as school performance (Martins 2017a,b). The Fast Track program – a multifaceted program consisting of a formal curricula, home visits, parent training groups, tutoring, friendship groups, and peer pairing – has been shown to improve aggression control, emotion recognition, general self-efficacy, self-control, social competence, and social cognition, with downstream effects on adult behaviors such as crime (Bierman et al. 1999a,b, 2011). Finally, an in-school intervention in Norway focused on shaping students' beliefs in their abilities – teaching them to have a gritty or perseverant mindset – was found to improve perseverance, tenacity, and grit and had downstream effects on academic performance (Bettinger et al. 2018). One might have the sense from these studies that noncognitive skills can only be moved in one direction – perhaps raising questions about the potential inevitability of improvement over with age and maturity; however, we find in our longitudinal study of WCPSS that the transition across schools – from middle school to high school, for instance – often corresponds with a decline in grit.

Meta-analyses of the existing research further confirm that noncognitive abilities are potentially malleable. A meta-analysis of thirty interventions in twenty-three countries shows that early childhood programs are quite effective at moving students' noncognitive abilities (Nores and Barnett 2010). Another meta-analysis of both experimental and nonexperimental comparisons likewise concludes that early child education programs can improve noncognitive abilities (Camilli et al. 2010). Finally, a meta-analysis of fifty-two field experiments concludes that various noncognitive skills can be taught, even when the interventions don't start until adolescence (Taylor et al. 2017). A 2014 report by the OECD – a must-read for those interested in noncognitive attributes – offers a comprehensive review of the effect of various early childhood, childhood, and adolescent programs on noncognitive abilities (Kautz et al. 2014). The report shows that programs including the Nurse Family Partnership (targeted in utero), Syracuse Family Development Research Program (early childhood), Houston Parent-Child Development Center (early childhood), Jamaican Supplementation Study (early childhood), Chicago Child-Parent Center Program (early childhood), Turkish Early Enrichment Project (early childhood), Seattle Social Development Project (childhood), Dominican Youth Employment Program (adolescence), and Self-Sufficiency Project (adolescence) all had an impact on individuals' noncognitive abilities. In another broad review piece, Fryer (2017) provides evidence – from a host of field experiments using various treatments and measures – that noncognitive abilities can be improved, and often noticeably so.

In sum, a host of causal studies have shown that noncognitive skills can be malleable, especially during childhood but perhaps into adolescence and adulthood with targeted interventions (e.g. Blattman, Jamison, and Sheridan 2017; Heller et al. 2017; Schilbach 2016; Taylor et al. 2017). To be sure, there is more to learn about when and how noncognitive attributes can be changed and for whom programs targeting these attributes are most effective, but it seems clear that these are not permanent characteristics out of the reach of well-designed social interventions. Put differently, these attributes are not "traits set in stone at birth and determined solely by genes" (Kautz et al. 2014, 2). Given this, we believe it is better to conceptualize noncognitive atttributes as skills or competencies to help distinguish them from stable individual-level traits. These skills can be taught, reinforced, and activated. As a result, noncognitive skills offer promise for school programs desiring to affect later life social behaviors including – we argue – civic behaviors.

3.2 OPERATIONALIZING NONCOGNITIVE SKILLS

Given the conceptual issues just discussed, it is perhaps not surprising that the operationalization of noncognitive skills is often inconsistent and varied across the literature. Noncognitive competencies vary not only in what they are labelled, but also how they are measured. Perhaps most common are survey-based scales of an individual attribute (e.g. grit) that are created through the combination of multiple self-assessment items, but there exist a variety of other measurement methods and approaches that have been used. We start by reviewing the benefits and limitations of different measurement approaches – survey self-reports, third-party evaluations, and observed behavioral techniques – and then we introduce the data and measures we use in our analysis.[6] As will become apparent, more work is clearly needed to develop explicit measures that are grounded in theory and empirically validated. We hope future researchers will do more to develop a valid and reliable measurement instrument of noncognitive skills in much the same way that has been done for cognitive aptitude. At the same time, we have to recognize that the measurement of cognitive aptitude, a historically well-studied topic, is also far from controversy-free.[7]

The first approach asks people to evaluate their own noncognitive capacities through a survey-based self-assessment. There is considerable variation in the exact items and response options measured. For example,

[6] These measurement types sometimes blur together – for example, when teachers are providing factual-based reports of students' observed behaviors.

[7] There are a wide range of different cognitive tests that are used, including the various Woodcock-Johnson measures (Woodcock, Johnson, and Mather 1989, 1990; Woodcock et al. 2003), the Kaufman Ability Battery (Cahan and Noyman 2001; Kaufman, Raiford, and Coalson 2015), the Peabody scales (Dunn et al. 1965), and the British Ability Scales (Elliott 1979), to name a few.

psychologist Angela Duckworth measures grit with a Likert-type scale created from survey items asking respondents to identify with statements like "Setbacks don't discourage me," "I am a hard worker," and "I finish whatever I begin" (Duckworth et al. 2007). A similar self-reported technique can be seen for measures of delayed gratification (Hill 2018), general self-efficacy (Condon and Holleque 2013), and the ability to empathize with others (Davis 1994). As Shechtman et al. (2013, 37) explain, this approach has strengths and weaknesses:

> Practically speaking, self-report surveys have the advantages of being easy to administer to large numbers of students, and data from surveys often can be interpreted with conventional statistical methods. Numerous studies show that well-constructed and well-validated self-report instruments can capture facets of dispositions and experiences that are closely aligned with behaviors and other performances. There are, however, several challenges, both theoretical and methodological, with self-report surveys. Self-reports [are] troubling to many researchers because people are not always valid assessors of their own skills (Jones and Nisbett 1987; Maki 1998; Winne et al. 2006). For example, people often claim to have skills that they do not have when the skills are valuable and desirable. Moreover, the explicitness of targeted skills as asked in surveys may compromise an intervention designed to promote these skills.... Alternatively, if completed post-task or at the conclusion of an experience or course, they require students to recall their perceptions, potentially introducing failures of memory. Surveys may not be sensitive enough to detect changes over time or across situations, possibly contributing to false assumptions about their relative stability within and/or across contexts.

The second approach to measuring noncognitive skills asks third parties (i.e. child psychologists, teachers, parents, siblings, etc.) to evaluate students' noncognitive skills. For example, in the Fast Track program that we analyze in the next chapter, teachers and experts evaluated children on their ability to control their emotions, thoughts, and behaviors and integrate within a classroom setting. Again, Shechtman et al. (2013, ix) explain that this approach comes with tradeoffs: "Advantages are that they can sidestep inherent biases of self-report and provide valuable data about learning processes. The main disadvantage is that these measures can often be highly resource-intensive – especially if they require training observers, time to complete extensive observations, and coding videos or field notes." Implicit biases linked to race or socioeconomic status can also plague third-party assessments (Boysen et al. 2009).

The final approach infers individuals' abilities from their observed behaviors, often (but not always) from administrative datasets. This can be done in a number of ways. First, scholars have shown that behavioral measures such as absences, tardies, and suspensions load on a common factor that is separate from cognitive ability and socioeconomic status (Holbein and Ladd 2017; Jackson 2018). The idea here is that individuals who exhibit these behaviors tend to have lower levels of self-control, independent of their underlying levels of intelligence or socioeconomic status. In a similar way, one may be able to generally infer noncognitive ability based on the gap between one's performance on standardized tests of cognitive aptitude and their performance in the classroom. Or, one might give an individual a tailored task to see whether and how well they complete that task; for example, to measure self-regulation one might give subjects a task to complete – say a survey or an unsolvable problem – and see how long they persist in that activity (Hitt, Trivitt, and Cheng 2016; Pitcairn and Wishart 1994).[8]

Some of these behavioral measures are quite creative; for example, in the "Reading the Mind in the Eyes" test individuals are asked to identify what emotions people are exhibiting based only on images of eyes. This approach has been used to capture individuals' ability to recognize and relate with others' emotions – a key component in being able to empathize with others (Baron-Cohen et al. 2001). Another common approach to measuring delayed gratification involves a revealed preference task that elicits how willing individuals are to wait (Fowler and Kam 2006; Schafer 2016). Shechtman et al. (2013, ix) explain the advantages and disadvantages of the observed-behaviors approach; "[The] advantage [is] the capacity to identify students who are struggling to persevere and new possibilities for rich longitudinal research. [The] disadvantage [is] that these records themselves do not provide rich information about individuals' experiences and nuances within learning environments that may have contributed to the outcomes reported in records."

Cognizant that there is no perfect way to measure noncognitive ability, we use all three of these measurement techniques in our own analyses. Each has their own limitations, but including all three techniques offers the most comprehensive approach to evaluating our expectations. We are careful to see if our results depend on the way noncognitive ability has been measured. We outline these specific measures in the subsequent section and the Appendix for this chapter.

[8] However, one has to be especially careful with how they use this completion task, as it has the chance to pick up on other constructs, like cognitive ability or (if, say, the survey is about political issues) political motivation.

3.2.1 Data about Noncognitive Skills

We use nine key data sources to explore the role of noncognitive ability in voting – a unique combination of longitudinal student surveys, school administrative records, and voter registration files. We outline these datasets in greater detail in the appendix of this chapter, but provide some highlights here.

Our nine datasets come from a mix of existing data sources, original data sources, and secondary data matched to voting records. These datasets include

- the Wisconsin Longitudinal Study (WLS),
- the National Longitudinal Survey of Youth of 1979 (NLSY79),
- the National Education Longitudinal Study of 1988 (NELS:88),
- the Fast Track Intervention,
- the National Longitudinal Study of Adolescent to Adult Health (Add Health),
- the National Longitudinal Survey of Youth of 1997 (NLSY97),
- the Education Longitudinal Study of 2002 (ELS:2002),
- the Wake County Public Schools System Longitudinal Student Engagement Survey (WCPSS), and
- a 2014 module of Cooperative Congressional Election Study (CCES).

Together, our nine data sources span seven decades and use a wide variety of ways of measuring noncognitive ability.[9] To our knowledge, no study of noncognitive skills – regardless of the outcome examined – has used data from this many sources. This is intentional: We want to be as

[9] Of the nine datasets, six are available for unrestricted public use. The WCPSS data used in this article is proprietary, and confidentiality agreements prohibit disclosure, as the data contains sensitive individual-level school records. However, interested scholars can apply for access through the WCPSS. For eligibility rules, restrictions, data security provisions, and how to apply to access the data, please contact the WCPSS Data, Research & Accountability Department (http://myworkplace.wcpss.net/d-and-a/index.htm). The Fast Track data is also proprietary and confidentiality agreements prohibit disclosure, as the information contained therein includes sensitive information about program participants. However, interested scholars can apply for access through the Fast Track organization. For eligibility rules, restrictions, data security provisions, and how to apply to access the data, please visit: http://fasttrackproject.org/request-use-data.php. The Add Health data are publicly available; however, we have a restricted-access license. Public versions of the data contain a 50 percent sample of the entire restricted-access file. To apply for the restricted-access data, please visit: www.cpc.unc.edu/projects/addhealth/documentation/restricteduse.

comprehensive as possible in exploring whether or not noncognitive skills help contribute to voting.

Among these nine datasets, one – the National Longitudinal Study of Adolescent to Adult Health (Add Health) – receives particular attention given its unique sample size, richness, and design features. As we discuss in more detail in the next chapter, the Add Health data contain a diverse set of control variables and a sample design that allows us to account for a host of unobserved confounders at the family and neighborhood level. We use the data in this chapter to describe the characteristics of noncognitive skills and to compare our measure to other individual-level characteristics known to predict turnout. Additional analysis of our noncognitive measures in our other data sources can be found in the Appendix.

Add Health is a high-quality longitudinal study that has been used in publications across a variety of disciplines and research topics, including a handful of political behavior topics (e.g. Fowler, Baker, and Dawes 2008). Wave 1 of this national probability sample of adolescents was conducted during the 1994–1995 school year. Within sampled schools, students in grades 7–12 were invited to complete an in-school questionnaire, with a random subset given an in-home interview. In total, the first wave included 20,745 students.[10] The original cohort of students has been followed through three subsequent in-home interview waves, the most recent occurring in 2008–2009, when subjects were twenty-five to thirty-three years old.[11]

The Add Health data allow us to build a scale that captures individuals' adolescent noncognitive skills using nine survey items (some reverse-coded) related to self-regulation.[12] These items include:

- **Item 1:** "When you get what you want, it's usually because you worked hard for it"
- **Item 2:** "You can pretty much determine what will happen in your life"
- **Item 3:** "You usually go out of your way to avoid having to deal with problems in your life (reverse coded)"
- **Item 4:** "When you have a problem to solve, one of the first things you do is get as many facts about the problem as possible"

[10] The Wave 1 in-home questionnaire response rate was 79 percent.

[11] Panel attrition was quite low given the duration of time between waves. In Wave 4, 79 percent of the remaining eligible panelists were interviewed.

[12] Doing so offers the cleanest test of the direct link between noncognitive skills and turnout, but given likely correlation with measures of interpersonal skills, we also examine the potential mechanisms for the observed relationship in the next chapter.

- **Item 5:** "When you are attempting to find a solution to a problem, you usually try to think of as many different ways to approach the problem as possible"
- **Item 6:** "When making decisions, you generally use a systematic method for judging and comparing alternatives"
- **Item 7:** "After carrying out a solution to a problem, you usually try to analyze what went right and what went wrong"
- **Item 8:** "You are assertive"
- **Item 9:** "When making decisions, you usually go with your 'gut feeling' without thinking too much about the consequences of each alternative (reverse coded)"

The resulting scale combines to capture individuals' ability to (1) plan for and assess a task at hand, (2) believe that they have the capacity to complete that task, and (3) put in the effort needed to actually finish what they set out to do. It conceptually and empirically captures the combination of self-regulation and effortfulness that we expect predicts one's ability to follow through on their behavioral intentions.[13] Together, these items create a scale that has an acceptable level of reliability (Cronbach's $\alpha = 0.6$; $\alpha = 0.7$ if we omit reverse coded items), loads on a single factor (Eigen 1: 1.8, Eigen 2: 0.3), and benchmarks well with other measures of noncognitive ability. Indeed, there are overlaps with our Add Health scale and the Duckworth Grit Scale (Duckworth et al. 2007). Using a sample recruited through Amazon's Mechanical Turk platform, we explicitly compared the Add Health scale with the Duckworth Grit Scale – an increasingly-used proxy for individuals' noncognitive abilities – to make sure we were tapping into a similar construct. Empirical checks suggests that we were. The combined scale had a Cronbach's $\alpha = 0.88$, the β from a bivariate OLS model predicting Duckworth from the Add Health scale was $\beta = 0.8$ ($p < 0.01$), and the Pearson's r was 0.63 ($p < 0.01$).[14] The close overlaps between scales are consistent with our broader categorization of noncognitive abilities as a family of related attributes.

Add Health's measure of noncognitive skills also has considerable variability. When rescaled to range from 0 to 1, our noncognitive skills scale

[13] These individual items have been used in the past to measure noncognitive abilities (e.g. Paternoster and Pogarsky 2009).

[14] Results come from an MTurk survey of 400 conducted in May 2015; additional details reported in the Appendix. Reported statistics are from items administered with equivalent response categories on a five point scale ranging from "very much like me" to "not like me at all." As a reference point, when we measured the Duckworth scale items among WCPSS students one year apart (8th graders in 2015 were administered the survey as 9th graders in 2016; to our knowledge, the only panel measure of the grit score available), the Pearson's r was 0.60, without any corrections for measurement error.

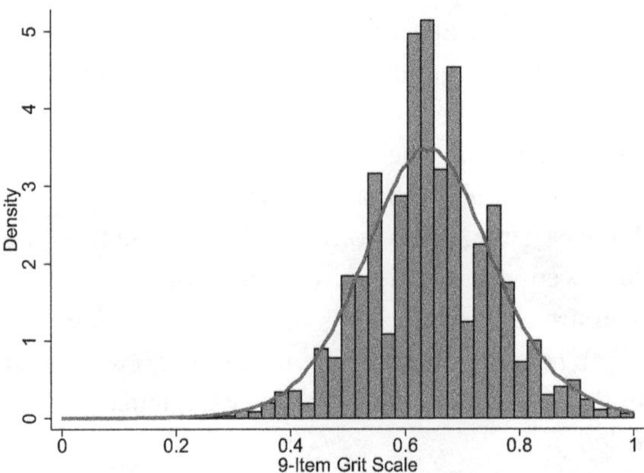

FIGURE 3.1 Distribution of the Add Health Noncognitive Skill Scale
The distribution of the Add Health grit scale with a normal distribution overlaid.

has a mean of 0.64, median of 0.63, and standard deviation of 0.11.[15] Figure 3.1 shows the distribution of the Add Health noncognitive abilities scale. As can be seen, the scale is slightly skewed toward higher values; though this is consistent with other studies using similar scales (e.g. Holbein et al. Forthcoming). This pattern is consistent across our other datasets, as shown in the Appendix to this chapter.

3.3 WHAT NONCOGNITIVE SKILLS ARE NOT

Although there remains some inherent murkiness about what exactly noncognitive skills are, we can more clearly say what they are not. A reasonable question about noncognitive skills – especially in light of their conceptual messiness – is if they are in fact a proxy for some factor already recognized as a predictor of political participation. In this section, we use the Add Health data to look empirically at the relationship between our measure of noncognitive skills and other individual-level characteristics, including cognitive ability, socioeconomic status, race, and personality measures.

3.3.1 Comparison to Cognitive Ability and Socioeconomic Status

We start by examining the relationship between noncognitive skills, cognitive skills, and socioeconomic status. It is well-documented that more privileged students perform better on achievement tests – so much so that measures of income are sometimes considered proxies for

[15] By racial group, the mean (standard deviation): White 0.64 (0.11), Black 0.65 (0.11), Asian 0.65 (0.10), Other 0.64 (0.11).

cognitive skills (Sirin 2005; White 1982). This strong correlation between socioeconomic status and cognitive skills raises obvious questions about how measures of socioeconomic status relate to noncognitive skills. Figure 3.2 – a correlation heatmap – plots the relationship between noncognitive skills and other individual-level characteristics related to cognitive ability and socioeconomic status.

Figure 3.2 shows that noncognitive ability is only weakly related ($r =$ 0.11) to cognitive ability – measured through the Add Health Picture Vocabulary Test, which captures competencies in logic, reasoning, memory, and word skills. Figure 3.2 also shows that noncognitive ability is only weakly correlated with measures of family income ($r =$ 0.02) and mother's education ($r =$ 0.07). In contrast, cognitive ability's is more strongly related to socioeconomic status.

This distinctness is not just an Add Health phenomena; empirical evidence from other datasets also supports a similar conclusion.

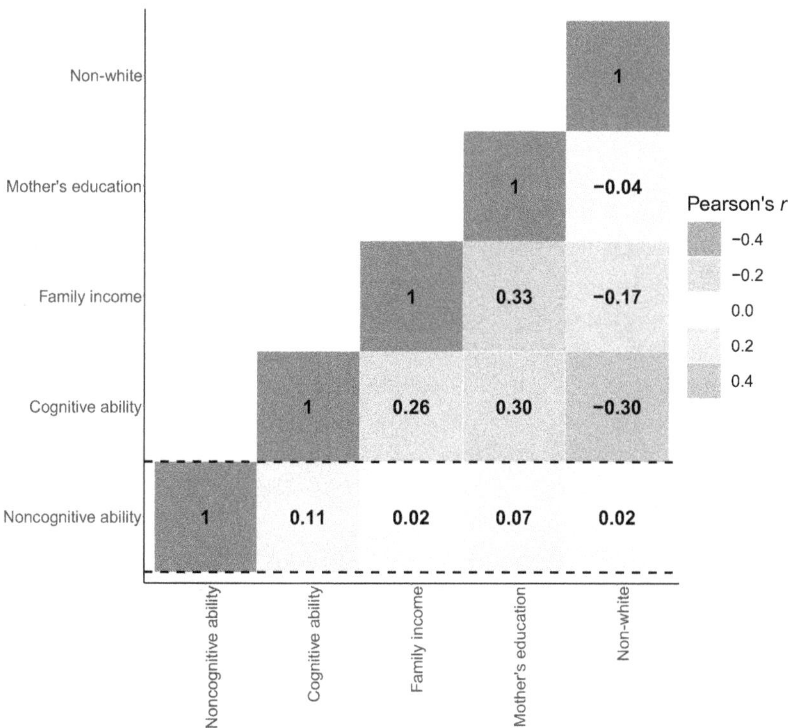

FIGURE 3.2 Correlations with other individual characteristics

This heatmap displays the correlation between noncognitive skills and various variables capturing race, socioeconomic status, and cognitive ability from the Add Health sample. The numbers in the cells are the Pearson r correlation coefficients. For a longer list of correlations with noncognitive skills, see Table A.1 in the Appendix.

For example, previous scholars have documented time and time again with multiple diverse data sources that measures of cognitive ability/ socioeconomic status and measures of noncognitive ability load onto separate factors (Heckman, Stixrud, and Urzua 2006; Jackson 2018; Park et al. 2017; Sorensen and Dodge 2016). We replicate this finding in the Appendix for this chapter, where we show that all our measures of noncognitive ability are distinct from these other two foundational constructs. Another way to see the distinctness of these constructs is to look at fMRI studies, which show that noncognitive and cognitive abilities require different areas and networks within the human brain (e.g. Yang and Raine 2009). Moreover, as we show in the next chapter measures of individuals' noncognitive ability also predict a number of adult outcomes (education, income, health, etc.) above and beyond measures of cognitive ability (Farrington et al. 2012). Finally, as our own evidence will show, various noncognitive measures are simultaneously improved through intervention, even as cognitive ability remains stable (Bierman et al. 2011).

Relevant to this discussion is the distinctiveness between cognitive and noncognitive skills in terms of their malleability. Earlier we provided evidence that noncognitive skills are malleable into early adulthood. However, the malleability of cognitive abilities is much less clear; indeed, a long literature has evaluated just how malleable cognitive abilities are. On the one hand, human intelligence is often viewed as a fixed trait (e.g. Deary, Johnson, and Houlihan 2009; McClearn et al. 1997; Neisser et al. 1996). Recently, however, others have argued that cognitive aptitude is actually quite malleable (Dweck 2000, 2006; Dweck and Leggett 1988; Mueller and Dweck 1998). Striking somewhat of a middle ground, James Heckman and his colleague conclude that "what used to be regarded as traits fixed at conception are now understood to be skills that can be augmented through guidance and instruction. Raw intelligence is not fixed solely by parental genes, although heritability plays an important role" (Heckman and Kautz 2013, 6).[16]

Cognitive abilities appear to be more difficult to move in a meaningful way over the long-term. Short of large programs targeted very early in the

[16] In a recent meta-analysis, Ritchie and Tucker-Drob (2018) provide evidence from various quasi-experimental techniques that an additional year of education increases "cognitive abilities [by] approximately 1 to 5 IQ points." They conclude that "education appears to be the most consistent, robust, and durable method yet to be identified for raising intelligence." While this would suggest malleability, we note the overall modest size of these effects and the fact that the authors specifically frame these effects as an upper bound.

life course, cognitive ability rarely moves substantively for an extended period of time (Kautz et al. 2014). And, even when large early life investments are made, cognitive ability often remains rigidly in place, or, at best, improves for a short time but then returns to its original levels. For example, several of the multifaceted interventions discussed previously were aimed at improving both cognitive and noncognitive skills, but often showed more success in moving noncognitive competencies. For example, the Nurse Family Partnership cited earlier as being effective at improving noncognitive skill development had limited long-term effect on cognitive ability (Olds et al. 1997). Similarly, follow ups of the seminal Perry Preschool study show that immediate gains in cognitive ability quickly tapered off to levels indistinguishable from the control group (Borghans et al. 2008; Heckman and Masterov 2007; Heckman, Stixrud, and Urzua 2006). A similar tapering-off can be seen with the Fast Track program (Bierman et al. 2011) that we use in our analyses and, to a lesser extent, with the Head Start program (Currie and Thomas 1995). This phenomenon is not limited to the United States. In fact, one recent study concluded that despite early childhood education in the United Kingdom having durable effects on noncognitive skills, effects on cognitive ability fade by the time an individual is eleven years old (Cornelissen and Dustmann 2019). In a systematic review of the literature, Kautz et al. (2014) conclude that "noncognitive skills are more malleable … than cognitive skills." This distinction is critical: *even if* cognitive ability appears to be a stronger predictor of later-life outcomes, cognitive aptitude may have limited use in efforts to improve those outcomes, given its rigidity.

In sum, existing empirical research indicates that noncognitive skills are distinct from cognitive ability and socioeconomic status. Moreover, it shows that cognitive skills are less malleable than noncognitive skills, which the reviewed research shows can be developed or reinforced through targeted intervention.

3.3.2 Comparison to Personality

We are also able to explore the relationship between noncognitive skills and personality measures in the Add Health data. The most common and reliable measure of personality is called the Big Five personality test, which captures the characteristics of openness, conscientiousness, extraversion, agreeableness, and neuroticism. Not surprisingly, some noncognitive measures are conceptually linked to some of the Big Five personality dimensions (Dawes et al. 2014; Gerber et al. 2011; Littvay,

Weith, and Dawes 2011; Mondak 2010; Mondak et al. 2010). Indeed, both tend to be measured using similar techniques and related metrics (the most common way to measure the Big Five is through survey self-reports). However, there are several reasons to treat these two types of attributes as conceptually distinct.

First, while there is an empirical relationship between measures of noncognitive ability and the Big Five, it is quite variable and often fairly weak. For example, estimates of the relationship between noncognitive skills and conscientiousness vary considerably across data sets: In the Add Health data the correlation is low ($r = 0.12$); see Table A.1, but others find a stronger relationship: $r = 0.44$ (Ivcevic and Brackett 2014), and $r = 0.77$ (Duckworth et al. 2007). Economic research consistently finds that noncognitive factors are predictive of various outcomes even when conditioning on the Big Five (Bandura et al. 2001; Caprara, Alessandri, and Eisenberg 2012; Duckworth et al. 2007; Park et al. 2017). Moreover, the observed relationship between personality measures and turnout is quite mixed, with the theoretical links quite under-developed. For example, research finds inconsistent relationships between conscientiousness and voter turnout – sometimes positive effects (indirectly channeled through civic duty), but other times null or even negative effects (Gerber et al. 2011). Nonetheless, we include measures of the Big Five in our analyses when available.

Beyond the clear empirical distinction revealed in our analysis, there is also an inherent conceptual one. Political science research using the Big Five often views personality traits as stable *traits* (Gerber et al. 2011, 265), even "biologically influenced and enduring" (Mondak et al. 2010, 6). In contrast, the literature on noncognitive attributes conceptualizes these additional attributes as *skills* that "are not set in stone at birth" but are instead teachable (Heckman and Kautz 2013, 4). Put differently, while Big Five research strives to describe *who one is*, research on noncognitive attributes describes *what one can do*.[17] This is a broader assumption that deserves elaboration and empirical justification, so we next turn to a discussion of the needed separation from (or updating to) the conceptual framework regarding the potential malleability of psychological attributes.

[17] Some Big Five scholars have held out hope that psychological characteristics could be improved (e.g. Bandura et al. 2001; Caprara, Alessandri, and Eisenberg 2012) and some scholars of noncognitive abilities and personality traits have suggested that these attributes' malleability "lies on a spectrum" (Kautz et al. 2014, 8).

3.4 MEASURING AND TESTING THE EFFECT OF NONCOGNITIVE SKILLS

Our analysis evaluating the link between noncognitive abilities and voter turnout draws its evidence from a unique combination of longitudinal student surveys, school administrative records, and voter registration files. These come from a mix of existing data sources, original data sources, and existing data sources that we have matched to voting records.

Our nine data sources vary in the sample that they target; however, each pairs measures of individuals' noncognitive abilities with measures of voter turnout.[18] The specific measures of noncognitive abilities vary across data sets, although many of them have been used in previous research examining the effects of noncognitive skills (often a specific attribute like "grit") on other nonvoting outcomes (e.g. Dee and West 2011; Deming 2017; Duckworth et al. 2007; Heckman, Stixrud, and Urzua 2006). While each sample measures different aspects of individuals' noncognitive ability, they all pick up a latent ability dimension that is separate from cognitive ability (and socioeconomic status, for that matter) – a point we show later. We describe the specifics of the measures in each data set in this chapter, but we broadly label them as noncognitive skills. We do so to avoid the jingle-jangle fallacy mentioned earlier (Kelley 1927). As we will show, these measures typically overlap with one another both conceptually and empirically. The core point is to realize that we are capturing components of latent individual ability separate from measures of cognitive skills.

Table 3.1 provides a brief overview of the key data sources that we use in the observational analysis in the next chapter. The WLS uses the self-reported approach to measuring noncognitive ability. Respondents were asked a battery of questions designed to measure their levels of individual autonomy, environmental mastery, positive relations to others, general self-efficacy, and tenacious goal pursuit, to name a few. Likewise, the NLSY79 uses self-reports to measure noncognitive ability. This dataset contains the Rotter Locus of Control scale and the Rosenberg Self-Efficacy Scale, both of which have been used in the past to measure noncognitive ability (e.g. Deming 2017; Heckman, Stixrud, and Urzua 2006). The NELS:88 is unique in that it uses all three types of measurement strategies – survey self-reports, observed behavioral measures of

[18] Reassuringly, the data sets are not primarily political surveys. We have concerns that seemingly "nonpolitical" variables – such as the Big Five personality items – are hard to view as nonpolitical when measured in the context of a 180-minute survey about politics.

TABLE 3.1 *Overview of data sources measuring noncognitive ability and voting*

Data source	*N*	IV: Noncognitive skills (source)	Citations for IV	DV: Voting measure (source)	Sibling/ twin/etc.
WLS (1957)	≈10,300	Self-control/ Social (self)	Henselmans et al. (2011) Herd et al. (2014)	2000–2012 (validated; Catalist)	Sibling
NLSY79 (1979)	≈12,700	Self-control (self)	Heckman, Stixrud, and Urzua (2006); Heckman et al. (2018)	2006 (self)	No
NELS:88	≈12,000	Self-control (self and teacher/ behavioral)	Dee and West (2011)	1992–1996 (self)	No
Add Health (1995)	≈20,000	Self-control (self)	Paternoster and Pogarsky (2009)	2000, 2008 (self)	Sibling
NLSY97	≈8,900	Self-control (self)	Deming (2017)	2004–2010 (self)	No
ELS:2002	≈16,000	Self-control (self/teacher)	Fredricks (2012)	2004–2011 (self)	No
Adult Sample (2014)	≈1,000	Self-control/ Social	Duckworth et al. (2007)	Validated vote	No
WCPSS (2015–2016)	≈50,000	Grit (self)	Duckworth et al. (2007)	Vote intentions	Sibling/ twin/ individual
Fast Track (1992)	≈900	Self-control (teacher/behavioral)	Sorensen and Dodge (2016) Holbein (2017)	2004–2012 (validated; state-files)	RCT

Table 3.1 provides an overview of the data sources we use in Chapter 4. The first column lists the data source, the second gives the reader an idea of the sample size, the third outlines the noncognitive measure used, the fourth provides citations for the noncognitive skill measure we use, the fifth outlines the voting data that we use as our outcome, and the last provides information on whether the data includes information on siblings, twins, or individuals themselves over time.

students' levels of absenteeism and tardiness, and teacher-evaluations of students' levels of behavioral control, task completion, and attention control. The NLSY97 uses the self-report technique for measuring levels of effortful control. The Add Health data uses measures of self-regulation from self-reports as discussed earlier in this chapter. The ELS:2002 contains both self- and teacher-evaluations of noncognitive ability. The 2014 CCES survey has self-reported measures of grit, emotion control, and sociability. In an original data collection effort, we administered a survey to a large sample of students in the Wake County Public School System (WCPSS) – one of the largest and most diverse school districts in the United States. This longitudinal survey contained questions used to elicit students' noncognitive abilities (Duckworth et al. 2007) and their levels of civic and political participation. This dataset contained these measures from children as early as fifth grade and as late as ninth grade and was matched to school administrative records. We provide further detail regarding the samples, measures, and methods in the Appendix for this chapter, including the specific measures that go into the scales that we use to create our measures of noncognitive ability. Table A.2 summarizes the measures that go into our composite noncognitive scale for each study.

Table 3.1 also shows that our measures of voting likewise vary across data sources. When possible, we rely on measures of validated voting – indicators of turnout from official government records. Other times we have only self-reported voting, and in our study of younger students, future voting intention. As we show later, regardless of how we measure voting, the results remain largely the same. Finally, we note that most of these data sources include a longitudinal component, thus allowing us to place time-ordering between our independent and dependent variables: a prerequisite in approaching causal inferences (Angrist and Pischke 2008) and one that allows us to explore the role of pre-voting attributes for later-life voting – an area in which there is a paucity of contemporary research (Almond and Verba 2015; Niemi and Hepburn 1995; Sapiro 2004).

The last column in Table 3.1 indicates the methodological techniques available in each of our datasets. Though we outline these methods in greater detail in Chapter 4, we provide a quick overview here as well. Given the relative lack of research linking noncognitive abilities and voting, we start by focusing on whether any observational relationship exists using observational analyses. This does not reflect our indifference toward causality in any way. On the contrary, we care very much about whether noncognitive abilities truly influence turnout, or instead reflect other factors or processes. While we firmly believe in the value of field-experimental approaches for studying political behavior, we simultaneously recognize that these tools might not be necessarily ideal for evaluating new theories of voting. Moreover, experiments that directly change noncognitive skills take a lot of time and money, with many of these starting in childhood and following individuals into adulthood. In seeking to understand the role noncognitive attributes play (or do not play), the first step is to determine whether an observational relationship does or does not exist.

With our observational analyses, we will control for possible confounders available in each data set. For example, all analyses with the Add Health data include the following model controls: educational attainment and verbal skills, the standard measures of cognitive ability, which are often presumed to explain the enduring relationship between education and turnout (Denny and Doyle 2008).[19] Cognitive ability is not only recognized as a key predictor of voter participation in the political science literature but also the most common foil for noncognitive skills in that literature (e.g. Duckworth et al. 2007). We also control for the standard NEO-FFI scales of the Big Five – openness to experience, conscientiousness, extraversion, agreeableness, and neuroticism (McCrae and Costa 1989). Church attendance and income help to capture the respondent's level of social connectivity, another potential confounder for the relationship between educational attainment and turnout (Nie, Junn, and Stehlik-Barry 1996).[20] In our models, we also include data quality controls to ensure that the observed patterns are not an artifact of attentiveness to the survey.[21] We might be concerned, for instance, that individuals with weaker noncognitive skills were also less attentive to the survey – i.e., more likely to satisfice in answering questions.[22]

[19] Measured in W1 using the Peabody Picture Vocabulary Test (Dunn and Dunn 2007).

[20] The results remain the same if we use religiosity in W1 instead of church attendance in W4.

[21] Indeed, survey data quality measures have been previously used as behavioral proxies for conscientiousness (Hitt, Trivitt, and Cheng 2016). Our controls include an indicator for straight-lined responses on the grit items and indicators for item nonresponse on the following items: cognitive ability, mother's education, initial grade in school, and income.

[22] Panel attrition in the survey was reasonable ($\approx$ 21 percent). Included in the models are the most common predictors of panel attrition (Frankel and Hillygus 2013). Reassuringly, we also find similar results across different survey waves.

We also include a wide range of individual-level demographics and geographic/contextual variables.[23] In addition, we include the best available proxies for political motivation. First, we include ideological strength as our closest direct measure of a respondent's political interest.[24] Second, we include commonly used proxies for parental political interest – family income and mother's education (e.g. Nadeau, Niemi, and Amato 1995).

In addition to controlling for a host of observable characteristics, we are able to go one step further and leverage design features that allow us to identify siblings, twins, and individuals themselves over time. Among nonexperimental studies of nonpolitical characteristics, these are some of the strongest robustness checks that can be run, as they control for a host of unobservable factors that conditional-on-observables approaches cannot. As such, these modeling techniques are commonly used to eliminate many sources of potential bias. Only after doing so do we turn to experimental evidence that links noncognitive skills and voting. In the second part of Chapter 4, we provide evidence from a small-scale experiment and a large-scale experiment that we analyze ourselves, as well as a set of experiments run by others. These help us explore the potential mechanisms linking noncognitive skills and voter participation, and provide us policy-relevant information about whether investing in noncognitive skills has an effect on voting.

Together, these multiple measurement techniques, samples, and design tools provide us with multiple ways to examine the relationship between noncognitive skills and voting.

23 Geographic controls measured at the census tract level include population, % urban, % white, % Hispanic, median age, standard deviation of age, % males never married, fertility rate, abortions per 1,000, residential stability, % foreign born, death rate per 1,000, infant death per 1,000, low birth weight, % in shelters, % in correctional institutions, % in college dormitories, median household income, standard deviation of household income, % houses on public assistance, % below poverty, % with HS diploma, prop with college degree, unemployment rate, % employed in construction, median *N* houses built, prop of houses moved into, % at-risk school children, total physicians per 100,000, total arrests per 100,000, % of population that is religiously adherent, % conservative, % voting Republican in 1992, and the % of state spending toward education.

24 Unfortunately, Add Health does not have a direct measure of political interest or political knowledge. Our results remain the same if we include belonging to a political party or majoring in political science in college – imperfect, but still useful proxies of these constructs.

3.5 THE BIG PICTURE

In this chapter, we have introduced the concept of noncognitive skills and have shown that they consist of a constellation of abilities, beliefs, and strategies related to self-regulation, effortfulness, and interpersonal interactions. Previous research has used a variety of methods and metrics to measure noncognitive skills, albeit often with different individual scales and items. We show that various noncognitive constructs closely hang together, but are separate from cognitive ability and personality. Noncognitive abilities have received less attention in studies of political behavior than have constructs like political interest, political knowledge, and cognitive ability, which have played a central role in explanations for what makes people vote. We have argued that there are reasons to suspect that these noncognitive skills are a critical resource that helps to determine who votes and who does not. We turn to our empirical test of this hypothesis in the next chapter.

4

Evidence Noncognitive Skills Increase Voting

We have argued that political motivation is not sufficient to get young people to engage in politics. Most young people *want* to participate and *intend* to do so, but many fail to actually *follow through* on their political goals or ambitions. We contend that a missing piece of the puzzle is noncognitive abilities – competencies involving self-regulation, effortfulness, and interpersonal skills. Among other things, these attributes are foundational in helping individuals overcome the obstacles, barriers, and distractions that can stand in the way of turning their civic attitudes into civic action.

In the last chapter, we explored what noncognitive skills are and what they are not, discussed the tricky issues involved with measuring these skills, and outlined the datasets that we use to test our expectations. In this chapter we use the multiple data sources outlined in the last chapter to examine the impact of noncognitive skills on voter participation. We show that the observed relationship cannot be explained by other well-known predictors of political participation, like political interest, cognitive ability, parental involvement, socioeconomic status, and other relevant, but difficult to observe, individual and contextual factors. We provide further experimental evidence, which shows that noncognitive skills can be taught or reinforced in schools, with increases in these attributes leading to noticeable downstream increases in voter turnout. Finally, we test for potential mediators and moderators in the relationship of interest.

We cover a lot of ground in this chapter – evaluating our hypothesis across multiple data sources, diverse methodological techniques, and various robustness checks. The conclusions all point to the same conclusion: Noncognitive skills help to make young voters.

4.1 METHODOLOGICAL APPROACH

Given the imperfect nature of the available data and the challenges of the empirical task at hand, no single dataset or methodological approach can concretely answer the question of whether and how noncognitive skills influence voter participation. As such, we use multiple methodological approaches to give a clearer picture of the robustness of conclusions across different assumptions, measures, and datasets.

Following the lead of research on noncognitive skills in other disciplines, we leverage a variety of observational and experimental methods to evaluate the impact of noncognitive skills on youth turnout. As with that literature, we start with observational comparisons (Cunha and Heckman 2007; Cunha, Heckman, and Schennach 2010; Heckman 2000) and then move to experimental ones (Kautz et al. 2014). This approach also resembles the standard phasing of medical research – in which the initial step focuses on evaluating whether a relationship exists and then experimental methods are used to better evaluate the nature of the relationship, evaluating the effect in smaller-scale survey experiments and, eventually, in larger interventions (Lieberman 2016). Our view is that exploring the relevance of noncognitive skills for political participation requires models with the best possible controls, panel methods, natural experiments, short-run randomized control experiments, and larger, more expensive longer-term randomized control experiments. Even with all of these different analyses, it is not our intention to provide the last word on the topic; rather, we hope to provoke a broader inquiry in political science – similar to that which is being had in economics, psychology, and education research – as to when and how noncognitive abilities matter.

4.1.1 Observational Methods

Our observational analyses draw on nine different datasets: the National Longitudinal Study of Adolescent to Adult Health (Add Health), the Wisconsin Longitudinal Study (WLS), the National Longitudinal Survey of Youth of 1979 (NLSY79), the National Education Longitudinal Study of 1988 (NELS:88), the Fast Track Intervention, the National Longitudinal Survey of Youth of 1997 (NLSY97), the Education Longitudinal Study of 2002 (ELS:2002), the Wake County Public Schools System Longitudinal Student Engagement Survey (WCPSS), and the Cooperative Congressional Election Study (CCES). Details on the samples and measures can be found in Chapter 3 and the Appendix to that chapter. As in Chapter 3, a great deal of our analysis will focus on the National Longitudinal Study of Adolescent to Adult Health (Add Health) because of its large sample size, rich set of covariates, and unique design that allows us to account for a host of unobserved confounders at the family and neighborhood level.

In our observational data, we do our best to move beyond simple correlations and approach causality as close as is possible. To evaluate the importance of noncognitive skills for political participation, we employ a number of identification strategies. We first start with models that control for the standard predictors of political participation – such as age, educational attainment, socioeconomic status, political interest, and, importantly, cognitive ability. These models allow us to rule out some of the standard alternative explanations of voting participation. While these models allow us to account for factors previously shown to predict voter participation, they are limited in that they do not control for unobservable characteristics that might influence both noncognitive skills and voting, such as one's life and school experiences, personal networks, or complex set of individual motivations.

To help purge out these potential sources of bias and further approach causality, we leverage design features available in a few of our datasets. Specifically, we are able to leverage comparisons between siblings (in the WLS, Add Health, and WCPSS datasets), twin pairs (in the WCPSS dataset), and across individuals themselves over time (in the WCPSS dataset). These modeling approaches include either family fixed effects, twin pair fixed effects, or individual fixed effects (respectively). For those unfamiliar with these approaches, fixed effects force comparisons to be made within groups. For example, in a model with family fixed effects we are making comparisons within families – that is, we compare the voting patterns of siblings who have higher noncognitive abilities to siblings with lower noncognitive abilities. As a result, these fixed effect models absorb difficult to observe factors that remain constant within these groups.

There are a number of advantages to this modeling approach. The sibling fixed effect model accounts for a host of shared observable (e.g. socioeconomic status; political socialization; family members' levels of political interest or political motivation; political discussion within families; family members' levels of engagement; parents' cognitive and noncognitive ability; etc.) and unobservable (e.g. parenting style and personality; shared inherited personality traits; etc.) factors that remain constant within families. Some political behavior studies have deemed this method sufficient to infer causality (e.g. Burden et al. 2017), and it is commonly used in education studies when randomization is not readily available (Ashenfelter and Zimmerman 1997; Currie and Thomas 1995). Still, this approach comes with assumptions and limitations – having a limited ability, for example, to account for features that are not shared within siblings.

Hence, to go one step further, we estimate models among twin pairs in the data source in which that is available (WCPSS).[1] This allows us to account for another batch of observed and unobserved factors that may be biasing our relationship of interest. This approach accounts for some of the factors that sibling models do not – forcing comparisons within individuals with the exact same age and cohort, for example (Freedman, Collier, and Sekhon 2010, chapter 15; Hart et al. 2009; Medland and Hatemi 2009). As such, this approach has often been used in studies exploring the relationship between personality traits and political behavior (e.g. Fowler, Baker, and Dawes 2008). While longitudinal datasets that contain measures of noncognitive ability and voting among twins are few and far between, we are able to use our original WCPSS data to make this comparison.[2]

Given that even twin pair studies have limitations (Charney and English 2012), as a final robustness check, we leverage the fact that we have an individual-level panel component embedded in the WCPSS data from Waves I and II. With this data, we are able to estimate individual fixed-effects models that approach causality even more so than the sibling and twin pair models. These models take advantage of growth and depreciation in individuals' levels of noncognitive ability

[1] Add Health has twin pairs; however, their sample is considerably smaller than what one would want to use to have adequate statistical power to test relationship of interest. We note that controlling for age in our sibling fixed effect specification likely achieves the same objective as twin pair models, as virtually all siblings born in the same year are likely twins. (This approach does not allow us to account for zygosity.) In both the Add Health and the WLS data, such an analysis results in the same conclusion.

[2] In the WCPSS data, there are about 30,000 siblings and 1,700 twins (1.8% of the sample). The prevalence of twins in our sample is roughly equivalent to what can be observed nationally in the United States (about 2–3 percent, according to National Vital Statistics). Siblings and twins are identified based on home address and, in the case of twins, being born on the same day, month, and year. Thus, we are unable to distinguish step-siblings, half-siblings, or unrelated children living in the same household with the same birthday. We also cannot account for the zygosity in twins.

over time.[3] Given the individual-level panel nature of our data, the individual fixed-effect approach might be thought of as analogous to a difference-in-difference specification. In this case, (roughly speaking) the first difference is between individuals whose noncognitive abilities change over time (i.e. the "treatment" group) and the second difference is between those that do not (i.e. the "control" group). This difference-in-difference is especially powerful as it controls for *all* observable and unobservable factors that remain constant within individuals over time. For example, given the stability of genetic features and personality traits over time (Cobb-Clark and Schurer 2012; Mondak 2010; Soldz and Vaillant 1999), our individual fixed-effects models will absorb all of these. This provides a very stringent robustness check in exploring the relationship between noncognitive ability and voter turnout; indeed, among nonexperimental studies of individual characteristics, this is one of the strongest robustness checks that can be run. Given its virtues, this approach has often been used in education studies that lack randomization (e.g. Hanushek, Kain, and Rivkin 2004; Ladd, Clotfelter, and Holbein 2017). However, to our knowledge, this strict specification has rarely (if ever) been leveraged in observational designs to study citizens' propensity to vote. Admittedly, while the individual fixed-effect approach is not perfect (it does not absorb time-varying individual-level unobserved heterogeneity), it goes a long way toward accounting for unobserved factors that may bias our estimates. With this final check, we are able to make our observational estimates as causally robust as possible.

While each of these approaches has their own limitations, together they provide us a variety of different ways to look at the relationship between noncognitive abilities and voter turnout.

4.2 OBSERVATIONAL RESULTS

We start by evaluating the role of noncognitive skills for voter turnout in the Add Health data, a longitudinal study of a nationally representative sample of adolescents in grades 7–12 in the United States during the 1994–1995 school year. The Add Health data include measures of individuals'

[3] The Pearson's r of the Duckworth grit scale among repeat survey takers was 0.60 – indicating a relationship at the individual level, but also a substantial number of individuals whose grit changed meaningfully over time. While the average change from one year to the next is approximately 0 (on our 0–1 scale), there is a substantial amount of variation over time. The standard deviation for change is 0.14.

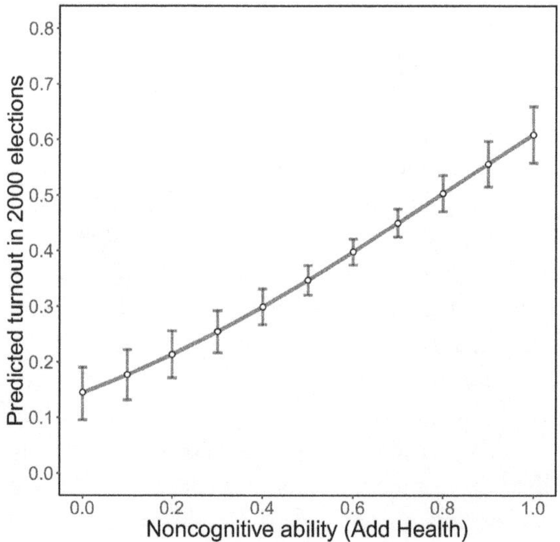

FIGURE 4.1 Bivariate relationship between noncognitive ability and turnout (Add Health)

Predicted turnout values from a simple bivariate model relating turnout in 2000 to noncognitive ability. Bars represent 95 percent confidence intervals.

noncognitive abilities using a self-reported scale that captures individual grit, perseverance, hard work, determination, and systematic thinking.

Our first results show the naive bivariate relationship between noncognitive ability and voter turnout. This gives a first glance at whether individuals with high and with low noncognitive ability differ in terms of their voter turnout. Figure 4.1 shows the predictive relationship between noncognitive ability and voter participation from an OLS model with no controls. It plots predicted probabilities from this model (the circles in the figure) as well as 95 percent confidence intervals (bars) from this model. As can be seen, there is a strong empirical relationship between noncognitive ability measured in the 1994–1995 school year and self-reported turnout in the 2000 presidential election. Individuals at the top end of the ability spectrum vote at a rate 40 percentage points above those at the low end ($p < 0.01$). This relationship holds – and is very similar in terms of substantive magnitude – across voting in presidential and local elections.[4] This difference in rates of self-reported voter participation is

4 Though not as strong in terms of sample composition and controls available, we find a similarly sized bivariate relationship among Mechanical Turk workers (68.5 percentage points).

striking. It shows that people with greater noncognitive skills are more likely to vote – and dramatically so.

To be clear, we cannot interpret this bivariate relationship as a causal one as there are surely omitted factors that help to account for variation in both noncognitive skills and turnout. We thus next look to see if the relationship holds once we account for a variety of observable factors. To test the robustness of the relationship and its sensitivity to the controls included, we estimate models with several control combinations. The individual controls in our Model 1 are cognitive ability, political motivation, mother's education, education, parents' income, gender, and church attendance.[5] This model allows us to control for the standard foil of noncognitive ability – cognitive skills – and one of the strongest predictors of political participation – political motivation – along with the core demographics known to predict voting. The controls in Model 2 are those in Model 1 plus measures of the Big Five: conscientiousness, extraversion, agreeableness, openness to experience, and neuroticism. This allows us to see whether our relationship of interest is actually explained by personality traits, separate characteristics that have already explored in voter turnout research (Gerber et al. 2011; Mondak 2010; Mondak et al. 2010). The controls in Model 3 are those in Model 2 plus census-tract controls for population, urban/rural, race/ethnicity, age, marriage rates, socioeconomic status, health, ideology, and religiosity, to name a few. This allows us to see whether any relationship we observe is really picking up on social context.

These model results are presented in Figure 4.2, which reports average marginal estimates across the distribution of noncognitive ability. To show our results, we use a coefficient plot, where the estimates are shown as points along with the corresponding 90 percent (wide) and 95 percent (narrow) confidence intervals. Across a variety of specifications, we see that adolescents with better developed noncognitive skills are more likely to vote in adulthood, even when controlling for these other observable factors. Individuals at the top of the noncognitive skill distribution are 19.1–21.0 percentage points more likely to have reported voting in the

5 Our measure of political motivation in the Add Health sample is not ideal. Being (primarily) a non-political survey, Add Health contains no measure of political interest, vote intentions, or civic duty. The best we can do is to measure ideological strength. When we use other proxies of political motivation, such as whether someone majors in political science or a related field, the results remain the same.

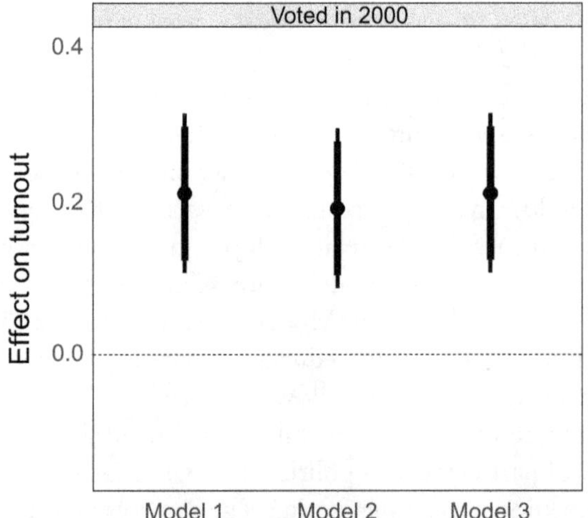

FIGURE 4.2 Noncognitive ability and voter turnout (Add Health, models with controls)

Average marginal effects for the noncognitive ability coefficient across models with several groups of controls. The dependent variable is whether an individual reported voting in the 2000 presidential election (W3). The individual controls in *Model 1* are cognitive ability, political motivation, mother's education, education, parents' income, gender, and church attendance. The controls in *Model 2* are those in Model 1 plus measures of the Big Five: conscientiousness, extraversion, agreeableness, openness to experience, and neuroticism. The controls in *Model 3* are those in Model 2 plus census-tract controls for population, urban/rural, race/ethnicity, age, marriage rates, socioeconomic status, health, ideology, religiosity, among others. For a full list and models with controls see Table A.2. For the results in local elections, see Figure A.6.

2000 election.[6] This suggests that while some (about half) of the relationship observed in Figure 4.1 can be attributed to observable characteristics that covary with noncognitive skills and voting, noncognitive skills still have a strong relationship with voting.[7] Moreover, in terms of substantive size, noncognitive ability compares well with other standard predictors of voting. For example, noncognitive skills' predictive strength is 83 percent of that for family socioeconomic status (i.e. mother's educational attainment); put differently, noncognitive ability appears to play a similarly

[6] A more modest comparison of the 5th and 95th percentile of the noncognitive skill distribution predicts a 8.1 percentage point increase in the likelihood of voting in the 2000 presidential election (Model 3).

[7] The controls in our models behave largely as expected, with higher average levels of turnout observed among those who are older, have more educated parents, are more educated themselves, attend church more regularly, have higher income, are extroverts and open to new experiences.

sized role to one of the foundational inputs of voting models. The noncognitive skills coefficient is roughly 60 percent of that of cognitive ability in this dataset. Given the rigidity of cognitive skills, this finding is also substantively significant. Moreover, the coefficient for noncognitive skills is also larger than any of the individual components of the Big Five; for example, noncognitive skills' coefficient is 4.2 times larger than that for conscientiousness – one of the most commonly used foils for noncognitive ability among individual characteristics. This distinction suggests that there are individual characteristics independent from the Big Five that may matter much more for voting. In sum, these results indicate a strong positive relationship between adolescent noncognitive ability and future levels of voter turnout, above and beyond a standard set of predictors of political participation.

4.2.1 Results from All Available Data Sources

To ensure the robustness and generalizability of the relationship between noncognitive skills and voting, we replicate our analysis using every existing dataset (of which we are aware) that contains measures of the two. These datasets span nearly seven decades and come from a variety of contexts, with many of these samples being nationally representative at the time the survey was taken. This compilation of data sources provides a unique breadth to our analyses. To our knowledge, no study of noncognitive skills – regardless of outcome, be it voting or measures of education, health, crime, or labor force performance – has utilized this many data sources together in one analysis.

Employing so many data sources, however, does come with the unique challenge of having the reader keep straight the exact details of each analysis. A summary of the datasets and specific noncognitive measures used can be found in Table 3.1, with greater detail in the Chapter 3 Appendix. Most of the datasets have self-reported voting behavior, with three exceptions: the WLS, CCES, and the Fast Track intervention, all which have validated voter turnout from administrative records. In the analyses in this chapter, we seek to keep our controls as parallel as possible across the datasets; models include controls for cognitive ability, mother's educational attainment, family income, race, gender, the number of civics courses one took in high school, and (when available) the Big Five personality traits.

Figure 4.3 presents the predictive relationship between measures of noncognitive ability and voter turnout across all of the data sources that

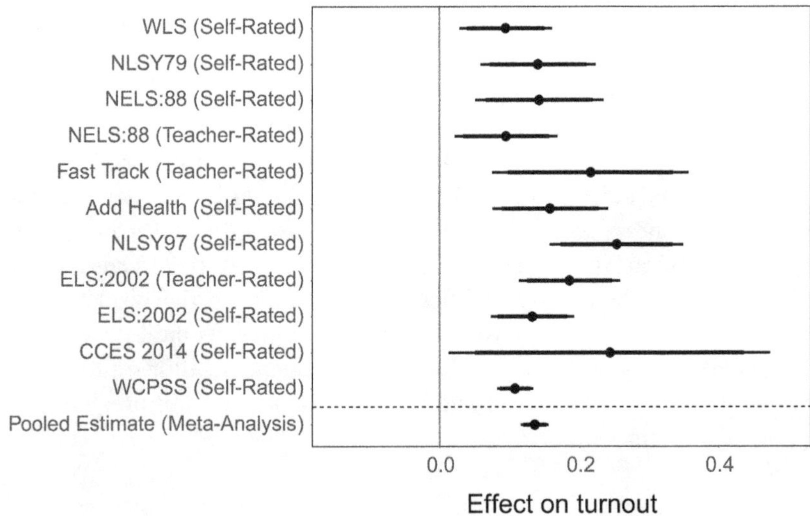

FIGURE 4.3 Noncognitive skills and voter turnout

Predicted relationship between noncognitive skills and voter turnout using data from the Wisconsin Longitudinal Study (WLS), the Wake County Public Schools System (WCPSS), the National Longitudinal Survey of Youth of 1997 (NLSY97), the National Longitudinal Survey of Youth of 1979 (NLSY79), the National Education Longitudinal Study of 1988 (NELS:88), the Fast Track Intervention Sample Control Group, the Education Longitudinal Study of 2002 (ELS:2002), the CCES (2014 Duke Module), and the National Longitudinal Study of Adolescent to Adult Health (Add Health). Points reflect coefficient estimates and bars represent 90 percent and 95 percent confidence intervals. Model labels indicate the data source and whether noncognitive ability was measured through survey self-reports or teacher evaluations (which are included in separate models regression models when these both were available). WLS and Fast Track use validated voting, WCPSS data use vote intentions, and all the other sources use self-reported voting. The last estimate comes from a fixed-effects meta-analysis of the studies included here.

have measures of the two.[8] The point estimates are ordered by the year in which the surveys were started – with the WLS having begun the earliest (in 1957) and the WCPSS having begun the most recently (in 2015). Most of these datasets pair a youth measure of noncognitive ability and a later-life measure of voting. The two exceptions are the WCPSS sample – which given the current age of the participants measures vote intentions concurrently with the measure of noncognitive ability – and the CCES – which measures noncognitive ability and validated voting among a small sample of adults. As shown in Figure 4.3, when multiple types of measures

[8] For full model results from the WCPSS sample, see Holbein et al. (Forthcoming).

of noncognitive ability are available in a given dataset, such as the individual self-evaluations or teacher reports, as is the case in the NELS:88 and ELS:2002 datasets – these measures are broken apart in separate models.

The data show, across all sources, a strong relationship between noncognitive ability and voter participation. All of the estimates are positive and statistically significant. Most of the samples are highly significant ($p < 0.012$ in 8/9 samples); the one closest to being insignificant ($p = 0.039$) is that from the CCES, which has a *much* smaller sample size than the others and includes all ages. Depending on the comparison used, these estimates are modest to large in size. The largest shift – which compares individuals with the lowest noncognitive ability to those at highest level – reveals estimates that range from 9.5 percentage points (WLS) to 25.3 percentage points (NLSY97).[9] If we compare individuals at the 10th percentile to those at the 90th percentile – the estimates across our nine datasets range from 5.8 to 13.1 percentage points. Shifting one standard deviation up the noncognitive ability distribution, the estimates range from 1.7 to 4.1 percentage points.[10]

The final row of Figure 4.3 shows the results when we pool all our estimates together. With our combined sample of just under 96,000 individuals the results suggest that noncognitive skills increase voter turnout by about 13.6 percentage points – an effect that is highly significant ($p < 0.0001$).[11]

For comparison, we again benchmark to the effect of cognitive ability.[12] In most cases, the estimates for noncognitive ability are a bit smaller, but quite comparable, to that for cognitive ability. Again, in the NLSY97 a one standard deviation change in noncognitive ability

[9] Heckman, Humphries, and Veramendi (2018) replicate the positive, strong, and significant effects of noncognitive skills on voting in the NLSY79.

[10] Across datasets, only the CCES result is sensitive to alternative model specifications, perhaps not surprising given the small sample size and known issues in measuring turnout among young people (Fraga and Holbein 2018; Grimmer et al. 2018). Given this, we urge some caution in interpreting the results from this dataset.

[11] Results from a meta-analysis with fixed effects. This meta-analysis treats each estimate separately. If we only include self-reported skills among the datasets with both measurement types, the pooled effect is 13.4 percentage points [11.2, 15.6]. If we only include self-reported skills among the datasets with both measurement types, the pooled effect is 13.6 percentage points [11.4, 15.8].

[12] As another substantive benchmark, across all data sources used, the coefficient for measures of young peoples' noncognitive ability are larger than those for the number of civics courses they take. For example, in the NLSY97 the coefficient for noncognitive ability is more than four times larger than that for civics courses taken. This pattern holds true across our other data sources.

leads to a 4.1 p.p. increase in turnout, whereas the coefficient for a one standard deviation change in the seminal predictor of cognitive ability is only a bit larger (6.9 p.p.). This pattern holds – in varying degrees – across our other data sources.[13] In most cases the two are statistically indistinguishable from one another. Moreover, in some samples the estimate for noncognitive ability is larger than that for cognitive ability.[14] Given the well-known connection between cognitive ability and social status, it is notable that noncognitive ability remains predictive of voter turnout. This indicates that *independent of where one starts in the social spectrum*, noncognitive abilities can help promote voting.

Moreover, it seems likely that our estimates of noncognitive ability's influence could be conservative. One bit of evidence that this is the case comes from varying our measure of noncognitive skills. In the two datasets where we have a self-rated measure and a teacher-rated measure for individuals in the same sample – NELS:88 and ELS:2002 – when we include both of these measures of noncognitive ability in the same model, both remain positive and substantively and statistically significant. For example, in the ELS:2002, the results show that individuals at the top of the teacher-rated noncognitive skill distribution vote at a rate 14.2 percentage points higher than those at the bottom and that *independently* those at the top of the self-rated noncognitive skill distribution vote at a rate 12.0 percentage points higher than those at the bottom.[15] This pattern also holds in the NELS:88.[16] Despite the fact that these measures appear to be part of the same family of abilities, both exhibit independent effects. This suggests each measure is picking up on slightly different aspects of noncognitive ability. As we have argued throughout the book, noncognitive skills are multifaceted – occupying a fairly large

[13] In the WLS (cognitive: 3.3 p.p.; self-rated noncognitive: 3.1 p.p.), NLSY79 (cognitive: 11.3 p.p.; self-rated noncognitive: 3.0 p.p.), NELS:88 (cognitive: 5.5 p.p.; self-rated noncognitive: 2.1 p.p.; teacher-rated noncognitive: 2.0 p.p.), Add Health (cognitive: 4.0 p.p.; self-rated noncognitive: 3.5 p.p.), and ELS:2002 (cognitive: 4.0 p.p.; self-rated noncognitive: 3.0 p.p.; teacher-rated noncognitive: 3.7 p.p.), data cognitive ability is a stronger predictor of adult voting.

[14] For instance, the Fast Track (cognitive: 2.1 p.p.; teacher-rated noncognitive: 4.1 p.p.) and WCPSS data (cognitive: 0.2 p.p.; self-rated noncognitive: 1.7 p.p.), noncognitive abilities are better predictors of voting.

[15] When teacher- and self-rated skills are combined into a single scale together, the models indicate a 20.5 percentage point increase in voting.

[16] When we do the same exercise with the NELS:88, those effects are 14.2 and 12.0 percentage points, respectively. When teacher- and self-rate skills are combined into a single scale together, the models indicate a 14.0 percentage point increase in voting.

space that is independent from cognitive ability and socioeconomic status. And our evidence here backs this up. Future work on noncognitive skills and political outcomes would do well to pay close attention to explicit psychometric work on the noncognitive skills construct.

To summarize, our analysis offers consistent and compelling evidence that the observed relationship between noncognitive ability and voting is not attributable to cognitive ability, one's level of political interest or motivation, socioeconomic status (measured by either parental education or family income), educational attainment, gender, age, race, dynamics of family arrangements (i.e. having a sibling or a male present in the home), or the Big Five personality traits. Simply put, noncognitive ability appears to be a contributor to promote voting even after we adjust for many of the standard predictors of political participation.

4.2.2 Robustness Checks

To evaluate if the relationship we just showed holds under careful scrutiny, we conduct a number of additional tests to see whether what we are seeing if our results are robust to alternative assumptions and models.[17] In the next section, we turn our attention to *why* the effect we observe exists.

Given that many of our analyses rely on a self-reported voting measure, we start by scrutinizing the Add Health results to make sure our observed findings are not an artifact of social desirability bias, which is well-known to affect studies of voter turnout (Abelson, Loftus, and Greenwald 1992). First, we note that in our data source that over-reporting does not appear to be as severe as many surveys. While youth turnout that year was about 36 percent, 43.5 percent of Add Health respondents indicated voting in the 2000 election.[18] (By contrast, the most recent ANES turnout rate exceeded the actual turnout rate by 14 percentage points.) This may reflect the fact that Add Health was not a political survey, thus reducing social desirability effects. Second, we attempt to account for susceptibility to over-reporting by controlling for illogical response patterns on engagement items – individuals who indicated that they had voted, but had not registered (< 1 percent of the sample). We

[17] Additional robustness checks are presented in the Appendix.

[18] See CIRCLE, "New Census Data Confirm Increase in Youth Voter Turnout in 2008 Election," April 28, 2009.

also note that our models include controls for many of the factors that are related to an individual's propensity to over-report, including educational attainment, race, and nonattentive survey taking (e.g. Silver, Anderson, and Abramson 1986). Finally, as an additional robustness check, we re-estimate our model on the two-thirds of individuals in our sample who do not report being organ donors (based on the logic that this act might also show social desirability effects, and, as such, individuals who give a negative response are also less susceptible to overreport civic behaviors) with similar results. All of this, combined with the fact that the results replicate in datasets in which voter turnout has been validated against government records, suggests that the relationship between noncognitive ability and voter turnout is not driven by social desirability bias.

Although not the primary purpose of the book, we also replicate our analysis on alternative measures of civic engagement. In the WCPSS data, we are able to look at the relationship between grit and volunteering. Depending on the particular model specification, the relationship between grit and volunteering ranges between 22 and 38 percentage points (top to bottom comparison).[19] This is also true for other forms of engagement in school, community, and democracy, which also survive the robustness checks listed here (Holbein et al. Forthcoming). It appears, then, that not only do noncognitive skills influence voting, but so too do they influence other forms of civic participation.

We next turn our attention to whether our effects are biased by some unaccounted-for factor. One concern might be that our measure of noncognitive skills is picking up another nonpolitical attribute, general self-efficacy, which has already been shown to predict voter turnout (Condon and Holleque 2013). Conceptually, general self-efficacy certainly relates to noncognitive abilities, but it seems unlikely to theoretically capture the full set of noncognitive skills needed to follow through on political goals. Nonetheless, to see if self-efficacy alone is doing the empirical heavy lifting, we re-estimate the Add Health models controlling for the full Pearlin Self Mastery Scale, a common measure of general self-efficacy (Condon and Holleque 2013). When we include general self-efficacy, our noncognitive skill scale remains positive, statistically significant, and substantively similar. To be sure, general self-efficacy is predictive, further confirming the relevance of noncognitive skills and

19 A one standard deviation change increases the probability of a young person volunteering by 3–6 percentage points.

highlighting the need for additional psychometric work.[20] At the same time, our results confirm that simply believing in one's self is not all that is needed to get a young person to the polls.

Any observational study leaves lingering concerns about possible unobserved factors that might affect the relationship of interest. The limited work that has been done in the past linking noncognitive abilities and political participation has relied on a conditional-on-observables approach, wherein the analysis adjusts for observed factors. We next turn to more rigorous analyses to see if the conclusions still stand when we account for potential unobserved confounders.

We first re-estimate the Add Health model including contextual fixed effects to account for possible unobserved social context variables such as school-level activities/curricula, school quality, neighborhood culture, or social capital. We know, for instance, that some schools and communities are more likely than others to organize voter registration drives or encourage civic activities. Moreover, we also know that students' noncognitive skills vary widely by school context (see West et al. 2016, and Figure 8.4). Ideally, then, our identification strategy would account for all sources of potential contextual variation that could be biasing our estimates. Although our models control for a host of geographic variables – many at a fine-grained level (census block or county) – we re-estimate the models with school and neighborhood fixed effects to better account for these observed and unobserved social context factors. Figure 4.4 shows our estimates with school fixed effects, which account for observed and unobserved contextual differences constant within schools. (For the results for turnout in local elections, see Figure A.8.) As can be seen, the relationship between noncognitive ability remains when accounting for these fixed effects. The school fixed-effect model indicates a 19.7 percentage point increase in the probability of voting for those at the top of the noncognitive ability scale relative to the bottom.

Offering the most compelling robustness check, we next leverage sibling, twin, and individual fixed-effect specifications. Among non-experimental analyses of individual-level attributes, this is one of the

[20] When we include the Pearlin Self Mastery scale and compare individuals at the 5th and 95th percentile our corresponding noncognitive skill estimates is $\beta_{2000} = 6.4$ p.p., $p = 0.001$. The Pearlin Self Mastery estimates from the same models are $\beta_{2000} = 6.0$ p.p., $p < 0.006$. The Pearlin results appear to be less robust than our scale. The Pearlin effect remains significant in models with family fixed effects ($p = 0.001$) but is somewhat sensitive to the inclusion of contextual covariates.

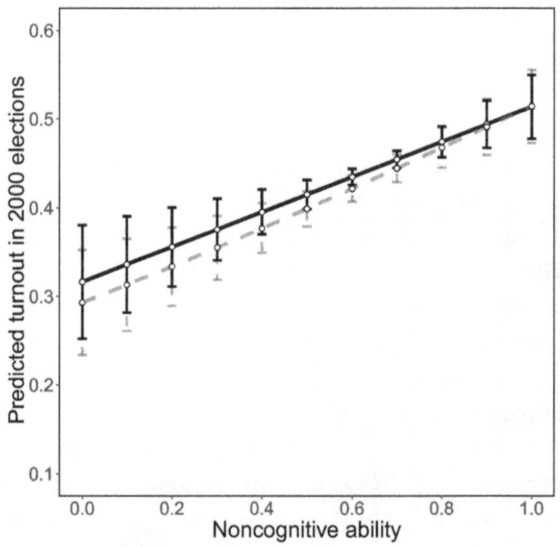

FIGURE 4.4 School fixed effects vs. controls (Add Health)

Comparison of predicted turnout values to those produced with no geographic controls and instead a school fixed effect. Solid black lines correspond to the school fixed effect; dashed lines correspond to the model with controls. Bars represent 95 percent confidence intervals. As can be seen, the two slopes are statistically indistinguishable.

strongest empirical approaches, since it accounts for a host of observable and unobservable factors that are shared within families, twins, and individuals themselves (respectively).

Figure 4.5 shows our results from these models. Here the estimates are grouped by modeling approach – with sibling pair models on the top and the twin and individual fixed-effects models below – and then by year that the survey started – with the earliest survey being grouped at the top. Figure 4.5 shows results consistent with the results in Figure 4.3. Across all modeling approaches, noncognitive abilities appear to be significant contributors to individuals' voting decisions. In all models, the results remain highly significant ($p < 0.003$ in all specifications). The WLS results are slightly smaller than those in Figure 4.3 – 8.4 percentage points (sibling FE) vs. 9.5 percentage points (controls only) – a difference that is not statistically significant. In the Add Health data, the effect also remains and is noticeable in size. Individuals at the top of the noncognitive ability distribution are 21.9 percentage points more likely to vote than those at the bottom. In the WCPSS data, the same holds in the sibling (26.3 p.p.), twin (32.8 p.p.), and individual (16.3 p.p.) fixed-effect approaches. When

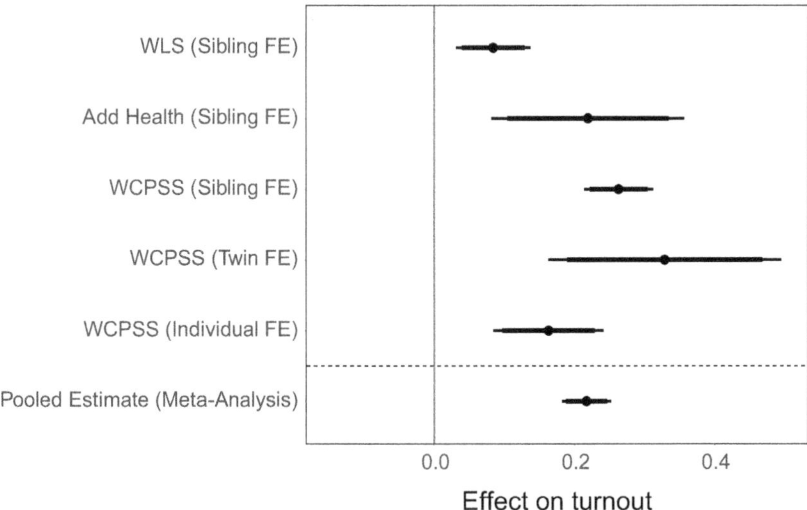

FIGURE 4.5 Noncognitive skill development and turnout (sibling, twin, individual FE)

Predicted relationship between noncognitive skills and voter turnout using data from the Wisconsin Longitudinal Study, the Wake County Public Schools System, and the National Longitudinal Study of Adolescent to Adult Health (Add Health). Points reflect coefficient estimates and bars represent 90 percent and 95 percent confidence intervals. All sources measure noncognitive ability using survey self-reports. WLS uses validated voting, WCPSS uses vote intentions, and Add Health uses self-reported voting. The last estimate comes from a fixed-effects meta-analysis of the estimates included here.

pooled together with a simple meta-analysis, the pooled effect (from the combined 50,000+ individuals total in these estimates) is 21.7 p.p. ($p < 0.001$).

In sum, these results show that noncognitive abilities are strong predictors of whether a young person develops into an active voter, or fails to do so. Regardless of the measure, method, or data source used, this previously unrecognized pattern remains. People with strong noncognitive skills are much more likely to vote.

4.3 EXPLORING THE MECHANISMS

The previous analyses offer consistent evidence that noncognitive ability is related to voter turnout, but they do not explore *why* noncognitive ability matters. Is the observed relationship between noncognitive skills and voter turnout about follow-through, as we have hypothesized? Perhaps individuals with greater noncognitive abilities are simply more likely to have good citizenship as a goal. Or perhaps it simply reflects the fact that noncognitive skills also promote educational attainment.

To get a sense of which of these competing hypotheses has the most supportive observational evidence, we start with mediation analyses using the Add Health data. Mediation analyses require three steps. The first regresses the dependent variable of interest (in this case voting) on the independent variable of interest (in this case noncognitive skills) to confirm that there is a direct relationship between the two. The second regresses the mediator(s) of interest on the independent variable of interest to confirm that the independent variable is a significant predictor of the mediator. The last step regresses the dependent variable on both the mediator and independent variable to confirm that the mediator is a significant predictor of the dependent variable. If there is a mediated relationship the previously significant independent variable of interest will likely be smaller, if not zero (Baron and Kenny 1986). This comparison is made by benchmarking the direct relationship (the ADE) to the mediated relationship (the ACME). In most common applications, this approach is done simultaneously. More recent applications have added a sensitivity analysis to the standard mediation analyses (Imai, Keele, and Tingley 2010). This procedure estimates a parameter (ρ) for how much the mediator would have to be related to the error term in order to make the mediation estimates zero.

This methodological approach allows us to get a sense of whether noncognitive skills have a direct relationship or one that is largely captured by its indirect relationship with well-established factors like education, financial resources, social connectedness, or political attitudes. While we – like Imai, Keele, and Tingley (2010) – argue that mediation models have value for exploring potential indirect pathways, we *strongly* emphasize that these results remain preliminary/descriptive due to the inherent risks in observational data of violating the ignorability assumption (Green, Ha, and Bullock 2010). Ultimately, mediation is best done when potential mediators can be completely isolated, one at a time, a high threshold across all methodological designs, experimental and nonexperimental.

The mediation results are shown in Table 4.1. The table reports three parts of the mediation models' output: the statistical significance of the mediation estimates, their substantive size (in terms of the ratio of the indirect estimates – the ACME – to the direct estimates – the ADE), and their robustness to unobserved heterogeneity (Imai, Keele, and Tingley 2010). Overall, the mediation analysis suggests that the relationship between

TABLE 4.1 *Potential mechanisms: Add Health*

	No controls			All controls		
	ACME/ADE(%)	95% C.I.	ρ	ACME/ADE(%)	95% C.I.	ρ
Registered (W3)	24.0	[20.9%, 28.4%]	0.4	14.6	[11.0%, 21.5%]	0.4
Educational attainment (W4)	20.5	[18.0%, 24.0%]	0.5	15.9	[12.7%, 22.1%]	0.5
Income (W3)	0.2	[0.1%, 0.2%]	0.0	0.3	[0.2%, 0.5%]	0.0
Income (W4)	6.3	[5.6%, 7.3%]	0.2	4.0	[3.0%, 5.7%]	0.1
# of close friends (W4)	6.0	[5.4%, 7.0%]	0.2	1.7	[1.3%, 2.5%]	0.1
Church attendance (W4)	5.8	[5.1%, 6.7%]	0.2	5.8	[4.4%, 8.3%]	0.2
Political motivation (W3)	7.2	[6.3%, 8.3%]	0.2	7.0	[5.3%, 10.1%]	0.2
Trust in government (W4)	2.2	[2.0%, 2.6%]	0.1	4.3	[3.3%, 6.3%]	0.1

Mediation analyses results from Add Health. The table provides the % of the direct effect estimates for noncognitive ability that are mediated through the variables listed for the wave 4 turnout measure. It also displays the sensitivity of these estimates to unobserved heterogeneity (i.e. ρ, see Imai, Keele, and Tingley 2010). The vote measure is from W4 (results similar for W3 measure). Mediation models include all controls, excepting political motivation (folded ideology) and education status in W3 when finishing college by W4 is the mediator. Church attendance (W4) is an indicator for whether an individual attended church twice a month (the median) or more.

noncognitive ability and voter turnout is, in part, attributable to the powerful role noncognitive ability plays in academic success – those who develop greater noncognitive abilities stay in school longer, receiving the participatory benefits of additional education. This predicted increase in educational attainment accounts for as much as 21 percent of the direct relationship between noncognitive ability and turnout – a sizable mediation estimate.

This is an important finding in its own right as it suggests that noncognitive skills are part of the explanation for the strong and enduring relationship between education and voter turnout, a finding that has not previously been explored in the large literature evaluating education and political engagement and one that offers a challenge to conventional wisdom, which focuses – almost exclusively – on cognitive ability (Luskin 1990; Nie, Junn, and Stehlik-Barry 1996). Young people who develop more noncognitive skills are more likely to stay in school, thus enhancing the chances that they vote in the future. This relationship may be mutually reinforcing, with noncognitive skills enhancing education, and education, in turn, also enhancing noncognitive skills. This feedback loop acts to increase the chances that young people participate in politics. This suggests a new, theoretically and empirically tractable reason for the long-studied relationship between education and participation: that is, that education enhances the noncognitive abilities that work to promote voting.

At the same time, the mediation analysis also shows that four-fifths of the relationship between noncognitive ability and participation is *not* explained by education levels. Likewise, the results suggest that the observed relationship is not fully explained by social connectivity, income, or political motivation. Besides the mediator of educational attainment, only registration is a large mediator – consistent with our argument that noncognitive ability matters because it helps voters overcome obstacles to turnout.

4.3.1 Heterogenous Effects in the Observational Samples

As a further check of the competing mechanisms, we consider whether the relationship between noncognitive skills and voting varies in theoretically predictable ways. If noncognitive skills help individuals follow through on a given intention to participate in politics, we should expect to see noncognitive skills having an effect among those who have at least a minimal goal to participate in the first place. After all, in order for follow through to be an issue, one has to at least have a goal, desire, or motivation to engage in that act. Individuals who are not even oriented toward participating may have very little use for noncognitive skills if the only channel is follow through. For politically disinterested citizens, perseverance and self-control may not be first-order concerns. For them, the challenge in the way of their participation is not about *following through*, but rather *starting up*. That said, as we've noted in Chapter 2, noncognitive skills could increase turnout by motivating disinterested citizens adhere to the social norm of voting. If noncognitive skills help orient people toward participating, we would expect to see their effect among low motivation individuals.

Unfortunately, testing this proposition is difficult given that most of the educational longitudinal studies do not have very good (or any) measures of political motivation.[21] One sample that gets close to having all the information needed to test the heterogeneity of interest is the WCPSS. This sample has a measure of noncognitive skills and a measure of political interest. However, as was mentioned earlier, given the age of the sample the voting measure in this sample is voting intentions. Hence, while this allows us to explore whether individuals who are differentially motivated to participate may use noncognitive skills to make plans to vote, we cannot see the end result of actually voting.

The adult sample from the CCES also comes close to having all the things we want to test for heterogeneous effects – having a single module (fielded by Duke University in 2014) that measures noncognitive ability, political orientations, and validated voter turnout. However, the CCES has a very small sample size; is not a sample of young people but rather all adults; has well-noted issues with accurately measuring voter turnout (especially among young people) even though this sample matches to Catalist's voter files (Fraga and Holbein 2018; Grimmer et al. 2018); and is an explicitly political survey that may have priming effects that influence all of our measures of interest. That said, it can be used to provide some relevant information as to whether noncognitive skills are about start up, follow-through, or both.

Given the limitations of these two datasets, we also use voting registration as a proxy for political motivation in reanalyzing our other surveys. The idea behind this approach is that individuals who take the time to

[21] For example, the Add Health has ideological strength as its best measure of political interest.

register to vote should, at minimum, be oriented to participate. Hence, registration could be thought of as a behavioral proxy for political interest. Registered individuals have signaled that they care about politics, but they have yet to fully follow through on their revealed interest in politics. If noncognitive skills were to affect individuals who have registered to vote, then we might infer that these abilities play a key role in getting people across the finish line. Given the strong relationship between registering and voting, this is a strict test of the relationship between noncognitive skills and voting. While all three methodological approaches we have just outlined are imperfect, they allow us to provide some preliminary tests of the primary channels behind noncognitive skills' effects.

For the first test, we use the WCPSS data and run our models by levels of political interest. If noncognitive skills like grit – the noncognitive skill measure available in the WCPSS data – matter because they help individuals who are somewhat motivated move toward the end goal of voting, we would expect to see a larger coefficient with individuals who have at least a minimum threshold of interest. Figure 4.6 shows this pattern visually – breaking the noncognitive (grit) estimates by political interest. As can be seen, noncognitive ability as measured in this sample is most useful for prospective voters who have a minimal orientation toward participating

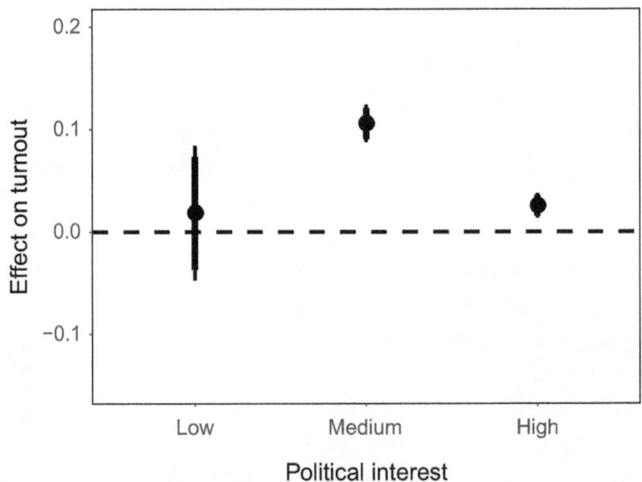

FIGURE 4.6 Noncognitive skills and vote intentions, by political motivation

The predicted relationship between noncognitive skills and intention to vote broken by levels of political interest. Figure made using data from the Wake County Public Schools System. Points reflect coefficient estimates and bars represent 90 percent and 95 percent confidence intervals. Here the measure of noncognitive abilities is the Duckworth grit scale.

and who are not so fully interested in politics that follow through is not an issue. For individuals in the middle interest category the estimates are more than five times larger than both the top or bottom interest groups. The difference between these coefficients are highly significant ($p < 0.001$ in both cases). Noncognitive skills are still predictive for individuals of high political interest, suggesting that follow through may still be a problem for individuals most politically motivated – a fact consistent with the large number of people who have high levels of political interest, but fail to vote. (The difference in effect sizes between high interest individuals and low interest individuals is not statistically or substantively distinct.) Our results suggest that noncognitive skills may be especially useful for those who are interested, but not die-hard political junkies.

Figure 4.7 shows the results from the adult sample. As in Figure 4.3, the effects here are the least precise given the small sample size in this adult sample. However, noncognitive skills – here measured as a composite of grit, emotion regulation, and sociability – appear to play a dual role. Not only do noncognitive skills correlate with vote intentions, they also appear to be related to whether individuals who plan to vote actually finish the task of casting a ballot. Noncognitive skills appear to be important for the start up and the follow-through. As also expected, noncognitive skills have little to no effect among individuals who are not

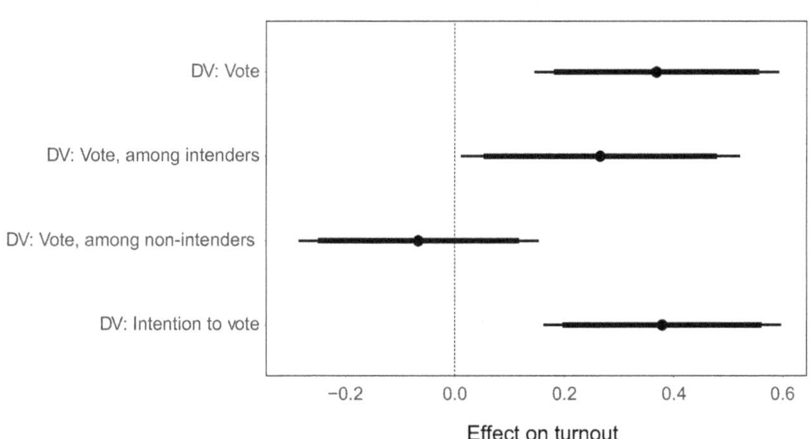

FIGURE 4.7 Noncognitive skills and voting, by intention to vote

The predicted relationship between noncognitive skills and voter turnout broken by various specifications involving intention to vote. Figure made using data from the CCES (2014 Duke University Module). Points reflect coefficient estimates and bars represent 90 percent and 95 percent confidence intervals. Here the measure of noncognitive abilities is a factor-weighted composite of grit, emotion control, and sociability.

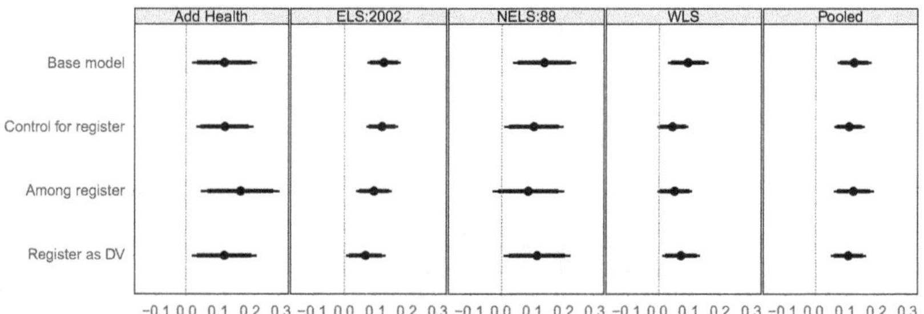

FIGURE 4.8 Noncognitive skills, registration, and voting

The predicted relationship between noncognitive skills and turnout/registration by various model specifications. The first contains no information on voter registration as in earlier models presented here. The second controls for whether a person is registered to vote. The third subsets the model results among those who are registered. The last uses registration as a dependent variable. Points reflect coefficient estimates and bars represent 90 percent and 95 percent confidence intervals. To make the results as comparable as possible across datasets, we report only the self-reported measures of noncognitive ability. The last facet pools our estimates using a fixed-effects meta-analysis.

political motivated and who have no intention to participate, helping to confirm that these measures are not an artifact of an unobserved political attitude.

Finally, we turn to our four samples that have measures of voter registration – Add Health, ELS:2002, WLS, and NELS:88. Figure 4.8 shows the conditional relationship between noncognitive skills and voting. To do so, it first presents our model results when we don't take into account the step of registering to vote (the first coefficient in each of the panels). It then turns to a model that controls for whether a person is registered to vote (the second estimate) and then, similarly, isolates the estimates down to individuals who are registered to vote (the third estimate). These provide slightly different ways of testing whether noncognitive skills help promote follow-through. The second estimate in the figure shows whether there are any likely channels, aside from voter registration (the classic voting obstacle), that link noncognitive skills to voting. If noncognitive skills are linked to voting when we condition on registration it could be because these skills help citizens avoid other distractions and diversions that get in the way of voting. The third provides us an opportunity to see whether noncognitive skills help individuals who are registered to vote to actually finish the task. The last model examines whether noncognitive skills are linked with registration – that is, that they also help to orient citizens toward participating.

As can be seen, our results suggest the importance of noncognitive skills for both registration and voting. In all cases, even when we account for registration, a relationship still holds – three-quarters of the coefficients are significant at the 5 percent level, the WLS relationship is significant at the 10 percent level; and the pooled estimate is significant at the 0.1 percent level. This suggests that registration is one, but not the only, barrier that stops individuals from voting. When we stratify on registration, noncognitive skills' ability to help individuals follow through comes into even clearer focus. Among individuals who have shown, through their actions, that they are interested or oriented toward participating, noncognitive skills still matter. While stratifying leads to much lower levels of statistical power, the coefficients are still large and positive – half are significant at the 5 percent level, one other is significant at the 10 percent level; and the pooled estimate is significant at the 0.1 percent level. This suggests that noncognitive skills may help individuals who have cleared the bar of registering to vote get to the finish line: to follow through on their intention to vote. However, this is not the only channel in play. Noncognitive skills are related to registration, indicating the importance of clearing this initial barrier – all four coefficients are positive and statistically significant (as is the pooled estimate).

Teasing apart mechanisms in an observational framework is difficult. We have provided cursory evidence that noncognitive skills matter because of their ability to help individuals follow through on their goals/orientations/intentions. But, there is also some evidence noncognitive skills matter because they help promote additional education and they might help individuals become oriented toward civic engagement in the first place. The exact channels are likely many and complex and may depend on the specific dimensions of noncognitive ability one is measuring. But this much is clear: Noncognitive skills developed early in life appear to predict who votes in adulthood.

4.4 EXPERIMENTAL METHODS

Although our efforts to purge out bias go a long way towards doing so, our estimates are not flawless. For example, they have not perfectly nailed down the potential mechanisms driving our relationship of interest. Moreover, though we discussed earlier the long literature that shows that noncognitive skills are malleable, we have yet to explore how exactly interventions might target noncognitive skills as a means to increase youth civic engagement. To help address these concerns, we next turn our attention to experimental comparisons linking noncognitive abilities and voting.

This approach leverages several relevant randomized control trials (RCTs). In an RCT, individuals are randomly assigned to a treatment or a control condition. In our case, we use RCTs to randomly assign individuals (over the short or long-term) to have higher or lower levels of noncognitive ability. Because of random assignment to these two conditions, RCTs have the virtue of dealing with selection bias, endogeneity, and other hard-to-control factors (Angrist and Pischke 2008; Gerber and Green 2012; Shadish, Cook, and Campbell 2002). We present a mix of smaller-scale survey experiments that activate individuals' noncognitive abilities over the short term and larger, long-term experiments that required significant resources to develop, implement, and evaluate.

The smaller scale experiment is designed to temporarily activate individuals' levels of grit, perseverance, or self-control. This approach is useful for two reasons. First, it allows us to get a greater handle on the mechanisms driving the relationship between noncognitive skills and voting. Second, this approach allows us to see whether noncognitive skills can be activated at critical decision points. In contrast, the larger scale experiment is designed to see whether noncognitive skills can be durably improved. While we have less control over the extant mechanisms mediating that relationship, this approach gives us a chance to see whether voting increases when people improve their noncognitive skills. These two types of experiments work nicely together. Where one experiment is weak, the other is strong. Together, they give us a more complete picture of the relationship between noncognitive skills and voting.

4.4.1 Short-Term Activation of Noncognitive Skills

Our first approach uses an experiment designed to activate or prime noncognitive skills in the short term; that is, we increase the salience of existing noncognitive abilities (specifically, perceptions of grit). This approach has strengths and weaknesses. On the one hand, this experiment may only have short term effects, being only designed to prime – not fundamentally change – noncognitive skills over a short period. That said, this design has distinct theoretical strengths. In contrast to longer-term, intensive interventions, where the exact mechanisms are typically unclear, this precisely controlled, short-term experiment helps us isolate the channels driving the connection between noncognitive skills and voting. By putting individuals into a (somewhat contrived) scenario, we can rule out some of the complementary channels that could link noncognitive skills and voting in the real-world. In particular, we attempt to compare the effects of noncognitive skills on start up vs. follow-through. To be sure, we cannot generalize these results into the real world of politics, but the design helps to shed light on the mechanisms linking noncognitive skills to turnout.

To evaluate whether priming noncognitive skills has an effect on voting, we designed an original survey experiment. This experiment was designed to specifically evaluate if activating individuals' grittiness – a well-known noncognitive attribute (Duckworth et al. 2007) – works in the short-term to move participants toward voting.

We fielded the experiment using Amazon's Mechanical Turk (MTurk) platform.[22] We recruited just over 1,500 respondents and randomly assigned subjects to a treatment ($n = 760$) or control condition ($n = 792$).[23] The treatment condition asked subjects to write about an experience working hard to achieve a goal, with the intention of priming grit, perseverance, or tenacity. The prompt asked subjects to write about the experience, what they did to keep going when things got difficult, and what individual attributes helped them achieve their goal. Those in the control group were asked to write about what they did on their typical morning. In the survey, there was not any mention of politics prior to measurement of our outcomes. This type of reflective writing assignment builds on work that has used writing tasks to target other individual attributes in the study of voting (e.g. Valentino et al. 2011).

Independent coding of a sample of responses found that MTurkers were highly compliant, with 99 percent of those assigned to the treatment group writing about a story that demonstrated grit, resilience, tenacity, or self-control.[24] By contrast, only one subject in the control group did the same. As a further manipulation check, we asked respondents in the

[22] We fielded the study twice – one in 2015 ($N = 535$) and one in 2019 ($N = 1,017$). The national nonprobability sample included U.S. residents over the age of 18 who were paid $0.60 for completion (first wave) or $1.00 (second wave) of the roughly seven-minute survey. We restricted eligibility to those with at least a 90 percent HIT approval rate in the first wave and 95 percent in the second.

[23] Randomization yielded balance across the two conditions on all our pre-treatment measures (joint $p = 0.91$).

[24] A research assistant blinded to the hypothesis read and coded all responses. Words coded as synonymous with grit included perseverance, pluck, fortitude, resolution, determination, persistence, tenacity, dedication, resolve, resilience, motivation, endurance, drive, hard work, focus, effort, commitment, and fight.

treatment condition what characteristics or attributes helped achieve the goal they wrote about, and 81.5 percent of subjects mentioned a synonym of grit. Importantly, none of the subjects in either condition mentioned anything related to politics in any of their open-ended responses. It appears that our treatment activated grit among the treatment group but did not cue politics for anyone in the treatment or control group.

Recall that we have theorized that noncognitive skills help citizens overcome the burdens involved with this foundational act of democracy and follow through on their civic intentions. Our key measure of follow-through is an original question asking how long the respondent would be willing to wait in line in order to vote.[25] Given the salience of long lines at the ballot box in recent elections and their negative impact on voter turnout (Pettigrew 2016), this measure provides a useful proxy in understanding whether the link between grit and voting is driven by follow-through. We also measured political efficacy, a known strong attitudinal predictor of voter turnout, and an outcome that is theoretically linked to grit through generalized self-efficacy. Here we think efficacy might be affected because individuals who have higher levels of grit may feel empowered to overcome the obstacles they face. Finally, we also asked a question measuring the respondent's general perception of voter registration as being easy or difficult.[26] We explore whether our treatment affected each of these three outcomes individually and, to reduce residual variance, as a combined factor-weighted scale meant to get a view into individuals' ability to overcome voting obstacles.

To test the alternative hypothesis – that noncognitive skills create a desire or orientation to participate – we also measured citizens' sense of civic duty, political interest, and turnout intention. We would expect a much smaller effect on these outcomes if noncognitive skills are about follow-through more than start up. To explore this possibility, our analysis looks at the effect of our treatment on individual items and on a combined factor-weighted scale meant to capture, with a greater degree of precision than one individual item can, political motivation.

[25] The question asked was, "As you may have heard, in previous elections some people have had to wait in long lines in order to cast a vote. Thinking ahead to the 2016/2020 presidential election, about how long do you think you would be willing to wait in order to cast your ballot?" Respondents gave an answer in minutes. We capped responses at 300 minutes.

[26] The question asked, "There has been a lot of attention lately to laws about voting and voter registration. From your perspective, how easy or difficult is it for a person to register to vote?"

TABLE 4.2 *Results of short-term experiment*

	Control ($N = 792$)	Treatment ($N = 760$)	Difference
Follow-through			
Willingness to wait (min)	47.1	54.5	7.4**
Voter registration easy (1–6)	4.50	4.55	0.05
Political efficacy (1–4)	2.55	2.60	0.04*
Combined follow through scale (std.)	−0.07	0.07	0.13**
Political motivation			
Political interest (1–5)	3.27	3.28	0.01
Civic duty (1–4)	2.54	2.60	0.06
Vote intentions (1–6)	4.16	4.18	0.02
Combined political interest scale (std.)	−0.02	0.02	0.04

$^{*}p < 0.1$, $^{**}\ p < 0.05$. This table shows the means and difference in means. One-tailed p-values are shown.

4.4.2 Short-Term Activation of Noncognitive Skills: Findings

The experimental results are shown in Table 4.2. We first focus on our measures of an individuals' ability to follow through (found in the top panel).[27] The results suggest that increasing the salience of grit increases attitudes related to following through to vote. Those in the treatment group exhibited a greater willingness to wait in line in order to vote. Individuals in the treatment group were willing to stand in line 7.4 minutes longer than those in the control group ($p = 0.017$; estimate with baseline controls: 8.8 minutes, $p = 0.005$). This effect is equivalent to 12.6 percent of a standard deviation shift in the dependent variable ($\sigma \approx 51$ minutes) and 15.8 percent of the mean base rate in the control group (control group $\mu \approx 47.1$ minutes). With baseline controls, the effect is equivalent to 14.8 percent of a standard deviation and 18.6 percent of the base rate.

We find similar results if we model wait times using a negative binomial or Poisson regression that is justified given the number of "0" responses in

[27] To maximize statistical power, we focus on the results that pool our two studies. The effects are similar when stratified by study, although a bit smaller in 2019 than in 2015, probably because levels of political interest are *much* higher in 2019, perhaps reflecting changes in the political environment. (Among the control group, levels of political interest are about 0.5 points higher on the five-item scale.)

outcome (about 9 percent of the sample). If we estimate a two-part model, we find that very little of the effect comes from moving someone from not being willing to wait at all to waiting a concrete amount of time. Most of the effect we observe comes from moving someone who is willing to wait a certain amount of time to a longer amount. This result suggests that our effect is being driven not by individuals who are totally disinterested in politics, but rather by individuals who have cleared a minimal threshold for interest in politics.[28]

The effect on political efficacy is a bit smaller (0.04 on a four-point scale) and less precise. This result suggests that noncognitive skills may help individuals believe they can overcome the obstacles they face and become more willing and able to do so. Our treatment had no effect on perceptions of how hard or easy it is to register to vote. In retrospect, however, we acknowledge this question was perhaps not as ideal for testing our hypothesis since treated respondents could have the same perception of difficulty but simply have been more willing to overcome it. When pooled together in a single scale – an approach that increases our statistical precision – we can see that our treatment had an effect on individuals' willingness to follow through. Individuals randomly assigned to treatment score about 13 percent of a standard deviation higher in their propensity to follow through than individuals randomly assigned to the control group ($p = 0.012$). With baseline controls included, the effect is equivalent to 14.5 percent of a standard deviation and is even more precise ($p = 0.005$).

In contrast, our treatment had little effect on our measures of political motivation. The second panel in Table 4.2 shows the estimates for our political motivation outcomes. If noncognitive skills simply worked to reinforce political motivation, we would expect large effects on political interest, civic duty, or vote intentions. Although the difference between treatment and control is positive in all of our measures, the difference is very small and not statistically different from zero in any case. Our short-term manipulation fails to change respondents' political interest ($p = 0.82$), attitudes about whether voting is a civic duty ($p = 0.22$), and

[28] We find similar results if we break up our sample by our only pre-treatment measure of interest – interest in the news. As with the two-part models, there appears to be no effect on individuals with low levels of interest in the news. Between those with moderate and higher levels of interest, the effect is largest among those in the middle interest category. However, this difference is not very large, nor is it statistically significant. Our treatment may have helped high interest follow through just as much as those who have moderate interest.

intention to vote ($p = 0.80$). This suggests that noncognitive skills like grit might not be so much about the start up (i.e. political motivation), as they are about the follow-through.

Our results suggest that noncognitive skills like grit are different from political motivation – with these attributes providing citizens with the ability to follow through on their political goals. To be sure, it's possible that not all noncognitive skills may operate in this way; some may also be useful for helping orient people toward participating in politics. But our observational and experimental results suggest that noncognitive skills help those who are politically motivated to convert their civic attitudes into civic action.

4.4.3 Long-Term Improvements in Noncognitive Abilities

Although the previous experimental analysis allowed us to scrutinize the mechanism by which noncognitive skills might influence voter turnout, it cannot test if directly changing one's level of noncognitive skills has consequences of political participation. To answer that question, we turn to a large-scale randomized control trial conducted by a set of developmental psychologists in the early 1990s, the Fast Track Intervention. We match respondents in that study to administrative voter records to evaluate the impact of changing noncognitive skills on future voter turnout.

The Fast Track program was explicitly designed with the goal of improving individuals' noncognitive abilities over the long term. Fast Track, having started in 1992, was one of the earliest and largest ($N \approx 900$) randomized-control trials to target children's noncognitive skills. Beginning when children were in first grade, this multi-site clustered intervention drew heavily from the broad developmental psychology literature to achieve the goal of "increas[ing] [children's] emotion regulation and social-cognitive skills" (Bierman et al. 1999a, 3). Children randomly assigned into the treatment group were exposed to a six-part intervention, which included a formal classroom curricula (PATHS), home visits, parent training groups, tutoring, friendship groups, and peer pairing. Students in the control group did not receive these program components. This program taught children, through hands-on applications, "skills for emotional understanding and communication (i.e., recognizing and labeling emotions), friendship skills (i.e., participation, cooperation, fair play, and negotiation), self-control skills (i.e., behavioral inhibition and arousal modulation), and social problem-solving skills (i.e., problem identification, response generation, response evaluation, and anticipatory planning)" (Bierman et al. 1999a, 7). Program components included discussions, stories, films, games, crafts, joint reading activities, and role-plays (Bierman et al. 1999a). The Fast Track program contained no expressly political content – it was not focused on developing political knowledge, political motivation, or many of the other factors thought to be relevant for political participation. While the program had several components, all were unified in their targeting of improvements in noncognitive skills. (For an even more detailed description of the program, see Holbein (2017); Bierman et al. (1999a,b); and Sorensen and Dodge (2016).)

From follow-up studies, we know that Fast Track helped children develop their noncognitive abilities and that these improvements lasted into adulthood (Bierman et al. 1999a,b, 2002, 2004, 2007, 2010, 2011; Sorensen and Dodge 2016). Table 4.3 documents some of the effects of the Fast Track program. Children assigned to the program had higher levels of empathy, self-efficacy, perseverance, self-control, and social-competence and lower rates of aggression, involvement with deviant peers, hyperactivity, delinquent behavior, and conduct disorders. These effects on noncognitive ability lasted into adulthood (Bierman et al. 2004, 2011; Holbein 2017; Sorensen and Dodge 2016). In short, follow up studies show that the Fast Track program had a long-run effect on children's ability to control their emotions, motivations, thoughts, and behavior and interact productively in social settings.

By way of contrast, Fast Track had only a small and limited effect on cognitive ability. Though the program appeared to increase cognitive

TABLE 4.3 *Fast Track's effect on noncognitive skills*

Noncognitive skills improved	Ages assessed	Citations
Emotional recognition/ regulation/coping	6–7	Bierman et al. (1999a)
Controlling hyperactivity	11–14	Bierman et al. (2010)
Behavioral control	5–6; 6–7; 8–9; 9–10; 11–12; 14–15; 17–18; 19–20	Bierman et al. (2004, 2007, 2010)
Social skills	6–7; 9–11	Bierman et al. (2002, 2004, 2007)
Social problem solving	8–9	Bierman et al. (2002)

Effects of the Fast Track intervention on noncognitive ability. The table shows the constructs affected, when the effects were documented, and the relevant citation for those effects. This table was adapted from that produced in Bierman et al. (2010, 20).

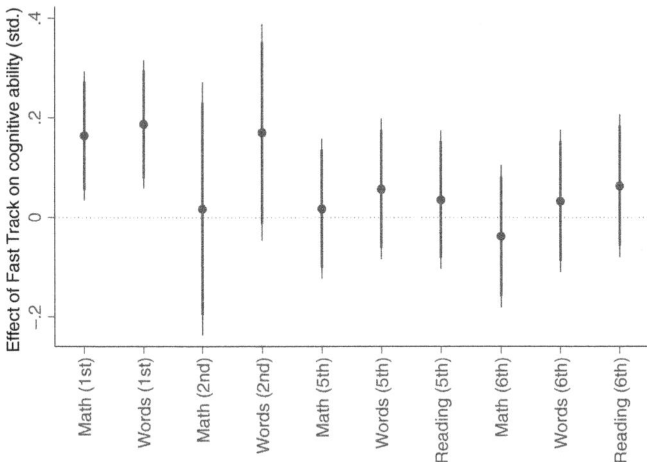

FIGURE 4.9 Effect of Fast Track on cognitive ability

The effect of the Fast Track intervention on measures of cognitive ability. These items come from the Revised Woodcock-Johnson Psycho-Educational Battery – a commonly used measure of children's cognitive ability (Woodcock and Mather 1989). The math items measure the child's skill in performing mathematical calculations such as addition, subtraction, multiplication, and division (59 questions). The words items measure word recognition using pictorial representations, isolated letters, and isolated words (58 questions). The reading items measure the child's ability to select a word that would be appropriate given the context of a written passage (38 questions).

skills in first grade, these gains disappeared by second grade. Figure 4.9 shows this visually. As can be seen, after first grade, none of the effects are significant and most are substantively small.[29] This post-treatment balance has the virtue from a design perspective of allowing us to expand our understanding of the skills that matter for political participation beyond cognitive ability. That is, given Fast Track's limited effects on cognitive ability, we can be reasonably sure that any effects on voter turnout that we observe are likely because of the program's noncognitive skill component. See Chapter 3 and the Appendix for more information on the match to voter files.

4.4.4 Long-Term Improvements in Noncognitive Abilities: Findings

We find that the Fast Track noncognitive skill program had a noticeable effect on adult voter turnout. Those randomly assigned to the Fast Track program voted at a rate 7–9 percentage points higher than the control

[29] Using equivalence testing, when we pool cognitive ability scores across years, we can confidently rule out effects as small as 8.54 percent of a standard deviation.

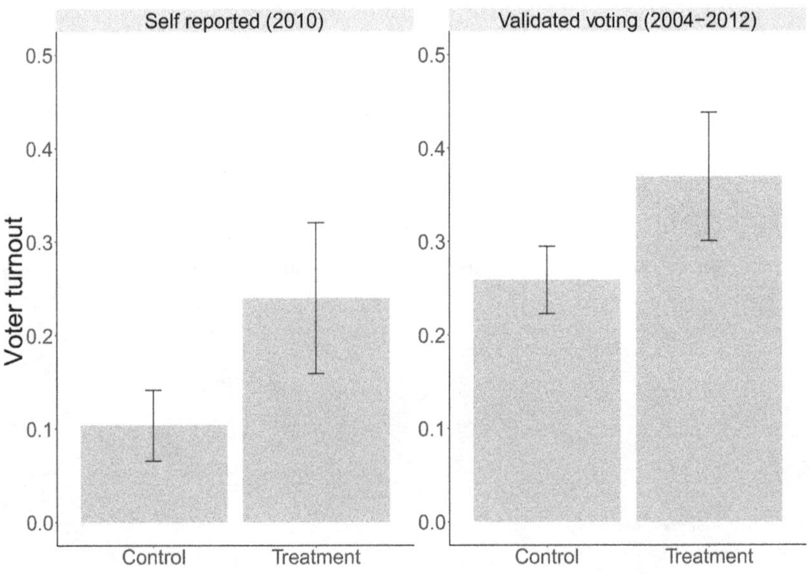

FIGURE 4.10 Effect of Fast Track noncognitive skills intervention on voter turnout

Bar graphs for the Fast Track treatment-on-the-treated (TOT) effect on validated and self-reported voter turnout. Ninety-five percent confidence intervals shown with bars. The plot on the right shows the effect on whether a subject ever voted from 2004 to 2012; the plot on the left shows the estimates for the effect on reporting voting in the past year as measured in 2010. Given that this survey measure was for one election year, we would expect voting rates to be lower (they are) than validated voting across multiple elections. Turnout rates are higher on the right because citizens had more opportunities to vote than in the left.

group. Figure 4.10 shows the effect of full exposure to the Fast Track childhood program on adult turnout (i.e. the treatment on the treated, or the TOT for short).[30] To do so, it plots predicted voter turnout rates across the two groups scaled by compliance rates along with corresponding 95 percent confidence intervals. Figure 4.10 shows that those exposed to the full Fast Track program voted at a rate 11–14 percentage points higher than the control group. This effect is statistically significant and large. Given that this group had a low propensity for voting at baseline (turnout among control group = 26.2 percent), this is a sizable estimate: representing at least a 30–40 percent increase in base voter turnout rates (depending on model specification). This effect is present regardless of whether we measure voting through a survey measure or a validated

[30] For the full model results, see Holbein (2017).

voting measure, suggesting again that our results connecting noncognitive abilities and voting are not confounded by social desirability.

Regardless of the exact mechanisms behind this result, these results are quite meaningful. They suggest that programs that target noncognitive abilities have a strong effect on whether a young person develops into an active voter, or fails to do so. It further suggests that noncognitive abilities are malleable to targeted school programs. When one successfully improves noncognitive abilities, they appear to also increase voter turnout as a result.

4.4.5 Fast Track's Heterogeneities

Who benefited most from Fast Track's noncognitive skills program? Fast Track was equally effective at mobilizing boys and girls, minority and nonminority participants, and children across the four implementation sites. That being said, there is some (albeit modest) evidence that those from low socioeconomic status (SES) benefited the most from this treatment. The effect estimate for low SES subjects is about 2.2 times larger than that for high SES subjects. The effect among low SES individuals represents 53 percent of the base rate of participation; while the high SES effect is only 13 percent of the base rate. This difference in treatment effects is not itself statistically significant ($p \approx 0.3$). However, from this sample it appears that there is at least some suggestive evidence that certain noncognitive skill programs could be most effective among especially low propensity citizens. While the Fast Track study has no measure of political interest, this result implies that some noncognitive skills may actually help individuals who fall in the lowest propensity category – that not all noncognitive abilities act like grit.

Finally, we would note that mobilizing young people – even disadvantaged young people like those in the Fast Track sample – does not have a clear partisan effect. We find that Fast Track had a precisely estimated null effect on party registration. This null effect is shown in Figure 4.11, which displays coefficient plots for the program effects on whether someone registered to be a Democrat, Republican, or a member of another party. As can be seen, being randomly assigned to the Fast Track program had no effect on party registration – those who develop their noncognitive abilities are just as likely to be a Republican as they are to be a Democrat. Despite mobilizing those treated to the program, this noncognitive skill program had no effect on what partisan group individuals chose to affiliate themselves with. Moreover, noncognitive skills appear to be spread

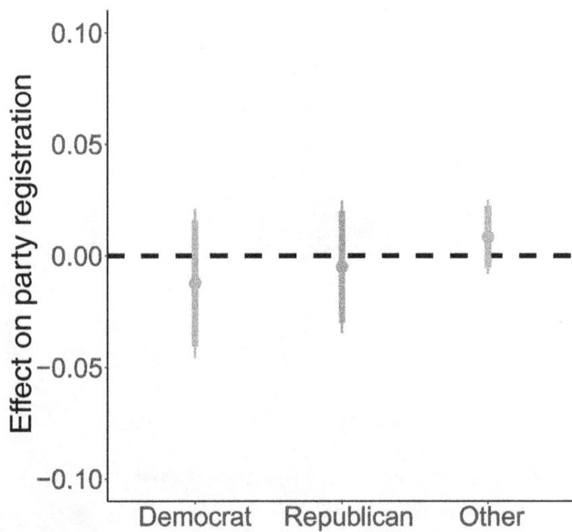

FIGURE 4.11 Fast Track's impact on party registration

Coefficients (points) and 90 percent and 95 percent confidence intervals (bars) for the Fast Track intervention's treatment effects on party registration. Party taken from the match to voter files of Fast Track's records with voter files.

relatively evenly across the ideological spectrum.[31] While not all noncognitive skill programs may work in this way, it suggests that investments in noncognitive skills need not advantage one party over another.

4.4.6 Fast Track's Potential Mechanisms

There are reasons to suspect that the effect of Fast Track on voter turnout was due, in large part, to the program's direct enhancement of students' noncognitive skills. After all, a strong descriptive relationship exists between Fast Track's measures of noncognitive ability and voter turnout (see Figure 4.3). Moreover, the Fast Track program was *explicitly designed* to target these skills and the program was successfully able to do so. Third, the program had no lasting effect on cognitive abilities – the

[31] Related to our discussion of distinctness in the last chapter, noncognitive ability is only weakly related to ideology (Pearson's $r = 0.02$), being a member of a political party (Pearson's $r = 0.09$), and the party one belongs to conditional on belonging to any (Pearson's $r = 0.00$). Individuals with highly developed skills (and less developed skills, for that matter) can be found among individuals at all points of the ideological spectrum. Our results do not change if we include ideology, belonging to a political party, or the party one belongs to conditional on belonging to any.

most likely alternate channel. Finally, other research has shown that Fast Track's other effects appear to largely channel through enhancements to noncognitive abilities (Sorensen and Dodge 2016). Still, the question remains: Did Fast Track increase turnout through the direct channel of noncognitive skill improvements, via indirect improvements of other outcomes that came as a result of noncognitive skill improvements, or because it moved some other factor independent of its effect on noncognitive skills?

Although the Fast Track program was not designed with the primary goal of eliciting causal mechanisms, we can lend some descriptive insights. Our approach estimates mediation models that allow for interdependence among multiple mediators (Kohler, Karlson, and Holm 2011). These models provide an estimate of what proportion of the treatment effect is explained by improvements in observed noncognitive skills or other factors. This approach is better suited for the Fast Track scenario than methods that examine single mediators one at a time (e.g. Imai et al. 2011), given the bundled nature of the program. While these mediation models are valuable, they are descriptive because of the inherent difficulties with unobserved mediators associated with violations of the ignorability assumption (Green, Ha, and Bullock 2010; Imai et al. 2011).

Figure 4.12 shows the results from these models. The mediation results reveal that the Fast Track effects were likely not driven by enhancements to social status, individual resources (i.e. income and attainment), cognitive ability, or enhanced adult attention provided to the participants. Instead, the results suggest that Fast Track's effect largely came from the bundle of noncognitive skills the program improved. Depending on the skills included, the mediation models show that improvement in students' measured noncognitive skills explains approximately 31–52 percent of the treatment effect. This mediation estimate is considerably larger than other potential channels and is consistent with previous work exploring the mediators of Fast Track's impact on crime (Sorensen and Dodge 2016). The strongest individual noncognitive mediators appear to be generalized self-efficacy, empathy, and ability to control one's emotions and behavior. Still, a significant amount of the treatment effect remains unexplained, suggesting that there may be other unmeasured noncognitive skills of importance or downstream consequences from targeting noncognitive skills in childhood that drove this effect.

The mediation estimates also provide some suggestive evidence for the indirect channels we articulated in Chapter 2. First, the mediation

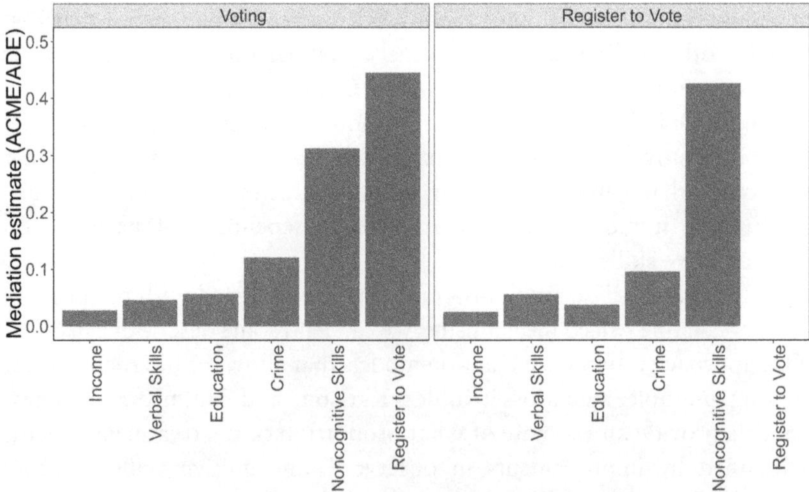

FIGURE 4.12 Potential mechanisms of the Fast Track program
Mediation estimates that allow for interdependence across multiple mediators using KHB decomposition (Kohler, Karlson, and Holm 2011). The mediators include: registration status from validated voting records ($N = 807$); educational attainment in year 19 ($N = 665$); income in year 19 ($N = 578$); the number of delinquent acts in years 8–13 based on public crime records ($N = 746$); scores on a verbal achievement test in years 5–6 ($N = 665$); and noncognitive skills.

models provide some evidence that noncognitive abilities help individuals overcome the obstacles to voting. If we think of one of the main barriers to voting as registration (which many have, see Leighley and Nagler (2013); Wolfinger and Rosenstone (1980)) we can see that noncognitive skill investments play a large role in overcoming this hurdle. Fast Track's effects on noncognitive skills explain about 42.5 percent of the increase in registration, with gains in registration explaining about 44.5 percent of the gains in voting. Second, the mediation analyses also suggest that the negative events hypothesis that we articulated earlier may have some value. The models suggest that Fast Track's effect on turnout can be partially attributed to the fact that participants spent less time in prison. This reduction in crime appears to be the result of upstream improvements in participants' noncognitive skills (Sorensen and Dodge 2016). This suggests that noncognitive abilities perhaps have indirect effects – channeling through registration and crime reductions – and direct effects that help individuals overcome the barriers, obstacles, and distractions that get in the way even after one has registered to vote and avoided time in prison. These multiple channels are consistent with what we showed in the observational data (see Figures 4.6–4.8).

In sum, Fast Track's effect on voter turnout appears to be largely attributable to improvements in participants' noncognitive abilities. This suggests that those who develop self-control and social skills are more likely to target those skills in mobilizing ways throughout their lives. Students who develop noncognitive skills are more likely to participate in politics in adulthood.

4.4.7 Evidence from Other Large-Scale Experimental Designs

While the Fast Track study is but one experiment, a related body of research offers supportive evidence that has been previously overlooked by researchers. Most notably, political scientists Rachel Sondheimer and Don Green find that the Perry Preschool program had a sizeable effect on adult turnout (Sondheimer and Green 2010). Those randomly assigned to quality preschools under the Perry trial voted at a rate 5.6 percentage points higher than those who were randomly assigned to the control group. Sondheimer and Green conclude that these gains are due to the fact that Perry increased participants' educational levels, but our results would suggest that Perry's effect was likely also driven (at least in part) by the fact that participants improved their noncognitive attributes in a lasting and durable way. Perry had the development of children's noncognitive skills as one of its central focal points. As Heckman, Pinto, and Savelyev (2013, 43) note, the "Perry Preschool program provide[s] some of the most compelling evidence that noncognitive skills can be boosted in ways that produce adult success." A core part of the Perry curriculum was to teach students to work well with others and to persevere through obstacles and distractions. For example, students were taught a "plan-do-review" sequence very similar to the PATHS curriculum in the Fast Track program. In this sequence children were taught what to do when they confronted obstacles. They learned to make a detailed plan of what to do, to execute that plan, and to then review their behavior. Research has shown that while Perry did *not* having lasting effects on cognitive ability (Cunha et al. 2006; Heckman and Masterov 2007) – the long assumed primary mover of educational attainment's effects on voting – it *did* have durable effects on children's noncognitive abilities (Heckman et al. 2010; Heckman, Pinto, and Savelyev 2013). Economist James Heckman and his coauthors have provided empirical evidence that many of the gains Perry participants had in income, health, and reduced arrests were attributable to improvements in noncognitive abilities (Heckman and Kautz 2013; Heckman, Pinto, and Savelyev 2013). While it's hard to know exactly how much of Perry's sizable effects on voter turnout are due to improvements in noncognitive skills, these results are consistent with what we have found with the Fast Track intervention. This provides a second example of a childhood intervention that, while having little effects on cognitive abilities, did have lasting effects on noncognitive skills and voting in adulthood. When you invest in kids' noncognitive skills, they are more likely to vote in adulthood.

A reexamination of another childhood program – the Tennessee STAR intervention – offers a similar conclusion. The STAR program was found to have increased voter turnout in adulthood by 2.3 percentage points, smaller than the other programs but still a statistically and substantively significant improvement (Sondheimer and Green 2010). Again, this effect was attributed solely to the education gain from program participation. However, students who were exposed to more conducive learning environments through this program also developed higher noncognitive skills. Other research has shown lasting effects on various proxies of self-control (with, again, little lasting improvement in cognitive skills) (Heckman, Pinto, and Savelyev 2013). Moreover, economics research has concluded that improvements in other adult outcomes (e.g. income) are attributable to improvements in noncognitive skills (Chetty et al. 2011). While Tennessee STAR is no different from other large-scale interventions in that we can never be 100 percent certain of the exact mechanisms driving the effect, this evidence, again, is consistent with what we find with the Fast Track intervention.

These two additional studies draw their evidence from large-scale interventions in early childhood. Can interventions targeted slightly later in the life course still affect voting? While this is an area for future research, we do have some cursory evidence that improvements in noncognitive skills (1) occur later in the life course (as we discussed thoroughly in Chapter 3) and (2) when improved during this later period can still potentially affect adult voter turnout. For example, an interdisciplinary team of economists, child psychologists, and political scientists recently explored whether an unconditional cash transfer program improved adolescents' noncognitive abilities (Akee et al. 2018a) and voter participation (Akee et al. 2018b). The income transfer program was shown to encourage disadvantaged families keep their children in school longer and to engage in parenting behaviors that promoted noncognitive skill development. Those children who improved their noncognitive skills showed large gains in their adult rates of voter turnout – on the order of a 8–20 percentage point increase. Those who received the income transfer, but did not improve their noncognitive skills, saw little to no increase in voter turnout. Likewise, adults who received the income transfer, but whose noncognitive skills are likely less malleable, also saw little to no effect on turnout. While the mechanisms of this cash transfer program are likely many and complex, the cursory evidence suggests that, again, noncognitive skills may have played an important role. These results provide some suggestive evidence that adolescent improvements in noncognitive skills can still affect voting.

In the next chapter, we provide evidence from a variety of other larger-scale randomized control trials related to civic education. We outline the nature and scope of these programs as these RCTs have direct bearing on the policy implications for civic education. For now, we simply note that each of these incorporated a variety of in-school programs to better engage students in more active learning and in noncognitive skill development. They were found to increase students' ability to problem-solve, work together in groups, and persevere when the going gets tough. Simultaneously, these programs have shown promising effects on young peoples' levels of civic participation.

As is always the case, more experimentation is needed, but these results suggest that noncognitive skills matter a great deal in determining who votes and who stays home.

4.5 THE BIG PICTURE

In this chapter, we provided extensive quantitative evidence – from multiple data sources and using multiple analytic techniques – that noncognitive skills promote voter turnout. An individual's general ability to control their thoughts, motivations, actions, and behaviors has consequences for civic behavior. This pattern holds across multiple data sources, various measures of noncognitive ability, alternative measures of participation (self-reports, validated voting records, and other civic behaviors), and multiple methodological approaches (observational and experimental). The results presented in this chapter suggest that in addition to not being explained by the standard observable predictors of political participation – such as political interest or motivation, socioeconomic status, educational attainment, gender, age, race, family dynamics, or the Big Five personality traits – the relationship between noncognitive ability and voter turnout is also not an artifact of the host of unobservable characteristics that remain constant within families, twin pairs, or individuals themselves. As such we can rule out the possibility that the relationship is driven by one's underlying propensity to participate, genetics, other stable or inherited personality traits, social desirability toward voting (given our use of validated vote records), parenting style, political socialization, family members' levels of participation in politics, parents' cognitive and noncognitive ability, or the sum total of one's family history. In so doing, the results we have presented are especially powerful because they suggest that as best we can tell from the available observational data sources, noncognitive ability appears to be a core contributor to whether young people develop into active voters, or fail to do so. Our experimental results help us to go further – allowing us to show that both short and long-term changes to noncognitive attributes can have consequences for youth turnout.

This finding makes several notable contributions for our understanding of what drives young people to vote. Most strikingly, and contrary to what others have argued (e.g. Hernstein and Murray 1994; Luskin 1990; Nie, Junn, and Stehlik-Barry 1996; Wolfinger and Rosenstone 1980), our results suggest that cognitive ability does not capture all the individual resources needed to vote. Indeed, noncognitive abilities remain strong predictors of voting when we include measures of cognitive ability. And when we subject individuals to a program that improves their noncognitive skills, but has *no effect* on cognitive ability, there are still sizable effects on voter turnout. These results imply that beyond cognitive aptitude, self-control and social skills make citizens more oriented toward participating, likelier to overcome the barriers that get in the way of their following through, and better able to avoid negative life events that make them unwilling, unable, or ineligible to vote.

In this chapter, we have stitched together the available empirical evidence linking noncognitive skills and political participation. While the data sources are many, and allow for various observational, quasi-experimental, and experimental methods, much more remains to be done. At present, the best we can do is to cobble together educational datasets that happen to have a few political measures, or to which we can merge in validated voting or a tacked-on survey. As such, our analysis has only scratched the surface of understanding the nature and influence of noncognitive skills for political attitudes and behaviors. Moving forward, political scientists would do well to measure and explore noncognitive abilities. In so doing, researchers should be cognizant of the multi-dimensional and interrelated nature of noncognitive skills and the fact that including these measures on political surveys may have the potential for priming effects to influence what exactly these surveys are measuring. Until noncognitive skills become a part of the general lexicon and measurement strategies of political scientists, our understanding of their relevance will be limited.

We will return to our thoughts on how these findings contribute to policy and practice in the concluding chapter. Suffice it to say, our findings have implications for how policymakers design the education system and where, when, and how scholars examine the antecedents to voting. Our work speaks clearly to both the timing of when we should target our efforts (childhood and early adolescence are key periods) and the factors that we target (noncognitive skills matter a great deal) to increase voting. Education policymakers are currently weighing the costs and benefits of emphasizing noncognitive skills in education curricula. However, these debates have narrowly focused on the potential benefits that noncognitive skills have for academic performance and labor force outcomes. Our results illustrate that noncognitive skills can have positive effects on other life outcomes, especially for measures of civic engagement that have vital importance for societal well-being.

PART II

PUBLIC POLICIES AND YOUTH TURNOUT

Thus far, we have made the case that noncognitive skills are an important piece of the turnout puzzle. These skills help individuals to follow through on their civic attitudes and intentions in the face of obstacles. The participatory barriers to registration and voting, including daily life distractions, tend to be greater for young people, so these skills help to explain why so many politically motivated young Americans fail to vote, even though they are interested in and want to participate.

Using a unique combination of longitudinal surveys, large-scale school administrative records, and public voter files paired with experimental, observational, and qualitative techniques, we provided comprehensive evidence that young people who develop noncognitive skills are much more likely to vote in adulthood than those that do not. This offers a fundamental shift in scholarly thinking about the factors that drive people to the act of voting. This perspective more fully accounts for the individual skills, attributes, and motivations that determine if individuals not only set, but also follow through on, their behavioral intentions in the political realm. In the past, research tended to focus on the importance of political motivation as a key contributor for overcoming the costs of voting. Yet, political motivation is not enough to help people follow through on their political goals. Other theories focused on cognitive abilities – especially political knowledge and verbal capabilities – as the key resource that individuals use to overcome the costs of voting. In contrast, we show that noncognitive skills are an overlooked factor that help young people to translate civic attitudes into civic action.

What are the practical implications for this finding? Recognizing that some individuals have a desire to participate but lack the skills to overcome the obstacles and distractions that prevent them from engaging in politics also offers a new perspective for thinking about policy solutions to help address low and unequal rates of civic participation. The finding that noncognitive skills predict turnout does *not* mean this is only an individual-level story. To the contrary, the observed relationship reflects both individual-level behaviors and the institutions that structure and constrain those behaviors. We thus shift our focus in this section of the book to key institutions that deserve scrutiny in light of our findings. The analysis in this section considers two complementary paths toward promoting youth turnout: one in the education system and the other through the electoral system.

First, our results highlight the need to reconsider the nature and content of civic education. As the rich literature on civic education recognizes, "schools are the only institutions with the capacity and mandate to reach virtually every young person in the country. Of all institutions, schools are the most systematically and directly responsible for imparting civic norms" (Gibson and Levine 2003, 5). At present, however, civic education – the predominant educational channel for teaching citizenship in schools – tends to focus on relaying knowledge and facts about government and politics – an approach consistent with the dominant theories of voting that have emphasized cognitive ability and political knowledge as the roots of voter turnout.

In the next chapter, we do a comprehensive analysis, using multiple datasets and methods, to evaluate if this approach has an impact on youth participation. Our work suggests that teaching political knowledge (as standard civics curricula traditionally does), getting young people interested in politics, and enhancing their verbal cognitive abilities, while noble goals, are not enough to see young people to the finish line of active civic engagement. Our analyses highlight the need for schools to help young people develop the skills required to convert civic attitudes into civic action. We discuss this all in greater detail in Chapter 5, where we also outline concrete steps that schools can take to help make young voters.

Second, the empirical results presented in the previous section underscore another path to increased youth engagement: electoral reforms aimed at lowering some of the key administrative barriers to participation. We explore the influence of these reforms in Chapter 6. In showing that individuals require a set of noncognitive abilities to overcome the obstacles that can stand in their way of participating in politics, our analysis draws attention to voting obstacles themselves. We show that the most effective electoral reforms are those that lower the obstacles for new voters, such as reforms that allow voter registration when citizens are most politically motivated. Rules like same-day registration (SDR) and preregistration appear to be the most effective because they work to bring in young voters at critical points. SDR allows young people who have procrastinated registering, perhaps as a result of a lack of self-control, to still participate in the electoral process. Likewise, preregistration allows young people to register well in advance of the election, when their eligible peers are excited and being mobilized. These reforms help remove the obstacles to voting when individuals are most attentive to politics, making it easier to then follow through with voting.

5

Rethinking Civic Education

> Since the achievement of American independence, the universal and ever-repeated argument in favor of free schools has been that the general intelligence which they are capable of diffusing ... is indispensable to the continuance of a republican government.
>
> — Horace Mann, 1846[1]

Scholars, activists, and policymakers have long looked to civic education as the most promising path for increasing political participation in American democracy. Civic education is thought to teach young people how to make sense of a complex political world and their rights and responsibilities as citizens, which in turn should make students more civically engaged. The structure and content of civic education in the United States, however, reflects cognitive-based assumptions about the link between education and turnout. Civics courses are often designed to bestow young citizens with knowledge and facts about government, political institutions, and democratic principles. Assessments of political knowledge – typically measured with standardized tests – are considered the primary metric of success for civic education and the education system more broadly. Civics, in short, has been myopically focused on developing young people's cognitive capacities.

Yet we have shown that cognitive ability is not enough to make young voters. In the previous section of the book, we showed that noncognitive skills – a cluster of attributes related to self-regulation, effortfulness,

[1] Quote from the "founding father of public education" in his tenth Annual Report to the Secretary of the Massachusetts State Board of Education (1846).

and interpersonal interactions – shape participatory behaviors. Citizens need not be automatons with infinite computing capacity and an endless reservoir of facts about government and politics. Rather, they need political motivation – the desire to participate – *and* they need the noncognitive skills to help them overcome the obstacles that might otherwise prevent follow through on those participatory intentions. This distinction between cognitive and noncognitive abilities is critical because the ways to nurture and develop them do not always overlap.

In considering the policy lessons to be learned from our theoretical framework and empirical results, we start by reflecting on the role of the education system. We do so because discussions and research on noncognitive skills have centered on schools and education policy. Education stakeholders are actively evaluating ways to shift education priorities to incorporate the development of noncognitive skills, but previous research has not considered the implications for civic engagement. As a result, civic education has not been reassessed in the same way as math, reading, and STEM curricula. Our results in the previous section indicate that a civic education system based on developing knowledge and facts is simply not enough to set young people on a path toward voter participation.

In making the case that we need to rethink civic education, we start by evaluating the impact of the current civic education system on youth turnout. Using a rich and varied source of data, we show that civic education does not have an impact on turnout, even if it might produce gains in political knowledge. Perhaps the most disheartening finding presented in this chapter is that civics has been ineffective at promoting active citizenship for *decades*. Based on this evidence, we contend that the standard approach to making young voters, and the models of citizen engagement on which it is built, need to be reconsidered.

We are by no means the first to conclude that civic education is broken (e.g. Gibson and Levine 2003). Our contribution is to make recommendations rooted in a more complete theoretical framework that has been rigorously and empirically evaluated. We conclude this chapter with suggestions for civic education reforms that should be more effective in preparing citizens for active citizenship. While no single approach will completely fix civics, there are some promising efforts afoot to help young people prepare for political participation. We believe it is time to rethink civics training informed by a more complete understanding of the factors that influence voter turnout. With the right theoretical framework and empirical evidence, we provide advice for creating civics curricula that will be more successful in preparing citizens for democratic engagement.

Before turning to our empirical analyses, we first lay the groundwork by (briefly) reviewing the history of civics in the United States, its basic rationale and objectives, and what we know about civics' status in contemporary America.[2]

5.1 CIVIC EDUCATION IN THE UNITED STATES

Scholars, philosophers, and other public thinkers have long emphasized the critical importance of civic education for the survival of democracy and society. In *Laws*, Plato implored his reader to "ask in general what great benefit the state derives from the training by which it educates its citizens, and the reply will be perfectly straightforward. The good education they have received will make them good men."[3] Plato goes on to explain that a vital goal of a state-provided education is to lead children to want to become what he calls "perfect citizens" who understand "how both to rule and be ruled righteously."[4]

From the very birth of the United States, civic education has been viewed as essential for the maintenance of our system of government. The founding fathers argued that education was needed to prepare citizens for civic participation by developing an understanding and acceptance of the principles, rights, and responsibilities of democratic governance. In *A Defense of the Constitution of the United States of America*, John Adams argued that instructing citizens

> in every kind of knowledge that can be of use to them in the practice of their moral duties, as men, citizens, and Christians, and of their political and civil duties, as members of society and freemen, ought to be the care of the public, and of all who have any share in the conduct of its affairs, in a manner that never yet has been practiced in any age or nation.
>
> —Adams (1788, 414).

President George Washington took a similar perspective in the early years of the new republic, arguing for

> the assimilation of the principles, opinions, and manners of our country-men by the common education of a portion of our youth from every quarter.... The more

[2] For a more thorough history of civics in America, see Schudson (1998); Ravitch and Viteritti (2003); and Smith (1997).

[3] Plato, *Laws*, 641b7–10.

[4] Plato, *Laws*, 643e4–6.

homogenous our citizens can be made in these particulars the greater will be our prospect of permanent union; and a primary object of such a national institution should be the education of our youth in the science of government.

—Washington[5]

Likewise, Thomas Jefferson asserted that among all of the possible arguments for public support of education, "none is more important, none more legitimate, than that of rendering the people the safe, as they are the ultimate, guardians of their own liberty."[6] Following this perspective, public education flourished in the young country, and the population had one of the highest literacy rates in the world at the time (Ravitch and Viteritti 2003; Schudson 1998).[7] After visiting early nineteenth-century America, French political theorist Alexis de Tocqueville observed that "it cannot be doubted that in the United States the instruction of the people contributes powerfully to the support of the democratic republic" (De Tocqueville 2003, Vol. 1, 329). Later, in the twentieth century, Franklin Roosevelt stated, "That the schools make worthy citizens is the most important responsibility placed on them."[8] It seems very clear that civics training was a primary motivation for the development of public education in the United States as a means of developing citizens to be actively engaged in democratic governance.

The centrality of civics to the mission of public schools continues to be in place – at least on paper. According to the National Standards for Civics and Government – a 2014 report commissioned by the US Department of Education – "the goal of education in civics and government is informed, responsible participation in political life by competent citizens committed to the fundamental values and principles of American constitutional democracy. Their effective and responsible participation requires the acquisition of a body of knowledge and of intellectual and participatory skills." At present, all fifty states mention the civic development of their students as a core part of the mission of public education, with 49/50 flagship universities doing so as well.[9] Almost all states acknowledge that schools are in place to "enable students to become informed, responsible

5 "Eighth Annual Message," December 7, 1796.

6 Epilogue to *Securing the Republic.*

7 Peterson, Paul E. (2010). Saving Schools: From Horace Mann to Virtual Learning, pp. 21–36.

8 White House Conference on Children in a Democracy (1942), as quoted in Crittenden and Levine (2013).

9 South Dakota is the lone exception.

participants in political life."[10] For example, a 1990 National Governor's Association statement affirmed the position that

> a well-educated population is the key to our future. Americans must be prepared to participate knowledgeably in our democracy and our democratic institutions. Today a new standard of an educated citizenry is required, one suitable for the next century .... [All students] must understand and accept the responsibilities and obligations of citizenship.
>
> —NGA Statement, 1990[11]

The perspective that education should promote civic engagement also permeates local school district governance. When asked, education officials readily agree that civics is a foundational part of their mission. For example, the Wake County Public Schools System (the fifteenth largest district in the United States) lists as part of its core mission the desire to help students be "ready for productive citizenship" on graduation.[12] Similar mission statements can be found for Chicago Public Schools (which has a mission to "prepare each [student] for success in college, career, and *civic life*."), Miami Dade Public Schools (which has a mission to see that "students are empowered to lead productive and fulfilling lives as lifelong learners and *responsible citizens*"), and Fairfax County Schools (which has a mission to make "global and ethical citizens"), to name a few.

While there may be some competing views on the specific citizenship outcomes that schools should be promoting (MacMullen 2015), there seems to be widespread agreement that voter participation is among them.[13] Justice Sonya Sotomayor recently asserted that "civic education is the key to inspiring kids to want to stay involved."[14] Likewise, former Justice Sandra Day O'Connor argued "the only reason we have public school education in America is because in the early days of the country, our leaders thought we had to teach our young generation about citizenship ... that obligation never ends. If we don't take every generation of young people and make sure they understand that they are an essential

[10] See Alabama Course of Study Outline, 2010.

[11] Quoted in "The Role of civic education" report, Margart Stimman Branson.

[12] See WCPSS Vision, 2020.

[13] Indeed, some scholars and advocates seem to devalue voting relative to other activities. For example, the Carnegie report, "Guardian of Democracy: The Civic Mission of Schools," emphasizes "Civic shortfalls extend beyond *mere* voting." (14, emphasis added)

[14] See "Civics ed key to equity, improving discourse," *Education Drive*, September 22, 2017.

part of government, we won't survive."[15] From our structured qualitative interviews with civics teachers, we heard instructors say again and again that civic participation was important. As one first-year social studies teacher explained, "Our end goal is to get [students] to be well-rounded citizens that ... participate in the community."[16]

In sum, making young citizens who are politically informed and engaged is a foundational mission of the education system. Public education was established in large part to teach an understanding of democracy (political knowledge), to instill a sense of civic duty (political motivation), and to promote engagement in civic and political life (voter participation).

5.1.1 The Decline of Civic Education in an Accountability Era

Civic education was a primary motivation for the creation of public education and appears to have the vocal support of prominent public officials today. However, it has been arguably neglected in the education system in recent decades. While it was common in the 1960s for students to take multiple courses in civics covering not only the structure of American government but also the role of citizens and the issues they and the government face, the topics are getting squeezed out of the current curriculum. In North Carolina, for instance, there is a single required civics course – American History: The Founding Principles, Civics and Economics – and it covers the history and development of national and state government, the US political and legal system, economic markets, and personal financial literacy. Only a small part of the course is focused on civic participation and voting. North Carolina is not unusual in this regard. With the rise of economic globalization, there are concerns that schools are increasingly serving the needs of the private marketplace rather than preparing citizens for democratic citizenship (Youniss and Levine 2009).

This decline in civics training may be at least partially attributable to the performance accountability movement and The No Child Left Behind Act of 2002 (NCLB). Signed into law with bipartisan support, NCLB requires schools to conduct assessments in math, reading/language arts,

[15] See "Former Supreme Court Justice Sandra Day O'Connor on the importance of civic education," *Washington Post*, April 12, 2012.

[16] Quote drawn from an interview with a first-year social studies teacher in North Carolina in May 2017.

and science, but not in civics or social studies (Ahn and Vigdor 2014; Dee and Jacob 2011; Holbein 2016; Holbein and Ladd 2017). Given the external forces that NCLB (and the more recent ESSA that replaced it) places on schools, it is not surprising that civics courses have often fallen by the wayside. In 2001, thirty-four states had assessments on social studies, but that declined to twenty-one states by 2012.[17] Among a recent survey of civics instructors, 70 percent report that civics has been crowded out because of pressure to show progress on statewide math and language arts tests.[18] A 2006 study by the Center on Education Policy found that 71 percent of districts reported cutting back time on social studies to make more space for reading and math instruction.[19]

In our qualitative interviews, civics teachers offered similar concerns about the negative impact of standardized testing. When asked "Can you think of anything that is preventing you from making your students more engaged in politics?" one teacher had a telling response, "Time. Always time. And the standardized testing."[20] Another teacher offered a similar take: "Standardized testing is a way to try to keep us accountable, but it really kind of narrows what we can do. You need to cover all this material within this amount of time, and then you have a 40 question test at the end .... It's difficult because I really like doing a mock election in my class. I think the kids really get a lot out of it and understand it [but] I don't necessarily always have the time because I'm held to making sure my students pass these standardized test[s]."[21] The counter-argument to this concern is that "what gets tested gets taught." In other words, a test would create incentives for schools to focus on civic education. While the debate about the role of education testing will surely continue, we would suggest that the common focus is on political knowledge.

[17] "Few States Test Students on Civics," *Education Week*, October 11, 2012. It is important to note, however, that a growing number of states require at least one civics course to graduate. The key distinction is that because the testing framework emphasizes reading and math, civics is viewed as less important.

[18] "High Schools, Civics, and Citizenship: What Social Studies Teachers Think and Do," *American Enterprise Institute Report*, September 30, 2010.

[19] See "Schools Cut Back Subjects to Push Reading and Math," *New York Times*, March 26, 2006.

[20] Interview conducted with Wake County Public School System social studies teacher, June 2017.

[21] Interview conducted with Wake County Public School System social studies teacher, June 2017.

5.2 ARE FACTS AND KNOWLEDGE ENOUGH?

At first glance, it might seem that simply placing a greater emphasis on civic education would help to remedy dismal rates of youth voter participation. One recent headline read, "Why Don't Young People Vote? Because Schools Teach Us Nothing about Politics."[22] Many scholars have called for renewed attention to civic education as the policy solution to declining civic engagement in the United States (Hanmer 2009; Hibbing and Theiss-Morse 2002; Hillygus 2005; Putnam 2000; Zukin et al. 2006). For example, the 2017 American Political Science Association publication, *Teaching Civic Engagement Across the Discipline*, declared the need for "quality civic education to foster the redevelopment of a knowledgeable, capable, and engaged citizenry .... Since the end of the Cold War, education policy has failed to invest in this foundation of our democracy"(4).

Yet, civics training has too often been equated with teaching facts and figures about politics and government – an approach that parallels cognitive-based models of voting behavior. As such, these courses emphasize factual knowledge of American government (e.g. the contents of the Constitution and the branches of government) and give considerably less attention to the *how* and *why* of civic participation. A recent nationwide survey conducted by the Carnegie-Knight Task Force found that civics teachers overwhelmingly see civics as being transformed into a narrow curriculum that is focused primarily on preparing students for state-mandated exams.[23] Statewide civics assessments are dominated by multiple-choice questions that require rote memorization rather than engagement in politics. One North Carolina teacher explained,

> I want to make sure kids are prepared for the state test because I know I'm judged on how well they do ... I understand why they need standardized testing because they like to measure and gauge and say we can prove how much growth the kids have and how much success they've had. But as a tool, honestly, if you saw how much – a lot of it's smoke and mirrors ... to be honest with you, what the tests really are, are reading tests at this point. If the kids are good at reading a historical

[22] See "Why don't young people vote? Because school teaches us nothing about politics," *The Guardian*, June 8, 2017, www.theguardian.com/commentisfree/2017/jun/08/young-people-vote-school-teach-politics-curriculum-election

[23] "Mandatory Testing and News in the Schools: Implications for civic education," *Carnegie-Knight Task Force Report*, 2005.

passage and pulling information from it, then they can do well on the test. They don't have to know a lot of content anymore for these tests.[24]

The problem, as political scientist Lance Bennett argues, is that "learning environments that emphasize old style, fact based, teacher-centered pedagogy may succeed in imparting abstract facts and skills of the sort that can be tested, but ... they do not help young citizens translate that knowledge into later civic practice" (Bennett 2007).

This cognitive-based focus of civic education is perhaps best captured by the structure and content of the Civics Assessment of the National Assessment of Educational Progress (NAEP), an exam mandated by the US Congress to collect and report information about student achievement in various academic subjects. Although civics exams were previously administered at grades 4, 8, and 12, it has been reduced to just 8th graders as of 2018. The 2018 NAEP framework explains that "to do well on this assessment, students will have to show broad knowledge of the American constitutional system and of the workings of our civil society. They will also be required to demonstrate a range of intellectual skills – identifying and describing important information, explaining and analyzing it, and evaluating information and defending positions with appropriate evidence and careful reasoning." Yet, as political scientist Arthur Lupia explains, NAEP "provides no evidence about the extent to which the topics covered on the civics exam actually cause people to perform important tasks [like voting] competently when they are legally old enough to do so" (Lupia 2016, 254).

Our qualitative interviews with civics teachers pointed to another factor, beyond the constraints of testing, that is shaping the content of civics training: political polarization. Teachers discussed the risk of talking about contentious political issues in the classroom. According to one teacher, "It's really hard when sometimes you have parents who don't want their child to hear different sides." Another explained, "I guess I worry that a parent will be like, 'Why are you in here having this kid present about gay marriage or abortion or police brutality?' Whatever it might be. I worry about parents. I think as a teacher I'm always gonna worry about parents." One teacher summarized the inherent tension as follows: "If you asked any administrator, any teacher, yeah, it's important for students to talk about [politics] and be engaged. You ask any school, and part of their mission statement is going to be [to encourage students to

[24] Interview conducted with Wake County Public School System social studies teacher,June 2017.

be] active members of their society [who] are engaged politically. But the problem is to put that on a standardized test is like political suicide ... if Johnny's mom and dad find out that gay marriage was being discussed in class, and they don't want Johnny talking about that in class ... they're going to start going up the chain and calling for somebody's head."[25] A fact-based civics curriculum fits within the accountability framework and helps to avoid the potential controversies of political discussion, but it might also mean that we are failing to live up to the civic mission of the educational system.

Criticisms of a fact-based civic education are not new. As far back as the mid-nineteenth century, John Stuart Mill made an appeal for experiential civic learning: "As we do not learn to read or write, to ride or swim, by being merely told how to do it, but by doing it, so it is only by practising popular government on a limited scale, that the people will ever learn how to exercise it on a larger."[26] More recently, education writer Rick Kahlenberg called the 2016 presidential election a "Sputnik moment" for civic education because it forced us to confront our failure "at what the nation's founders saw as education's most basic purpose," preparing students for thoughtful and competent self-government. Robert Pondiscio, a fellow at the conservative education think tank, The Thomas B. Fordham Institute, confirmed that "voices on the right and left critiqued the recent election as proof of the failure of civic education."[27] Conventional civic education has been criticized as too narrowly concerned with remedying deficits in historical facts about government (Youniss and Levine 2009). Pondiscio, for example, criticized the most recent redesign of the AP curriculum for requiring reading of dense formal language in court cases and the archaic writing structure of historical documents, leading to the conclusion that "Literacy, not content knowledge, is the most significant hurdle to widespread adoption of AP Government at present."[28] Many youth development organizations and civic education leaders have proposed action-centered civic learning, but these programs are often

[25] Interview conducted with Wake County Public School System social studies teacher, June 2017.

[26] John Stuart Mill, "Tocqueville [1]," Collected Works, xviii, 63.

[27] See "Making citizens: A 'Sputnik moment' for civic education?," *American Enterprise Institute*, February 22, 2017, www.aei.org/events/making-citizens-a-sputnik-moment-for-civic-education/.

[28] See "Making citizens: A 'Sputnik moment' for civic education?", *American Enterprise Institute*, February 22, 2017, www.aei.org/events/making-citizens-a-sputnik-moment-for-civic-education/.

explicitly apolitical (Zukin et al. 2006). Moreover, as Peter Levine and James Youniss observe, there has been mixed evidence on these programs' effectiveness, reflecting "variation in their quality and a lack of philosophical clarity in their driving rationale" (Youniss and Levine 2009). Nonetheless, these early efforts have spurred some program evaluation research that will inform our recommendations at the end of this chapter.

We contend that the system of bubble-sheet civics does not teach the skills necessary to actually participate in politics. The political information needed to vote is different than (and less than) assumed by classic models of voter turnout and the current structure of civic education (Lupia 2016). In criticizing standard political science measures of political knowledge and standardized civic tests like NAEP, Lupia argues that civic education should teach "content that not only corresponds to improved performance at important tasks with respect to well-defined competence criteria, but that is also perceived by prospective learners as helping them advance their core concerns" (Lupia 2016, 255). The fact that a core part of the mission of civic education is to promote voter turnout suggests that the knowledge needed to engage in politics might be more applied and practical – it might include information about the mechanics of voter registration, about when and how to cast a ballot, and about the two political parties and the issues surrounding contemporary political debates. It may also suggest the importance of helping young people develop the skills necessary to find and evaluate information themselves and to persevere when obstacles or distractions get in their way. Unfortunately, such skills are far removed from the standard political knowledge questions about policy and politics taught or asked about on NAEP or in political science surveys.[29]

To be sure, some research suggests civic education can increase those standard measures of political knowledge. One of the classic studies on this topic, Niemi and Junn (2005), finds that civics exposure has a positive (albeit small) relationship with civic knowledge. More recently, Campbell and Niemi (2016) used a unique dataset of individual-level data from the NAEP exam to show that civic education increases political knowledge, with more pronounced effects among minority citizens. Positive effects on political knowledge have also been found for specialized civics training programs, such as Kids Voting USA (McDevitt and Kiousis 2004),

[29] For a more extensive treatment on the inadequacy of the ANES political knowledge scale items, see Lupia (2016).

Student Voices program (Pasek et al. 2008), and a Bill of Rights Institute curriculum (Green et al. 2011). In sum, there is some evidence that civic education increases cognitive capacities about politics. When given more civics content – knowledge and facts about government and politics – individuals' levels of political information appear to rise.[30]

The critical assumption, however, is that any increase in political knowledge will also increase participation. In his book, *Cultural Literacy: What Every American Needs to Know*, E. D. Hirsch argues, "Only by piling up specific, communally shared information can children learn to participate in complex cooperative activities with other members of their community" (Hirsch Jr, Kett, and Trefil 1988, xv). It is true that empirical research shows that people with more political knowledge and cognitive capacity are more likely to vote – but the causal mechanism is less clear. Although there is a rich literature examining the relationship between civic education and political outcomes (e.g. political knowledge, interest, values, and attitudes), there are only a handful of studies that have considered voter turnout – perhaps because the training often happens long before voter eligibility. Among the few studies examining voter turnout, the results are quite mixed – some find a positive relationship (Bachner 2010; Kiousis and McDevitt 2008; Pasek et al. 2008), but others find no effect (Persson and Oscarsson 2010).[31] Again, we contend a civic curriculum that is successful at improving political knowledge is unlikely to have an impact on voter participation.

5.3 ASSESSING CIVIC EDUCATION EFFECTS

We have made the case that the current approach to civic education will not prepare young people to behave politically. It is, however, a challenging task to convincingly evaluate the impact of civic education on turnout for several reasons. First, and perhaps somewhat surprisingly given the civic mission of schools, not many data sources exist in which civics exposure and voter turnout are linked. Moreover, estimating the effect of civics is complicated because of concerns about selection bias – that those who are already likely to engage are more likely to

30 For other studies on this topic see, Carpini and Keeter (1996); Feldman et al. (2007); Howe (2011); McDevitt and Chaffee (2000); Meirick and Wackman (2004).

31 For older studies of civics' role in political behavior, see Langton and Jennings (1968) and Litt (1963).

choose to take civics courses.[32] Many of the aforementioned previous studies have used a conditional-on-observables approach, wherein civics exposure is simply related to civic participation outcomes with a few demographic controls included in the model. Only very rarely are experimental or quasi-experimental techniques leveraged to identify the causal effect of civic education, and most – if not all – of these occur outside the United States.[33] This leaves open the possibility that the simple relationship between civic education and civic participation is confounded by unobservable individual or contextual characteristics, including, for example, that young people who are more politically interested enroll in more civics courses. If this were the case, any positive relationship between civics enrollment and voting would be biased upward. That is, by filling civic education courses with individuals who would have been likely to vote already, it may make civic education look like it is having an effect on voting, when it is not – any supposed gains that we might attribute to civics courses might rather be attributed to selection.

With these challenges in mind, we attempt here a comprehensive analysis of the role of civic education on youth turnout. We take two approaches. We start with the conventional approach of looking at civics exposure in adolescence as it relates to voting in adulthood, conditional on observable characteristics. This approach uses all of the available longitudinal surveys that have measures of civics exposure and voting of which we are aware. These data sources include the Wisconsin Longitudinal Study (WLS), the National Longitudinal Survey of Youth 1979 (NLSY79), the National Education Longitudinal Study of 1988 (NELS:88), the National Longitudinal Survey of Youth 1997 (NLSY97), the Education Longitudinal Study of 2002 (ELS:2002), and the National Longitudinal Study of Adolescent to Adult Health (Add Health). We described these datasets in great detail in Chapters 3 and 4, as we used many of them to explore the noncognitive abilities that precede voting. We simply note here that each of these is nationally representative in the time period of study (with the exception of the WLS, which was designed

32 This is of particular concern for studies attempt to examine college curriculum effects (e.g. Hillygus 2005).

33 A few randomized control trials that have civic education components have been evaluated, but all of these have been done outside the United States. These too, however, find mixed effects – sometimes finding positive effects, sometimes null effects, and sometimes even negative effects on various measures of citizen participation (Finkel 2002; Gottlieb 2016; Mvukiyehe and Samii 2015; Sexton 2017).

to be representative at the state level for the given cohort it was studying and each has reported measures of civics course enrollment in adolescence and voting in early adulthood, along with formal controls that we can include in our models.[34] Going one step beyond previous research in this area, we are able to augment our conditional-on-observables models with family fixed effects in our Add Health sample, given that this contains a sibling over-sample.[35] This approach allows us to hold constant observed and unobserved factors that remain constant within families (e.g. parental voting, political socialization, parenting style, etc.), which helps protect us from some potential sources of selection bias.

We supplement these analyses with a second examination that uses panel techniques to explore the effect of civics on voter turnout. As we describe in greater detail, this approach leverages changes in civic education requirements and specific course availability over time. This analysis allows us to rule out any additional factors that might be biasing our estimates.

5.4 EMPIRICAL RESULTS

Figure 5.1 shows the results from our multiple survey-based datasets. It plots the estimates for each of the given datasets (vertically sorted by time, with the exception of the Add Health sample) with coefficient plots. Coefficient plots display the size of an effect estimate (with a point) and the statistical uncertainty around that estimate (with bars). In our figures here, we display two error bars: one representing the 95 percent

34 We attempted to include a similar set of controls across the datasets used in Figure 5.1; however, there were inherent constraints given variation in variable availability across data sources. WLS controls include cognitive ability, noncognitive ability (self-reported), the Big Five Personality Traits, gender, age, parents' education, family income, and number of siblings. NLSY79 controls for cognitive ability, noncognitive ability (self-reported), gender, age, parents' education, and family income. NELS:88 controls for cognitive ability, noncognitive ability (self-reported and teacher reported), race, gender, age, parents' education, family income, number of siblings, and whether the child reported discussing school with their parents. Add Health controls for cognitive ability, noncognitive ability (self-reported), race, gender, age, mother's education, family income, number of siblings, and the Big Five Personality Traits. NLSY97 controls for cognitive ability, noncognitive ability (self-reported), the Big Five Personality Traits, gender, age, parents' education, and family income. ELS 2002 controls for cognitive ability, noncognitive ability (teacher and self-reported), gender, race, age, parents' education, and family income.

35 The WLS also contains a sibling oversample. However, sadly, civics taking was not measured among siblings.

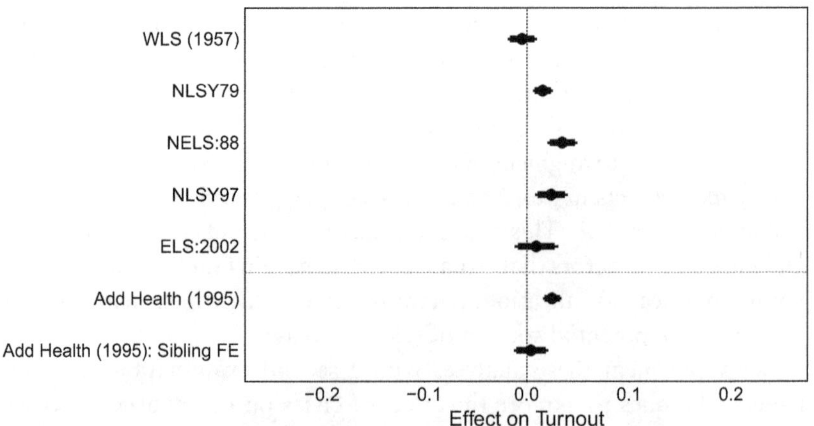

FIGURE 5.1 Civics exposure and youth voting

Predicted relationship between the number of civics courses taken in high school and the proportion of elections voting in adulthood. The WLS data leverages validated votes; the rest are self-reports. The figure shows point estimates (dots) and 90/95% confidence intervals (bars). *N* from top to bottom: 3,420; 4,443; 6,500; 5,428; 8,165; 9,882; 3,424.

confidence interval (thinner line) and one that represents the 90 percent confidence interval (with a thicker line). In a coefficient plot, positive effects would appear on the right side of the figure with negative effects falling on the left. Effects that are not statistically distinct from zero will have their confidence intervals overlap with the (dashed) reference line found at zero.

As can be seen in Figure 5.1, across all data sources, civic education has, at best, a small relationship with voting in adulthood, or, at worst, a precisely estimated null effect. This holds true across data sources that span from the 1950s to the 2000s. The largest estimate – that which comes from the NELS:88 survey – indicates that taking an additional civics course in high school is associated with an increase of early adult turnout of about 3.5 percentage points; although, we discuss later that this might be too optimistic an estimate.

For one, the estimate is something of an outlier. The rest of the estimates are much smaller, with the absolute value median estimate being 1.6 percentage points. Similarly, if we pool all our estimates together in a meta-analysis, the effect is 1.8 percentage points.[36] While some might argue that this effect is meaningful, we think it important to remember the scale

36 Results from a fixed effects meta-analysis. 95 percent confidence interval [1.2 p.p., 2.4 p.p.].

of this intervention. This effect size is roughly equivalent to the turnout effect of sending a moderately effective get-out-the-vote (GOTV) message in the mail (Green, McGrath, and Aronow 2013). Clearly, however, there is a difference in treatment intensity between these two interventions. In contrast to a GOTV intervention, which may touch voters for (at most) a few minutes, civic education exposure here involves an intense four-month treatment (the approximate length of an academic semester). Not surprisingly, the cost of staffing and implementing a civics course is an order of magnitude larger than sending a postcard in the mail. Retaining the same return on investment at a *much* higher cost is a poor way to run any public policy initiative. Simply put, civic education programs give little bang for the buck (when it comes to promoting the valued goal of political engagement).

Most importantly, the datasets that do show positive effects do not appear to be robust to alternate modeling approaches to address potential concerns about omitted variable bias. In the Add Health data, we are also able to add a family fixed effect, which purges out potential sources of unobserved bias that remain constant within families.[37] Results are reported in the bottom estimate in Figure 5.1. As can be seen, the civic education estimate is cut drastically and is no longer statistically significant – suggesting that individual selection may actually be driving the relationship of interest.[38] That is, the results in Figure 5.1 likely overstate the effect of civic education, giving pause to previous conclusions touting a positive impact.

Admittedly, voter turnout is just one type of civic engagement. While we do think that this outcome is deserving of such attention, given it is the foundational act of democracy and a vital component of societal well-being, we can look at a wider set of civic activities for some of the datasets. For example, virtually all of our samples also have a measure of how often one volunteers their time for civic or political causes. When we substitute these measures of volunteering into our models, however, we reach a similar conclusion. The median estimate size across the five datasets

[37] The Add Health dataset has several measures of the number of civics courses a student has taken – one that measures the total number of Carnegie credits earned in history/social science courses and a second that focuses exclusively on the number of credits earned in civics courses as defined by the National Council on Social Studies. Using either measure, we get similar statistical and substantive significance – with the estimates being very similar.

[38] In a new working paper, Dawes and Weinschenk (2019) find the same thing with the Add Health data: small positive effects with observable controls, but nulls with family fixed effects.

that have a measure of adult volunteering (ELS:2002, WLS, NELS:88, NLY97, and Add Health) is −0.005. Civic education exposure predicts a 0.5 percent decrease in the probability of volunteering as an adult. However, most of these estimates (again, the NELS:88 excepting) are not statistically significant. Unlike noncognitive skills in early life, the number of civics courses one takes in adolescence is not predictive of turnout in adulthood.

We think it is important to put these null effects in context. Ex-ante, there are strong reasons to suspect that student selection may give us an over optimistic view of the effects of civic education. Students who are likely to choose to take more civics courses are often more likely to engage in politics *before* they take these classes. If there is such selection bias – and it seems likely to us that there is – our analysis will over-estimate the effect of civics' exposure on youth engagement. The fact that we observe such small to null effect estimates with modest assumptions on our estimates is telling. The results point to the conclusion that civic education does not help to make young voters.

As a robustness check, we next leverage a panel design. This approach takes advantage of the fact that states vary in terms of the types of civics courses that are available to students and the number of civics courses they require their students to take to graduate high school. These vary both across states and within states over time, allowing us to estimate difference-in-difference models that absorb many sources of potential bias.[39] The advantage of this approach is that it helps minimize the role of individual student selection – accounting for the fact that children more predisposed to vote choose to take more civics courses.[40] In so doing, it helps us get closer to identifying the causal effect of civic education requirements on youth turnout.

Data for state civic education requirements come from the National Center of Education Statistics database on state civics requirements and our own individual review of states' laws regarding civic education over time. Figure 5.2 maps civics course requirements across states and time. As can be seen, there is considerable variation across states and within states over time in terms of the number of civics courses that are required – indeed, the intracluster correlation of this measure

39 Our data shows little signs of an Ashenfelter dip, whereby states respond to downward trends in youth voting (Ashenfelter and Zimmerman 1997).

40 Our approach here assumes that selection into a state (that is, the decision to move into or out of it) is orthogonal to civic education offerings/requirements.

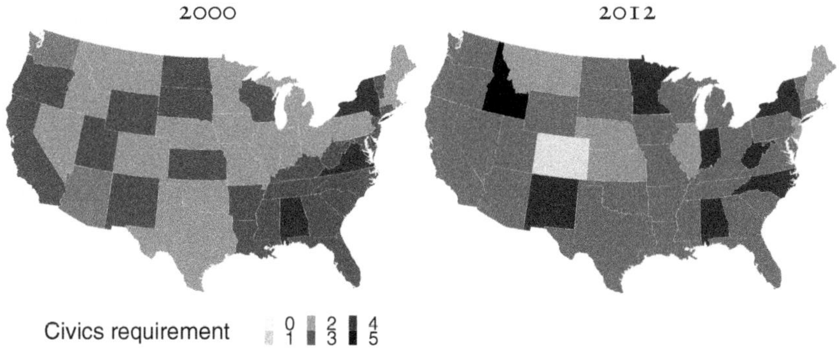

FIGURE 5.2 Civics course requirements across states and time
Variation in states' civics requirements in the first and last years of our panel. These range from 0 semesters to 6 semesters. Darker colors correspond to higher requirements.

(a measure of how much variation there is within states over the period of study) is 0.55.[41] This approach uses the best available proxy for states' overall civics course requirements (the number of social studies classes a student must take to graduate). For this proxy of civics exposure, we measure the number of social studies courses that are required when citizens were 14 – when, presumably, most students would have had their curricula expectations set for high school. However, the results are robust to variations on this coding decision – for example, if we use current year civics requirements, we find the same thing.[42] While this treatment measure is not perfect because it captures the average effect of all social studies classes, including those that would not be traditionally considered civics (e.g. geography), it is useful for getting a broad view of the cumulative effect of civics on turnout.[43]

We also collected data on Advanced Placement (AP) government and US history course-offerings – an increasingly common complement to standard civic education courses. Advanced Placement (AP) is a program that offers college-level curricula and examinations to high school students. Many universities offer course credit to students who

[41] In the data, 1994 rules are directly imputed for 1996 and 1993 rules are imputed for 1992, as data from these years are not available. The results do not change if we, instead, simply hold out these years.

[42] In our primary models, we restrict the sample to individuals who are eighteen years old. This allows our analysis to parallel that with our AP courses. Our results hold if we expand the sample to include older individuals (e.g. 18–22, 18–25, and 18–29).

[43] Unfortunately, state education statutes (often) do not include panel information about specific civics courses.

obtain high scores on the examinations. The advantage of considering AP courses separately is that AP courses are prevalent in all fifty states and offer a targeted, standardized curricula.[44] If teaching knowledge and facts about government and politics were to work, we should see an effect with these topical, standardized courses. Data for this approach comes from the National Student Clearinghouse, which has information on the roll-out and enrollment in these courses from 1997 to 2015. With this dataset, we are able to calculate the percent of students enrolled in these two courses in a given state-year, which we use as our proxy for civics exposure/penetration in a given location. As with civics courses, enrollments/availability of AP courses varies across states and within states over time.[45] Because these AP courses can be taken throughout high school, we use enrollments in the current year as our treatment variable. In all of our models shown here, we restrict the age of individuals to 18 (based on the logic that these individuals are those most likely to be exposed to AP courses in the current year). To us, this is the most straightforward way to link AP exposure treatments with voters.

To show that our results are not a product of the sample, or of the vote measure employed (be it self-reports or validated voting), we pair our civic education measures with turnout data from three sources. The first comes from the US Census Bureau CPS November Supplement from 1998 to 2012, which includes measures of self-reported voting.[46] The advantage of this dataset is that it is nationally representative, containing information from young people of all backgrounds. The disadvantage is that it relies on self-reports, which may be contaminated by social desirability. Scholars have argued that this design feature often has minimal impacts on effect estimates (Burden et al. 2014; Highton 2005); however, it remains unclear whether this holds in our context. Hence, our second approach uses administrative voter file data from the National Study of Learning, Voting, and Engagement (NSLVE) housed at Tufts University. This unique dataset matches college students at the individual level to nationwide voting records held by Catalist, a national voter file

44 At the same time, it clearly shares the same theoretical concerns we have emphasized in terms of focusing on preparation for testing of memorization of facts and figures.

45 AP government ICC = 0.77; AP U.S. ICC = 0.84.

46 The models adjust for individual income, age (excepting in the model with just eighteen-year-olds), marital status, gender, educational attainment, time living at the address, race, whether the CPS interview was conducted in person, and yearly statewide average AP scores in government and US history courses.

vendor.[47] This combined dataset provides us with a unique large dataset ($n \approx 10$ million per year) that has validated vote.[48] While this dataset is not as comprehensive as the CPS in that it omits noncollege students, young people in college are an important segment of the population. To get around the limitations of these two samples, our last approach looks at the effect of civics on overall youth turnout using validated voter turnout numbers from the Data Trust.[49] The advantage of these data is that they allow us to go one step beyond the NSLVE analyses and look for effects on validated turnout among the entire youth population, not just those who are in college. The disadvantage of this dataset is that it has been less studied/validated in the literature and, in drawing from public-use voter files, contains mostly individuals who are registered to vote.[50,51] In sum, each of these datasets has its own quirks, but together they give us a picture of the role of civic education on youth voting and tell a remarkably consistent story about the effect of civic education.

To estimate our difference-in-difference models, we include state and year fixed effects in our regression models. These force our comparisons to be within the same states over time and simultaneously account for shared time shocks. Figure 5.3 provides the estimates from the difference-in-difference models using data from the CPS. These results come from a difference-in-difference model that includes all three measures of civics exposure together; the model is run two ways – one with no controls beyond the fixed effects and the other with some background individual-level covariates (e.g. income, race, gender, etc.). As can be

47 Catalist is used by Democratic and progressive candidates and interests, but they also offer a subscription access for academic research.

48 For the full list of over 1,000 schools participating in the NSLVE match, see https://idhe.tufts.edu/nslve/participating-campuses. Data include 46/50 flagship institutions.

49 The Data Trust is the analytics arm of the RNC. This dataset comes from a nationwide snapshot from September 2017.

50 Our own validation of the file suggests that it is quite accurate. The Data Trust's nationwide data closely approximates official state turnout counts. For example, in 2014 the Data Trust turnout numbers miss the actual reported turnout by less than 0.8 percentage points on average (Pearson's $r = 0.9947$). The Data Trust's state turnout counts most closely approach official topline and state by state numbers from 2006 and beyond.

51 We run our Data Trust models at the state-year level weighted by number of voting age young people in the file to improve computation time and to avoid the potential for differential registration bias. To calculate the turnout denominator, we use estimates of the youth population (from the Census, via the Missouri Census Data Center) and the number of young people in the Data Trust files (with the results not changing with either approach).

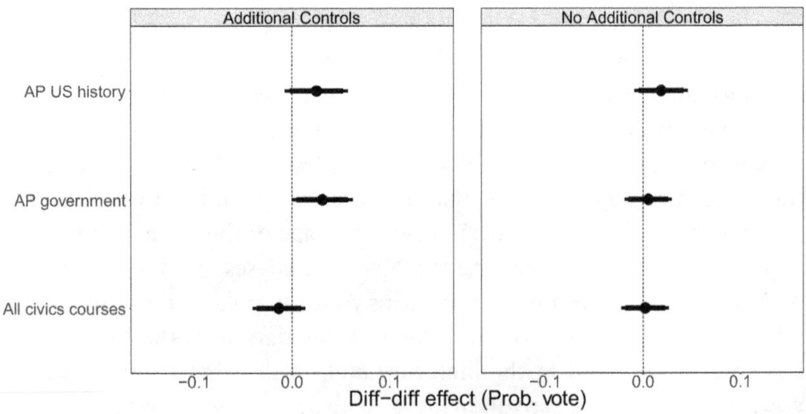

FIGURE 5.3 Civics course exposure and youth voting (CPS)

The estimated impact of civic education requirements, AP government exposure, and AP US history exposure on youth turnout. Each panel shows the results from a separate difference-in-difference model. Voting measured using the CPS November Supplement. Sample: eighteen-year-olds in a given year. Civic education exposure is quantified by the number of social studies years required to graduate. The models estimate the effect of a one standard deviation increase in civics requirements (an increase of about 0.7 semesters required), AP government enrollment (an increase of about 1 percent of high school students $\approx$ 8,800 students), and AP US history enrollment (an increase of about 1 percent of high school students $\approx$ 15,000 students). Models include state and year fixed effects and the models with additional controls add family income, age, marital status, gender, education, time at one's address, race/ethnicity, and whether the interview was in person. Points reflect coefficient estimates and bars represent 90 percent and 95 percent confidence intervals. $N = 11,625$ (right panel), 8,759 (left panel).

seen, when we leverage this comparison, we find no effect of a social studies requirement on turnout (estimates range between −1.3 and 0.2 percentage points, depending on model specification and are never close to being statistically significant). This null finding is not for a lack of statistical power; our 95 percent confidence intervals allow us to confidently rule out positive effects as large as 3 percentage points. This null finding extends to AP Government and US History courses. Given the intensity of treatment here – with exposure to civics classes lasting multiple months – these estimates are disappointingly small.[52]

[52] The coefficients for AP courses are a bit larger than our overall civics course estimate – with that for AP government ranging from 0.5 to 3.1 percentage points and that for AP US History ranging from 1.9 to 2.5 percentage points. These null effects are slightly less precise – but our 95 percent confidence intervals still allow us to rule our effects as large 5.7 percentage points (US) and 6.2 percentage points (Government). None of these estimates are significant at the 5 percent level.

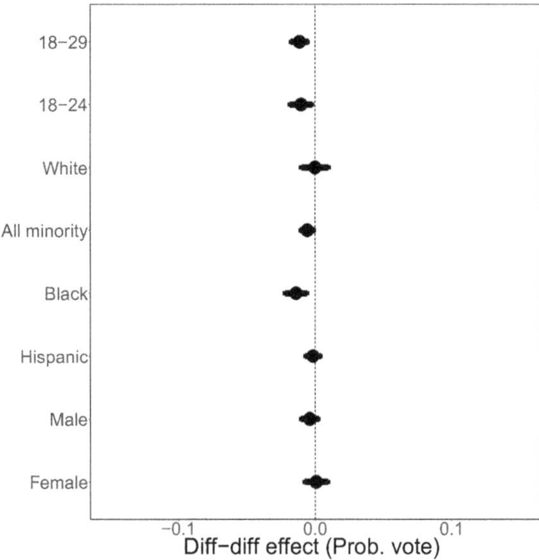

FIGURE 5.4 Civics course exposure and college student validated voting (NSLVE)

The estimated impact of civic education requirements on youth turnout. Turnout data comes from the National Study of Learning, Voting, and Engagement (NSLVE) housed at Tufts University. Civic education exposure is quantified by the number of social studies required to graduate. The models estimate the effect of a one class increase in civics requirements. Points reflect coefficient estimates and bars represent 90 percent and 95 percent confidence intervals. *N* from top to bottom: 18,133,031; 15,177,899; 9,518,034; 4,528,704; 1,625,349; 1,836,011; 7,590,697; 6,163,001

Figure 5.4 provides the difference-in-difference estimates from the NSLVE validated voter file data of college enrollees. For the sake of space, here we focus on the effect of the overall civics requirement measure. We break the results by various subgroups to see if our estimates are masking substantial heterogeneities of interest. They are not. As can be seen, the estimates all remain small. Again, our estimates are quite precise – allowing us to rule out effects as small as 2.5 percentage points. These results are consistent with those provided from the longitudinal surveys and CPS data, suggesting that the NSLVE data (despite containing only college students) might still provide us with insights that generalize to the broader youth population.

Finally, in Figure 5.5 we run the difference-in-difference models for the Data Trust nationwide voter file data. As can be seen, we run the difference-in-difference models several ways: varying whether we look at the effects of our three proxies for civic education exposure – social

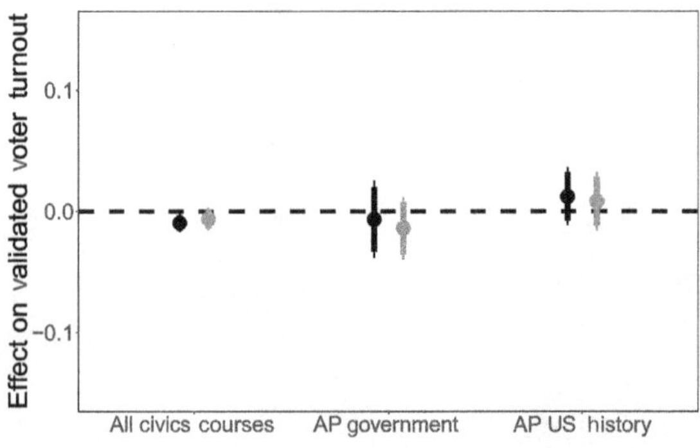

FIGURE 5.5 Civics course exposure and validated youth voting (Data Trust)

The estimated impact of civic education requirements on the validated voter turnout of eighteen-year-olds (source: the Data Trust, September 2017 snapshot numbers). Civic education exposure is quantified by the number of social studies years required to graduate when the sample was 14 and the percent of high school students enrolled in AP Government and AP US History. The models estimate the effect of a one standard deviation increase in civics requirements (an increase of about 0.7 semesters required), AP government enrollment (an increase of about 1 percent of high school students ≈ 8,800 students), and AP US history enrollment (an increase of about 1 percent of high school students ≈ 15,000 students). Points reflect coefficient estimates and bars represent 90 percent and 95 percent confidence intervals. Models estimated at the state-year level, with the weighted models frequency-weighted by the number of eighteen-year-olds in the Data Trust sample. Standard errors clustered at the state-year level. Unweighted *N* from left to right: 227, 250, 250; Weighted number of voters (and number of state-years) from left to right: 13,648,957 (227); 15,496,054 (250); 15,496,054 (250).

studies requirements, AP government, and AP US History – and whether we do or do not weight our state-level estimates based on the number of eighteen-year-olds in the sample. As can be seen, across all model specifications, the effects are all small and (with one exception) not statistically significant at traditional levels. The $|\text{median } \beta|$ is 0.9 percentage points. None of the estimates are close to being statistically significant, with the median p-value across the eight difference-in-difference estimates being $p = 0.31$. This lack of significance is not a result of a lack of statistical power. Indeed, our null estimates are quite precise – allowing us to confidently rule out positive or negative effects as large as 1.7 percentage points with the overall civics measure and 3.9 percentage points for the AP measures. This further corroborates the similarity of findings across the various datasets used to estimate the effect of social programs (in this case civics exposure) on youth turnout.

In total, these results show that traditional civic education appears to have little to no impact on whether young people vote when they come of age. Given the longstanding motivation for civic education, the evidence of positive effects on political knowledge, and the high cost that states bear to fund civic education instructors and curricula, it is disappointing to see that civic education has little downstream impacts on voter participation. On one of its primary goals – making active young voters – civic education (as currently constructed) falls short. When using the measuring stick of active voting (or volunteering), civic education appears to be broken and has been for more than sixty years. Even though the number of years one spends in school appears to strongly predict voting (Dee 2004; Henderson 2018; Milligan, Moretti, and Oreopoulos 2004; Sondheimer and Green 2010; Verba, Schlozman, and Brady 1995; Wolfinger and Rosenstone 1980), traditional civic education does not appear to account for the observed relationship. Civics has small, inconsistent, and virtually undetectable effects on youth turnout.

5.5 WHERE DOES CIVICS GO FROM HERE?

Providing young people with a high quality civic education is a core mission of the public education system. By many accounts, however, civics has lost this emphasis in recent years. That said, the empirical evidence we have presented suggests that simply adding more classically conceived civic education is not enough to make active voters. Across numerous datasets and several methodological techniques, we find that the relationship between civics and turnout is small to nonexistent. We argue that not only do we need a return to civic education but we need to fundamentally rethink the content and nature of civic education.

What specifically can education policymakers do to improve the status quo and meaningfully increase youth participation? Acknowledging the failed promise of civic education is the first step to improvement. Too long have we simply accepted an insufficient approach to civics. Simultaneously, policymakers should realize that this problem is *not* just about the quantity of civics training one receives. Rather, many of the problems in civic education come down to the content of that civics training. It is not enough to bemoan a lack of focus on civic education or to advocate that civics receive more emphasis in schools. What we need is not only more civics, but better civics; civics deserves more attention in schools but the curriculum also needs restructuring. We want to acknowledge that there are many uncertainties as to how best to integrate the development of noncognitive skills into civic education. As education scholars come to understand the particular pedagogical strategies that help to develop noncognitive skills, civics training will need to update and integrate those strategies. Although our analysis does not directly assess specific curriculum proposals, we can offer some tentative recommendations based on our findings and extensive review of the relevant literature.

Civics should be rooted in a clear understanding of voter turnout. Across decades of political science research, many scholars have emphasized the fundamental role of political motivation and political knowledge (Denny and Doyle 2008; Hernstein and Murray 1994; Jacobson 1983; Luskin 1990; Nie, Junn, and Stehlik-Barry 1996; Verba, Schlozman, and Brady 1995). However, these factors are not enough to make active voters. These are important elements in their own right, but they are not the only, nor the most, important skills and attributes one needs to become active in politics. In order to become a young voter, students need to develop the noncognitive skills that are important to their development in all areas of life. Civics needs to focus on giving students the experiences to develop noncognitive skills and the applied knowledge about the voting process that is relevant to putting them to use in the political domain.

5.6 WHAT SCHOOLS CAN DO: RETHINKING CIVIC EDUCATION

In showing that noncognitive skills matter for voting in Chapters 3 and 4, we join researchers in economics, psychology, and education in concluding that the development of noncognitive skills is critical for individual and societal well-being (Shechtman et al. 2013). Our analysis thus contributes to highly salient debates in education policy. Education policymakers are currently weighing the costs and benefits of emphasizing noncognitive skills in education curriculum (Farrington et al. 2012). However, these debates have focused narrowly on the potential benefits that noncognitive skills have for a select set of outcomes – academic performance, crime, health, and labor-force outcomes. Our results highlight that noncognitive skills can have positive effects on other life outcomes – especially for measures of civic engagement that have vital importance for societal well-being. That interventions targeting noncognitive skills produce such large positive civic externalities supports an increased emphasis on these skills as a part of school curricula. Such civic benefits are especially valuable to consider given the core role that active citizenship plays in the original mission of public schools (Brighouse et al. 2016; Ravitch and Viteritti 2003). Simply put, noncognitive skills play a key role in helping to accomplish the foundational mission of public education: the production of engaged citizens equipped to actively contribute to democracy and society as a whole.

Our work suggests that we need to reconsider the nature and content of civic education and education more generally. The null effects of traditional civic education on youth voting shown in this chapter suggest that the predominant approach for teaching citizenship in schools is insufficient. At present, civic education tends to (over)emphasize knowledge and facts about government and history, while overlooking practical information about the voting and registration process. Though this approach is consistent with the dominant theories of voting that have emphasized cognitive ability and political knowledge as the core roots of voter turnout, this approach (and the model upon which it relies) is insufficient. In an era of test-based accountability, civics may have placed too much emphasis on teaching students knowledge and facts that can be measured with a bubble sheet at the expense of helping them have the experiences and develop the skills they actually need to become active participants in democracy. Enhancing political knowledge and verbal cognitive abilities are simply not enough to see young people to the finish line of active citizenship.

We thus join the chorus of civic education scholars, policymakers, and advocates calling for civic education reform. Although many would agree that textbook civics is insufficient, we contend there is a need to focus on the myriad obstacles that can get in the way of young people following through on behavioral intentions to vote. Too often, previous reform efforts have overlooked the basics of voter registration and the mechanical aspects of voter participation that too often become the barriers that prevent young people from following through on their civic actions and intentions. For example, the well-regarded report *The Civic Mission of Schools* (2003) and its follow-up *Guardian of Democracy: Civic Mission of Schools* (2011) make explicit calls for schools to provide students with an opportunity to engage in community service but do not discuss voter registration and the potential value of in-class voter registration or preregistration efforts. To promote youth turnout, civics education should provide knowledge and experience grounded in awareness of the factors that shape voter participation.

5.6.1 What Schools Can Do, #1: Focus on Applied Learning

First, then, civics training should follow the advice of Lupia (2016) and focus on the practical knowledge and skills relevant to the registration and voting process. Researchers have long advocated for civics instructors to move toward applied learning (e.g. Bennion 2006; Elder, Seligsohn and Hofrenning 2007; Gershtenson et al. 2013; Huerta and Jozwiak 2008; McCarthy and Anderson 2000; McGuire and Waldman 2008; Morrell 2005; Oros 2007; Ravitch and Viteritti 2003) that includes the basic mechanics of voter registration and the voting process, and provides opportunities for students to experience political – not just apolitical – engagement. While there have long been calls to ensure that young people develop into more than just "walking encyclopedias of governmental news" (Schudson 1998), it's clear that applied learning has not become the status-quo approach to civic education (Carnegie-Knight Task Force 2007; Torney-Purta and Amadeo 2004). This represents one of the clearest ways that civics training can integrate lessons from research on the development of noncognitive skills.

Research suggests that even modest changes to civics curricula to incorporate more applied elements can have meaningful effects. For example, in a unique, in-class randomized control trial that spanned six states (Connecticut, Indiana, Kentucky, Nebraska, New Hampshire, and New Jersey), Addonizio (2011) tested the effect of providing students with a one-time applied voting demonstration in the classroom (through the First-Time Voter Program). Students randomly assigned to the First-Time Voter Program learned how to "register to vote, how to use a voting booth, and ... were given the opportunity to cast a practice ballot" (Addonizio 2011, 197). These demonstrations were low impact, taking only about 40 minutes of class time.

Addonizio (2011) shows that this program had a substantial impact on participant voting rates – increasing youth turnout by 5.7 percentage points, which represented a 23 percent increase over the base turnout rate in the control group (25 percent). Figure 5.6 shows a visualization of the effects reported by Addonizio (2011). It plots mean levels of voter turnout (with bars) broken by the treatment and control groups and flags the effects that are statistically significant (with a *).[53] This finding suggests that taking the step of integrating a small amount of applied learning into curricula goes a long way; indeed, this simple, low-cost approach of adding voting demonstrations to classrooms is much more effective than traditional civics curricula that focus on knowledge and facts about

[53] Addonizio (2011) reports one-tail p-values based on the rationale that there was a strong directional hypothesis in this program.

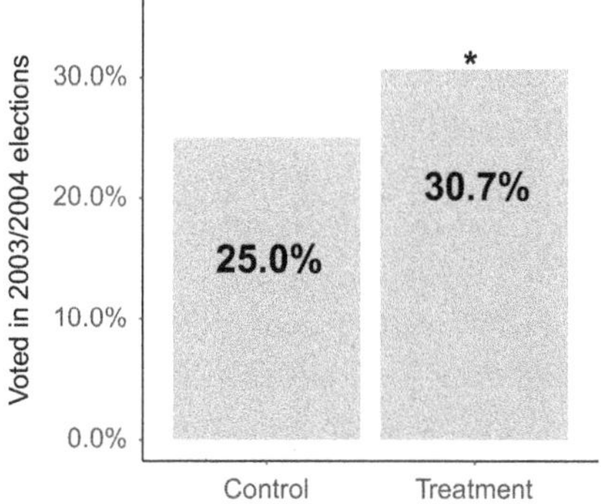

FIGURE 5.6 Effect of First-Time Voter Program on youth voter turnout
Mean validated voter turnout levels for the first-time voter program. Comparison is between those randomly assigned to the program and those randomly assigned to the control group. Effect estimates are intention-to-treat (ITT). * $p < 0.05$. Analytic sample is any student who was in one of the 14 schools in Connecticut, Indiana, Kentucky, Nebraska, New Hampshire, and New Jersey ($N = 840$). Recreated from Addonizio (2011, 222).

government and politics alone. Indeed, there is complementary evidence that parallel approaches that encourage students to register to vote and show them how to do so may also be beneficial (Bennion 2009b; Gershtenson et al. 2013; Syvertsen et al. 2009).

Further research shows that efforts to more fully incorporate applied learning into civics classrooms can perhaps pay even bigger dividends. An especially pronounced example of such an approach can be found in Democracy Prep charter schools. Democracy Prep is a growing network of open-enrollment charter schools founded in 2005 that currently has twenty-two schools educating approximately 6,500 students in five locations: New York City, NY; Camden, NJ; the District of Columbia; Baton Rouge, LA; and Las Vegas, NV. In 2012, Democracy Prep received a grant from the US Department of Education to open fifteen additional schools. As their name implies, Democracy Prep schools place a great deal of focus on active citizenship; the stated mission of Democracy Prep schools is to "educate responsible citizen-scholars for success in the college of their choice and a life of active citizenship." To accomplish this goal, Democracy Prep schools focus on exposing their students to an applied civics curriculum that is incorporated across all classes – not just in civics courses, but also in English, math, science, and extracurricular activities. In Democracy Prep schools, students visit with elected officials, attend public meetings, testify before legislative bodies, and hold active in-class discussions on timely political issues. Even though many students in Democracy Prep schools are not yet eligible to vote, Democracy Prep students participate in a get out the vote (GOTV) campaign each Election Day. In these campaigns, students have discussions with potential voters, providing them (nonpartisan) information about elections and encouraging them to be active in democracy. As seniors, high school students "develop a 'Change the World' project to investigate a real-world social problem, design a method for addressing the issue, and implement their plan" (Gill et al. 2018, 1). Beyond its integrated applied civics curriculum, another thing that makes Democracy Prep schools unique is that they enroll a particularly disadvantaged student body, with 76 percent of students being eligible for free-reduced price lunch, 69 percent of the student body being African American, and 23 percent speaking no English at home (Gill et al. 2018). Based on their demographics alone, it wouldn't be unreasonable to say that before enrolling in Democracy Prep schools, these students are unlikely to participate in politics.

Democracy Prep students are admitted via a lottery, as many of the schools are oversubscribed. This feature allows for a well-controlled evaluation of the effect of the Democracy Prep approach to civic education by comparing students who are randomly admitted to Democracy Prep schools (lottery winners) with those not accepted (lottery losers) in terms of their later-life voter participation since all selected to be treated.[54] To match Democracy Prep lottery entrants to vote files, Gill et al. (2018) contracted with the (well-respected) voter firm Catalist. The match was conducted with standard matching inputs (first and last name, gender, date of birth, address and phone number). This match paired Democracy Prep lottery data with voter turnout data from the 2016 general election.[55] This allows estimation of the causal impact Democracy Prep schools had on early patterns of voter turnout.

Figure 5.7 shows the estimated effect of being admitted to a Democracy Prep school, all else equal. The figure plots mean levels of voter turnout (with bars) broken by the treatment and control groups, labels these mean turnout numbers (overlaying the bars), and flags the effects that are statistically significant (with a *). As can be seen, students who are admitted to Democracy Prep schools have (unadjusted) rates of voter

54 Gill et al. (2018) show that the treatment and control groups show balance on observable covariates.

55 Because of data restrictions, this match could only be conducted for students in the New York City Democracy Prep schools. For more details on this match, see Gill et al. (2018).

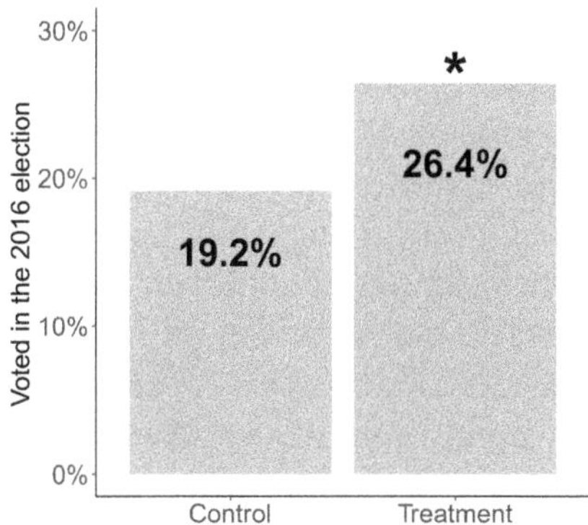

FIGURE 5.7 Effect of Democracy Prep admittance on youth voter turnout
Mean validated voter turnout levels for the democracy prep program. Comparison is between lottery winners and lottery losers. Effect estimates are intention-to-treat (ITT). * $p < 0.05$. Voter turnout from a match of Democracy Prep student files to Catalist records for the 2016 general election. The match was conducted with standard matching inputs (first and last name, gender, date of birth, address, and phone number). Analytic sample is any student who entered the lottery to attend any Democracy Prep school in New York City from 2007–2008 through 2015–2016 who was 18 by election day ($N = 1{,}060$). Recreated from Gill et al. (2018)

turnout that are 7.2 percentage points higher than students who are not lotteried into the school system. This difference is statistically significant ($p < 0.01$) and substantively large; it represents a 38 percent increase over voter turnout at baseline. If we isolate our comparisons down to students who win the Democracy Prep lottery *and* accept this offer, the effect on voter turnout is even more noticeable; the effect of attending a Democracy Prep charter school (i.e. the treatment on the treated estimate, or the TOT) being equivalent to a 24 percentage point increase in voter turnout.[56] This result shows that even though this group of disadvantaged young people is unlikely to vote overall, Democracy Prep schools make a meaningful difference – helping to incorporate a sizable group of young people into democracy who wouldn't have engaged otherwise. This result suggests that if schools do more to promote applied civics – incorporating students into active political discussions and activities across courses and extracurricular activities, as Democracy Prep does – there is a chance for a substantial change to the status quo.

Further evidence of the effectiveness of applied civic learning comes from the United Kingdom, which in recent years has experimented with

[56] The rate of compliance is just under 30 percent (Gill et al. 2018).

various forms of active learning programs, often called "social action programs." Such interventions emphasize discussion of salient political issues and implementation of challenging, youth-led political engagement projects. Here we focus on three social action programs that are conducive to evaluation: the Citizenship Foundation program, the Envision program, and the Voluntary Action Within Kent program (VAWK/IMAGO). Each of these programs is unique, but they are held together by a common thread of active, applied civics curricula. For example, students (usually eleven- and twelve-year-olds) who are exposed to the Citizenship Foundation program participate in applied learning in the form of mock trials, a curriculum (Go-Givers) that encourages group discussion and learning on salient political issues, and a school-wide campaign (the Make a Difference Challenge) in which pupils identify, research, and write a proposal to address a social cause (local or international) that they want to do something about. In this last part of the program, students are taught to follow through by fundraising or taking some other form of direct action in this area.

The Envision program works in a similar way. Designed to be a supplement to current curricula, Envision provides students (usually ages 16–19) with an opportunity to engage in political action. Over a school year, students focus on a real-world local community issue (e.g. decreasing crime or improving race relations). Students are grouped in teams and develop proposals/videos/presentations to try and think about how to address the issue. This program is structured around a multi-school competition in which proposals are judged and given prizes. Like the other two, the VAWK/IMAGO program is an initiative that focuses on having students (ages 15–18) develop proposals to address social issues.[57] These programs vary in their form and substance, but are all designed to help students go beyond volunteering by engaging in a way that develops the skills, attitudes, and experiences that they need to work for political change.

Are these applied learning social action programs effective? That is, do they help students develop the skills that they need to meaningfully engage? In a recent innovative report by the Behavioral Insights Team, Kirkman et al. (2016) evaluate the effect of the Citizenship Foundation, Envision, and VAWK/IMAGO programs. To do so, they used randomized control trials wherein some (randomly assigned) students took part in

[57] For more information on the Citizenship Foundation program, see www.youngcitizens.org/. For more information on the Envision program, see www.envision.org.uk/. For more information on the VAWK/IMAGO program, see www.imago.community/.

these programs and some (randomly assigned) students did not. To assess the effects of these programs, they looked at five skill measures: cooperation, empathy, grit, problem solving, and sense of community.[58] These skill measures are close to the noncognitive abilities that we explored in previous chapters. To measure engagement, they looked at an individuals' willingness to volunteer in the future. Unfortunately, they were not able to link the programs to voter records.

Figure 5.8 looks at the effect of the Citizenship Foundation, Envision, and VAWK/IMAGO programs on five measures of noncognitive ability. The figure plots mean levels of our outcomes of interest (with bars) broken by the treatment and control groups, labels these mean values (overlaying the bars), and flags the effects that are statistically significant (with a *). As can be seen across all three interventions, noncognitive abilities are higher in the groups that were exposed to the applied learning social action programs. These effects vary in size across the Citizenship Foundation (0.7–9.4 percent of the base rate), Envision (7.0–16.8 percent of the base rate), and VAWK/IMAGO (5.5–14.6 percent of the base rate). In the Citizenship Foundation program 4/5 of the effect estimates of interest are statistically significant at the 5 percent level, with 5/5 being significant in Envision, and 3/5 in the VAWK/IMAGO program. Another way of looking at the effects is within noncognitive constructs. Cooperation increases significantly in 2/3 of the programs (Envision and VAWK/IMAGO), empathy increases significantly in all 3, grit increases significantly in 2/3 (Citizenship Foundation and Envision), problem solving increases significantly in 2/3 (Citizenship Foundation and Envision), and sense of community increases significantly in 3/3.

Though the statistical precision and size of these effects vary across interventions, it is clear these social action programs that emphasize active learning improve noncognitive abilities. Simply put, when students are challenged to work in their communities – to go beyond the dry, rote presentation of facts and knowledge about government and politics – they develop the practical skills and experiences needed to engage in politics. Not only do social action programs instill habits of participation but they also instill skills that will payoff across various forms of civic participation.

Figure 5.9 confirms this visually by showing the effect of social action programs on willingness to volunteer in the future. Figure 5.9 plots

[58] See the Appendix for measures.

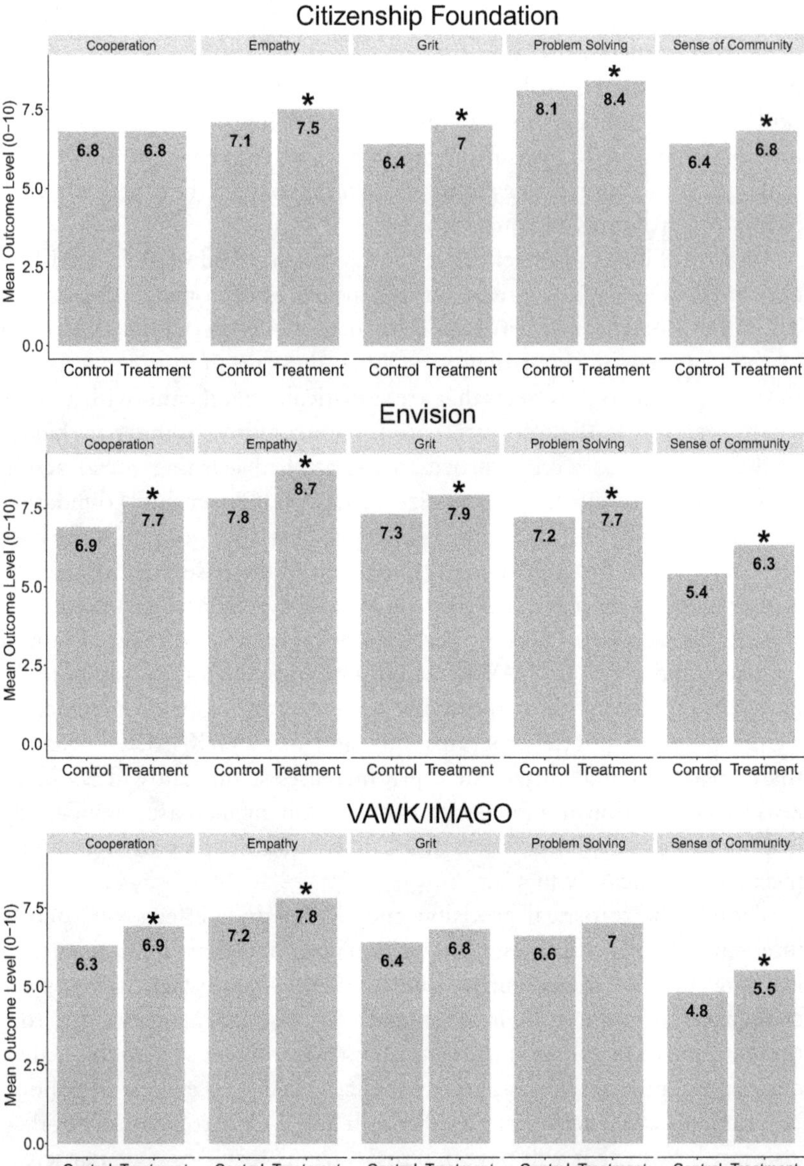

FIGURE 5.8 Effect of Social Action Programs on students' noncognitive skill development

Mean noncognitive skill levels across the treatment and control groups for the three social action randomized control trials (Citizenship Foundation, Envision, and VAWK/IMAGO). Effect estimates are intention-to-treat (ITT). * $p < 0.05$. Analytic sample is Citizenship Foundation ($N = 1,074$), Envision ($N = 364$), and VAWK/IMAGO ($N = 2,190$) participants in the United Kingdom. Recreated from Kirkman et al. (2016).

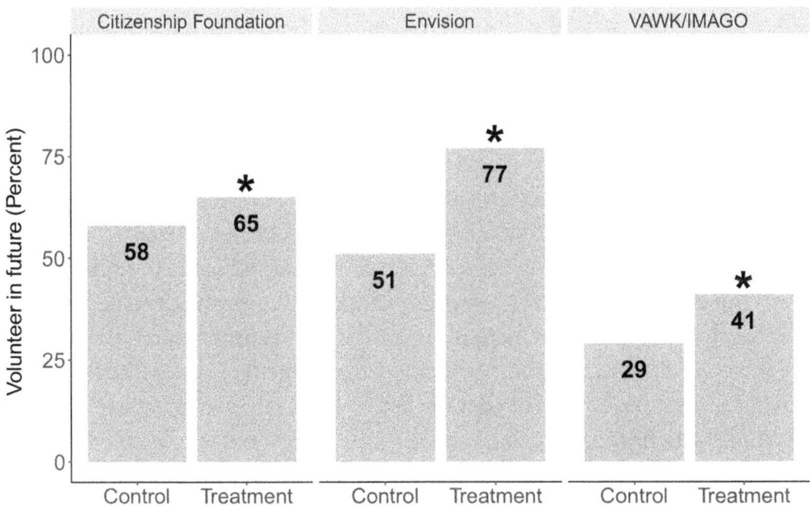

FIGURE 5.9 Effect of Social Action Programs on students' volunteering in future
Mean levels of volunteering in the future across the treatment and control groups for the three social action randomized control trials (Citizenship Foundation, Envision, and VAWK/IMAGO). Effect estimates are intention-to-treat (ITT). * $p < 0.05$. Analytic sample is Citizenship Foundation ($N = 1{,}074$), Envision ($N = 364$), and VAWK/IMAGO ($N = 2{,}190$) participants in the United Kingdom. Recreated from Kirkman et al. (2016)

mean levels of volunteering (with bars) for the treatment and control groups, labels these mean volunteering levels, and flags the effects that are statistically significant (with a *). As can be seen across all three programs, willingness to volunteer increased. These gains are all statistically significant at the 5 percent level and are substantively meaningful with the Citizenship Foundation program increasing volunteering willingness by 12.1 percent, the Envision program doing so by 51 percent, and the VAWK/IMAGO likewise increasing engagement by 41.4 percent over the base rates. While we cannot be sure if these gains in civic participation will last, these early results are promising. They further support our argument that there is a connection between noncognitive skill development and youth engagement. When young people develop the ability to work well with others and to channel their thoughts, emotions, motivations, and behaviors in appropriate ways, they are more likely to be set on a path toward engaging in their communities and democracy more generally.

Taken together, these results suggest that engaging young people in active learning programs while they are in school noticeably increases levels of civic participation. Programs that focus on deliberation and discussions of current political issues (Gershtenson, Rainey Jr., and Rainey 2010; Huerta and Jozwiak 2008; Longo, Drury and Battistoni 2006; Mendelberg 2002; Morrell 2005), engage students in service learning/social action campaigns (be those voter canvassing or designing proposals to address real-world social problems), hold mock elections or trials, or facilitate interaction with elected officials have great potential to meaningfully increase youth civic engagement (Gill et al. 2018; Kirkman et al. 2016). Although the current nature of civic education might be the easiest path, it is clearly not the most effective. Programs that incorporate applied learning serve to increase noncognitive abilities that have payoffs in the civic domain. To be sure, there are challenges and research gaps. The teachers we interviewed raised the risks of talking about current politics, which suggests that teacher training needs to do a better job of addressing how to navigate political discussion. More experiments are needed to identify which curriculum changes will best scale and have long-term effects. Still, based on the weight of available evidence at present we can say that applied political learning shows much more promise than the status quo civics approach of memorization of facts about government and politics.

5.6.2 What Schools Can Do, #2: Timing Matters

We recommend that education officials carefully consider the timing of civics training. The status quo in many school districts is for formal civics training to only start in earnest when a young person has reached high school. Before that point, students are mainly taught history; very rarely does their training expand into topics of social science. Yet, theories of human development and political socialization predict that many of the resources needed for life success are most malleable in childhood and early adolescence. During these critical periods, children develop the skills, attitudes, and habits needed to integrate in society. Delaying most of one's civics training until high school may miss a key window of opportunity.

This recommendation connects to our findings on noncognitive abilities and voter participation. While research suggests that noncognitive skills may be malleable into late adolescence, effects are clearest at a younger age. Waiting comes with a risk because for a nontrivial portion of the population, noncognitive abilities and civic habits may lock in by the time they reach voting age. The sizable effect the Fast Track intervention had on voter turnout (outlined in Chapter 4) shows that early investments – including those that start as early as kindergarten – pay significant rewards in the civic domain, even many years later. In the last section, we discussed five other randomized control trials that show that childhood and early adolescent interventions, when they are well designed, have the potential to greatly increase youth turnout. These programs also illustrate that designing civics programs for young people is possible; indeed, in some school districts, well-designed civic education programs that incorporate best principles are already being implemented at scale among children as young as ten years old.

Timing matters in another way: It is critical for schools to capitalize on spikes in political attention among students. Flexibility can be difficult in today's education system, but civics training should follow the ebbs and flows in political events to engage students in politics, and importantly, to remove barriers to participation when students are more attentive to the political environment (e.g. in political campaigns). Currently, there is wide variation in the extent and timing of school-led voter registration efforts. Putting a table in the cafeteria in presidential elections years is simply not sufficient to live up to the responsibility to prepare young voters because it relies on student initiative to know when and how to complete the form. Schools in states with preregistration for individuals as young as sixteen should be using classroom time and instruction to help remove the registration barrier to voting. Even for those states without preregistration, there is often a large pool of students eligible to register to vote in the days after an election (since eligibility is defined relative to the next election). For example, students who disliked the outcome of the 2016 presidential election should have been given the opportunity to register (or preregister) to vote in the days *after* the election. Civics training that corresponds with student eligibility to register or pre-register and with political events is likely to have the most direct effect on voter turnout.

5.6.3 What Schools Can Do, #3: Integrating Civics

So far, we have focused on ways to integrate noncognitive skill development and barrier reduction into training in civic education. At the same time, we recommend that education policymakers consider ways to integrate civics into other courses and extracurricular activities. Based on the Democracy Prep, Citizenship Foundation, Envision, and VAWK/IMAGO experiments – which all incorporate active civics learning throughout the school day – we recommend that education officials not be afraid to outsource some of this new type of civics instruction to venues outside of civics classrooms. After all, the bulk of previous research into the programs that improve noncognitive skills takes place outside of the civics classroom. Indeed, a recent experimental study found that arts classes help students develop valuable noncognitive skills (Bowen and Kisida 2019). There are reasons to suspect that noncognitive skills may be best developed when they are reinforced in an integrated curricula.

5.7 THE BIG PICTURE

Schools are a critical institution for making young voters. Our research on the link between noncognitive skills and voter turnout helps to inform ways that the education system can better promote political participation. The other institutional context that is fundamental to youth turnout: The rules and procedures that govern voter registration and voting. In the next chapter, we scrutinize potential electoral reforms in light of our findings.

6

Promoting Follow-Through by Reducing the Cost of Voting

> [Registration] . . . presents significant barriers to citizens voting.
>
> Wolfinger and Rosenstone (1980, 88)

> Non-participants are not likely to flood the polls simply because [voting] barriers diminish.
>
> Timpone (1998, 155)

Contrary to popular wisdom, the dismal levels of youth turnout in the United States are not due to a lack of political interest or the absence of a sense of civic duty. When surveyed, the vast majority of young adults say they intend to vote. Unfortunately, too many young Americans fail to follow through on their civic attitudes and intentions in the face of obstacles and distractions. Our analysis has shown that participatory behavior is more likely among those with strong noncognitive skills – competencies related to self-regulation, effortfulness, and interpersonal interaction – providing a missing piece to the turnout puzzle. Of course, the observed relationship between noncognitive skills and voter turnout reflects not only the characteristics and behaviors of individuals but also the institutional and electoral context that constrains and structures individual choices. In other words, in showing that individuals require a set of noncognitive abilities to overcome the obstacles that can stand in their way of participating in politics, our analysis shines light on the voting obstacles themselves. In the previous chapter, we consider ways in which the education system could help reduce the costs of voting; in this chapter, we evaluate electoral reforms that would to reduce institutional barriers to participation.

A rich literature in political science has examined the way that different aspects of context can shape political participation. We focus here on the way electoral institutions and rules can influence whether and how civic attitudes are expressed (e.g. Atkeson et al. 2010; Brians and Grofman 2001; Erikson and Minnite 2009; Hanmer 2009; Hanmer et al. 2010; Herrnson et al. 2008; Mycoff, Wagner and Wilson 2009; Neiheisel and Burden 2012; Niemi et al. 2009; Ponoroff and Weiser 2010; Vercellotti and Anderson 2006). Electoral rules should matter because they can make it easier or harder for citizens to participate. If the act of voting requires perseverance and self-control to overcome the costs of voting, reducing the costs of registering and voting might therefore increase voting. While electoral reform is unlikely to totally resolve low patterns of youth turnout given the complex nature of voting costs, including the distractions of daily life, we evaluate the extent to which specific electoral reforms might be effective at promoting turnout, specifically among young citizens.

In this chapter, we turn to a logical extension of our broader model of youth turnout, exploring electoral reforms that might reduce the costs of registration and voting.[1] We make the case that it is necessary to evaluate the effect of electoral reforms on youth turnout, not just overall levels of turnout in the population. Using panel data from 2000 until 2012, we evaluate the effect of electoral rules like no-excuse absentee voting, early voting, preregistration, same-day registration, online registration, Election Day registration, and combinations of these reforms. To preview, our results show that some – but not all – electoral reforms work to increase youth turnout. When we consider the effect of no-excuse absentee balloting and early voting, we find that these reforms have virtually no influence on youth turnout. Our analysis suggests that the most effective reforms are those that make registration easier – and particularly those designed to reduce the cost for new voters when they are more likely to be paying attention to politics. Among registration reforms, same-day registration and preregistration laws have the largest impact on youth turnout. Finally, when we consider electoral reforms as a package – rather than as separate pieces of legislation, as is common in previous research – we find the clearest evidence of the link between electoral institutional hurdles and levels of youth turnout. Models that combine the six electoral reforms that we consider reveal that easing registration and voting burdens together increases youth turnout substantially.

[1] Although we focus only on reforms that might ease the burdensome of registration and voting, it is also critical to evaluate recent efforts that might make it more burdensome – namely, voter identification laws (See, for instance, Cantoni and Pons 2019).

We conclude this chapter by acknowledging the challenges of widespread electoral reform and the realistic limits of their impact.

In short, the analysis in this chapter shows that young people are responsive to the external voting costs that they face – particularly the cost of registering to vote. While electoral reforms don't work to completely close the age gap in voting on their own – perhaps necessitating further reforms in other venues, such as schools (see Chapter 5) – they can and do influence youth turnout, illustrating the importance of both contextual and personal factors in shaping political participation, separate from levels of political motivation.

6.1 WHY EXPLORE THE EFFECT OF ELECTORAL RULES ON YOUTH TURNOUT

As the first step in evaluating the potential for electoral reforms to increase youth turnout, we look at the extent to which there is state-level variation in youth voting. Figure 6.1 shows wide differences in rates of voting among first-time eligible voters across states and elections–shown are a midterm election and presidential election from the years in our analysis. For example, in the 2012 election, among first-time voters rates of voter participation ranged from 3.3 (Idaho) to 44.0 (Iowa) percent of eighteen-year-olds.[2]

Even though there is a rich literature on the effect of electoral reforms on *overall* rates of voter turnout, little work has focused on how these reforms affect *youth* specifically. This is unfortunate as voting obstacles are expected to be especially burdensome for young people who are just learning about the registration and voting process, as discussed in more detail in Chapter 2. Whereas for older, habitual voters the barriers to registration and voting may be negligible, our qualitative interviews revealed that young people find the process daunting. As such, reforms that lighten or remove voting obstacles may have a noticeable impact on young people.

A handful of empirical studies have scrutinized the impact of various electoral laws on young people, and have found that law changes that have only modest effects overall can have more sizeable effects on young

[2] These numbers are calculated by dividing the number of eighteen-year-olds who vote by the number of eighteen-year-olds in the state. Unfortunately, there are no estimates of the VAP/VEP by year of birth. The lower midterm election estimates reflect the much lower levels of turnout in these elections. Alaska and Hawaii are omitted from graph, but their rates of turnout among eighteen-year-olds from 2006 to 2014 follow: Alaska: 6.9 percent, 12.5 percent, 6.2 percent, 8.7 percent, and 5.2 percent & Hawaii: 3.3 percent, 6.6 percent, 4.7 percent, 5.0 percent, and 2.7 percent.

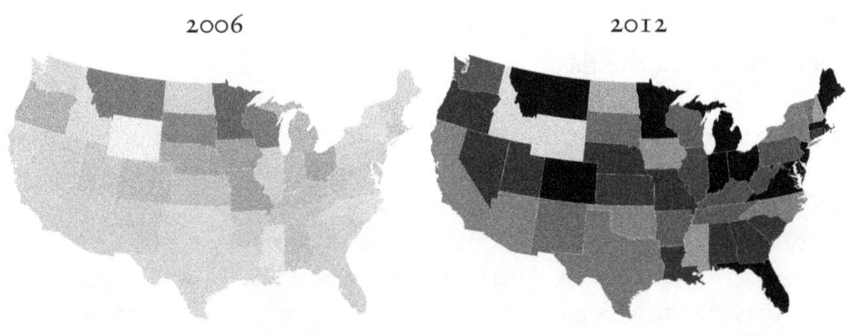

FIGURE 6.1 Mapping youth turnout by state

State-level rates of validated voter turnout for first time eligible young voters in the 2006 and 2012 elections. Data come from the Data Trust's nationwide voter file.

people. For example, one study found that election law reforms in California that exogenously changed individuals' distance to their polling location resulted in a noticeable decrease in rates of in-person turnout among young voters, which – unlike among their older counterparts – was not offset by increases in absentee voting (Brady and McNulty 2011). Another study found that allowing people to register when they get to the polls – same-day registration – has a modest impact on voter turnout writ large, but was quite effective at increasing turnout among young adults (Leighley and Nagler 2013, ch. 4). It is unclear if this pattern holds for other types of electoral reforms that make registration or voting less burdensome. Given our previous evidence that young people are especially sensitive to having their turnout intentions derailed, we see clear motivation for evaluating the effect of electoral reforms on young people specifically. Our analysis will help to fill this glaring gap in the literature.

Here we focus on six popular electoral reforms – no-excuse absentee voting, early voting, preregistration, same-day registration, Election Day registration, and online registration. For those unfamiliar with these reforms, we provide a brief description:

- **No-excuse absentee voting**: voting that does not happen in person on Election Day but instead occurs another way – usually by mail or over the internet. No-excuse absentee voting allows individuals to vote absentee without an excuse.

- **Early voting:** expands the window of the days/hours that someone may vote. This reform allows people to cast a ballot at a polling place prior to an election.
- **Preregistration:** allows young people who are 16 or 17, and not eligible for the next election, to register to vote, so that they are automatically added to the registration list when they turn 18.
- **Same-day registration (SDR):** allows individuals to register whenever they show up at the polls (be it on Election Day or during an early voting period).
- **Election Day registration (EDR):** more restrictive than SDR; allows individuals to register when they get to the polls on Election Day only.
- **Online registration:** allows citizens to register to vote online.

6.2 DATA AND METHODS FOR THIS CHAPTER

To evaluate the effect of these policies, we pair panel data on these electoral rules with pooled cross-sectional data from the Current Population Survey (CPS), a monthly government survey of 60,000 US households.[3] With these data, we employ a statistical design called a difference-in-difference that leverages variation in election laws across states and time to estimate the impact of the electoral rules on voter turnout rates among young adults in the state. Using this technique, we explore the effect of individual electoral rules, conditioning on other electoral rules available in the state, and the combined effect of rules bundled together. For this second task, we create a combined scale – the ease of voting scale (EOVS) – to indicate the overall ease of registration and voting in a given state at a given time. Previous research has tended to evaluate the impact of only a single election law at a time, thereby missing potential complementarities between laws.[4]

Our independent variables of interest come from panel data on state-level electoral reforms. We draw this information from a thorough review of several sources, including the National Conference on State Legislatures (NCSL), the Pew Trust, the Correlates of State Policy Project (Jordan and Grossmann 2016), data from Biggers and Hanmer (2015), data from

[3] The CPS is conducted by US Census Bureau for the Bureau of Labor Statistics. In election years, the November supplement of this rotating panel asks questions about voter registration and voting of adult citizens in the sample. Like others (Burden et al. 2014), we code voting as 1 if the individual indicated she voted in the most recent election and as 0 if she answered "no," "don't know," "refuse to answer," or has no response recorded.

[4] A notable exception is Burden et al. (2014).

TABLE 6.1 *Overview of electoral reforms (2000–2012)*

	'00	'01	'02	'03	'04	'05	'06	'07	'08	'09	'10	'11	'12
Absentee voting	19	22	22	23	24	27	28	28	28	29	29	29	29
Early voting	18	20	21	24	25	29	30	30	30	31	31	31	31
SDR	6	6	6	6	6	8	8	9	9	9	10	10	11
Preregistration	2	2	2	2	2	2	2	2	3	3	9	9	10
Online registration	0	0	1	1	1	1	1	1	2	3	8	9	13
EDR	.	.	6	.	6	.	7	.	8	.	9	.	11

The number of states with each of the electoral reforms that we use in this chapter. No-excuse absentee voting and early voting data from Biggers and Hanmer (2015, see figure 1). Preregistration data from Holbein and Hillygus (2016). SDR data from the National Conference on State Legislatures (NCSL). Online registration data from the Pew Trusts. EDR data from Fraga (2018), who only has even-year data from 2002 onward.

Keele and Minozzi (2013), and our own review of state-level statues on election laws.[5]

Table 6.1 provides a view of how the electoral reforms that draw our focus have changed over time within our window of study. As can be seen, once electoral rules catch on, they tend to spread. No-excuse absentee voting and early voting are by far the most prevalent; however, preregistration, same-day registration, and online registration have also increased in recent years.

With this panel information on electoral laws, we are also able to construct two composite scales. The first creates a simple mean scale of these six reforms.[6] The second is a simple three-item mean scale with the registration-based reforms – preregistration, same-day, registration, and online registration – that end up showing the most promise below. These measures give us a feel for the overall ease in registering and voting in the state. We term these the ease of voting scale (EOVS). As with any scale construction exercise, as long as we are picking up with a latent construct of interest, a combined scale will reduce noise in our estimates. While the EOVS is not a perfect measure of registration and voting costs, it acts as a proxy that allows us to consider the combined effect of implementing these reforms as a bundle. This increases our degree of ecological validity, as electoral reforms are often implemented – and sometimes

5 See the Appendix for details.

6 This approach applies an equal weight to reforms that go into the scales. We deem this the best approach as there seems to be little ex-ante justification for weighting some election laws more than others. If we use a principal component factor analysis, we find results that lead us to a similar conclusion – that lowering the overall barriers in a state increases turnout (though by perhaps a bit less than the mean scale would suggest).

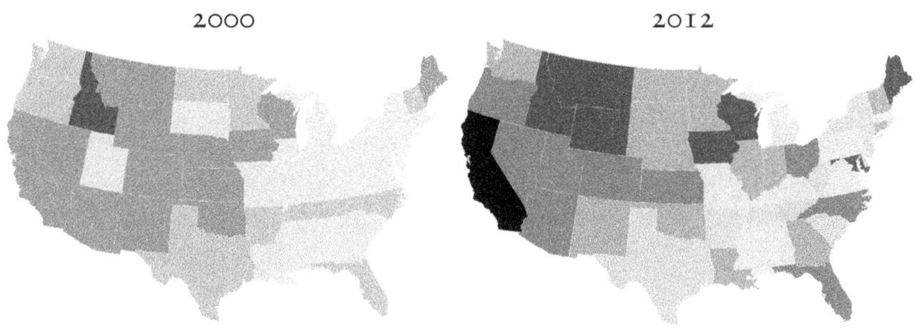

EOVS 0.00 0.25 0.50 0.75 1.00

FIGURE 6.2 Ease of voting scale across states and time

Variation in states' scores on the ease of voting scale in the first and last years of our panel. Those who have none of the six reforms are at 0, while those who have all of the reforms are at 1. Darker colors correspond to easier registration and voting rules.

repealed – in package legislation (e.g. North Carolina in 2009 and then again in 2013). This approach also helps us avoid the concern that estimating changes to individual election laws (say, same-day registration) may actually be picking up on simultaneous changes to other election laws (say, absentee voting).

Figure 6.2 maps where voting rules are least burdensome, with darker colors corresponding to less burdensome registration and voting rules. This allows us to estimate the effect of the overall easiness to register in a given state. With this scale, the states with the least burdensome registration standards in 2012 include California, Idaho, Iowa, Maryland, Maine, Montana, Wisconsin, and Wyoming, while Missouri, Mississippi, Alabama, Michigan, Virginia, Massachusetts, Kentucky, and Pennsylvania had the most burdensome requirements.

To be clear, it is not our intention to argue that these two scales are necessarily the best way to measure the "cost of voting" – even just the institutional costs. As we have argued in previous chapters, voting obstacles may be much more complex than just the electoral rules one must navigate. Voting costs – while theoretically tractable – can be hard to measure in practice. While this scale does not entirely capture voting and registration costs, it does allow us to get some view of how much of an effect voting and registration rules have.

We combine this state-by-state electoral rules panel with information from the US Census Bureau's November Voter Supplement to the Current Population Survey (CPS), which has been used in numerous studies on voting (e.g. Berinsky and Lenz 2011; Burden et al. 2014;

Milligan, Moretti, and Oreopoulos 2004; Oliver 1996). While this panel relies on self-reported voting, research shows that the CPS's youth turnout numbers are strongly related to validated voter turnout numbers (Fraga and Holbein 2018).[7] Here we specifically use data from the CPS in 2000–2012, but also use information from validated voter rolls to verify our results (as in the previous chapter). In addition to containing information on voting, the CPS contains information such as age, marital status, gender, family income, educational attainment, whether an individual lives in a metropolitan center, race, ethnicity, time living at current address, whether one is employed as a business or farm employee, whether the interview was done in person, and whether the person registered at the DMV, which we include as controls in our empirical models. Below we vary how we operationalize young people – employing both the 18–25 and 18–29 ranges that many organizations use (e.g. CIRCLE) – however, our results are not sensitive to this decision.

6.2.1 Methodological Approach

Our analysis leverages variation in adoption of electoral reforms and the panel nature of our data to estimate difference-in-difference models similar to those estimated in Chapter 5. Difference-in-difference models are the standard approach in electoral reform studies (e.g. Bertocchi et al. 2017; Fitzgerald 2005; Hanmer 2009; Knack 1995; Leighley and Nagler 2013). These models absorb a host of potential sources of bias left unaccounted for in cross-sectional models. Often, difference-in-difference approaches that utilize cross-state variation constitute the best available approach for estimating the effect of election laws, especially given that cutoffs, instruments, or random assignment in electoral laws are few and far between.[8]

[7] On this point, Burden et al. (2014, 101) argue that even though the CPS relies on voting self-reports, "the CPS is one of the most accurate among all election surveys," and that "although the [voting] over-reporting phenomenon is well known, the large literature on the problem has generally concluded that the consequences for statistical inference are minor." Moreover, research finds young people are less susceptible to misreporting voting than older people (Ansolabehere and Hersh 2012).

[8] Exceptions include population-based cutoffs for Election Day registration in Wisconsin and Minnesota (Keele and Minozzi 2013) – which we discuss further – age-based cutoffs for preregistration (Holbein and Hillygus 2016), and intra-state difference-in-difference specifications (Burden and Neiheisel 2013; Gerber, Huber, and Hill 2013), which may be preferable to cross-state comparisons in terms of their internal validity. However, these types of plausibly exogenous variation are few and far between and may struggle to produce estimates with an adequate degree of external validity.

Difference-in-difference models rely on two sources of variation: with the first difference removing all sources of heterogeneity that remain constant within states (e.g. state-level culture, other institutional rules, school quality, etc.) and the second difference removing all sources of heterogeneity that remain constant within years (e.g. competitiveness of a campaign, a specific candidate, economic conditions, etc.). In practice, these models are estimated by including a battery of state and year fixed effects to the regression models (Gerber, Huber, and Hill 2013; Leighley and Nagler 2013). In the difference-in-difference models, the key variable of interest is whether or not the individual state possesses the various electoral reforms in a given year, or not.[9]

The key condition for identification in the difference-in-difference model is the so-called parallel trends assumption, which asserts that the average change for the control group represents the change in the treatment group in the absence of treatment (Angrist and Pischke 2008). While this assumption is fundamentally untestable, comparing observed pre-treatment trends in the dependent variable offers at least suggestive evidence of whether it is satisfied. The parallel trends assumption would be violated if states selected into electoral reforms on the basis of prior year trends in the dependent variable: perhaps, for example, easing voting restrictions when youth voter turnout declined (i.e. the "Ashenfelter's dip" or the "pre-program dip," see Ashenfelter and Card (1985)). In our data, the evidence seems to suggest that this threat to causal inference is not occurring (see the Appendix). While some previous work has questioned if the parallel trends assumption holds among all adults (e.g. Keele and Minozzi 2013), pre-treatment trends in youth voter turnout specifically appear to be parallel. While not conclusive proof, this suggests that our models will do reasonably well at approximating the causal effect of the electoral reforms of interest.

To offer the most comprehensive analysis, we include the various electoral reforms together in shared difference-in-difference models. This allows us to account for the other aspects of electoral reform in a given state or year, something critical to understanding the effects of various electoral reforms, but only done in some select election law studies. However, we have also run models with these reforms individually, which

[9] Within our window of study (2000–2012), our five electoral rules do change (in varying degree) within states. This can be seen in the intra-state correlations (ICC) in these reforms ($ICC_{absentee} = 0.68, ICC_{early} = 0.62, ICC_{preregistration} = 0.49, ICC_{SDR} = 0.75, ICC_{online} = 0.16, ICC_{EDR} = 0.76$).

produced similar results. Finally, in an alternative model specification we include our election laws into shared scales. This allows us to estimate the effect of bundling electoral reforms together.[10]

With preregistration it makes sense to also slightly modify our difference-in-difference models in some specifications. In contrast to simply specifying whether a state has preregistration in a given period, which we also do to help make our analyses parallel across electoral reforms, here we also define preregistration exposure by coding individuals within a given state as either having been the right age to have been exposed to preregistration (i.e. 16 or, in an alternative specification, 16 or 17) or having been too old to potentially utilize this reform when it was in place (i.e. already 18), even if the state currently had preregistration. This more fine-grained specification of the independent variable of interest allows us to use age as a third source of variation. In practice, we estimate this model by adding age fixed effects to our difference-in-difference specification along with our updated, more fine-grained treatment variable.[11] This modeling approach purges out sources of potential bias that vary across age cohorts. Unfortunately, we cannot run similar specifications for our other electoral rules, as these are available to individuals of all ages.[12]

6.3 RESULTS: THE EFFECT OF ELECTORAL RULES ON YOUTH VOTING

Figure 6.3 shows the effect of the six different electoral laws. These come from a difference-in-difference specification with two-way fixed effects (state and year) and the individual-level controls just mentioned. We outline the effect of each of the laws in turn, taking time to mention additional robustness checks that we run when those are merited.

Absentee Voting: As can be seen in Figure 6.3, there is almost no effect of no-excuse absentee voting on levels of youth turnout. Substantively, the point estimates are all small: The model with no controls indicates an effect of -0.8 percentage points ($p = 0.58$) and the model with controls

[10] Unfortunately, the data do not have enough common-support to estimate models that include the full set of six way interactions. For this reason, we focus our attention on the combined effect, rather than the piece-by-piece comparisons.

[11] The results are unchanged if we allow these age fixed effects to flexibly vary by state and year.

[12] The results presented for this alternative specification remain unchanged if we add the other electoral reforms available in that state–year or if we control for lagged treatment.

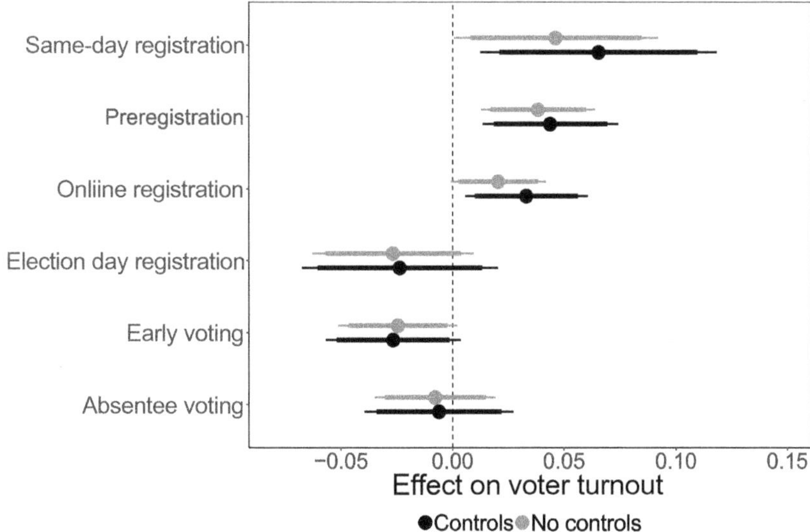

FIGURE 6.3 Effect of election laws on youth turnout

Difference-in-difference effect estimates for the electoral reforms listed. Points reflect coefficient estimates and bars represent 90 percent and 95 percent confidence intervals. Models with controls include age, marital status, gender, family income, educational attainment, whether an individual lives in a metropolitan center, race, Hispanic ethnicity, time living at current address, whether one is employed as a business or farm employee, whether the interview was done in person, and whether person registered in at the DMV.

indicates an effect of −0.6 ($p = 0.72$). Moreover, the confidence intervals are precise enough to almost completely rule any reasonably sized effects, with the largest upper bound of the 95 percent confidence interval being 2.8 percentage points. This suggests that among the potential electoral reforms available as a means of increasing youth turnout, no-excuse absentee voting is not likely to have a meaningful effect.

Early Voting: Similarly, Figure 6.3 shows that early voting appears to be a less than ideal strategy for increasing youth turnout, consistent with previous research that finds this law does not tend to increase overall turnout levels. Indeed, one study found evidence that adopting early voting in a state actually depressed overall voter turnout (Burden et al. 2014). The coefficients for our difference-in-difference models are all in that direction – ranging from −2.5 (no controls) to −2.7 percentage points (controls). However, none of these estimates is statistically significant at traditional levels, perhaps because the estimates among young people alone are slightly less powered than estimates that look at all adults together. Regardless, the corresponding 95 percent confidence intervals suggest that a meaningful positive effect is unlikely – with both models allowing us to rule out effects as small as 0.4 percentage points. Early voting alone does not appear to increase youth turnout.

SDR/EDR: Before presenting our results, we note that SDR is not the same as EDR (EDR). SDR is "the marriage of [Election Day registration] and early voting" (Burden et al. 2014, 97). So, SDR allows for registration whenever people show up to the polls – be it on Election Day or during an early voting period. Hence, SDR is less restrictive (and thus a more powerful treatment) than EDR. That said, they are highly correlated ($r = 0.9$) – many of the states that have EDR also have SDR. So, in models where we include both together, one of these coefficients is bound to lose significance.

With these caveats in mind, our models indicate that SDR increases youth turnout, but EDR does not. The positive effects of a state adopting SDR on youth turnout are sizable – an increase of 4.6 (no controls; $p = 0.048$) to 6.5 (controls; $p = 0.016$) percentage points. This finding is consistent with recent work conducted by Grumbach and Hill (2019), who use a CPS time series that is even longer than ours and a variety of identification strategies to estimate that SDR increases youth turnout by 3.5–10.1 percentage points. Keele and Minozzi (2013) likewise found overall turnout increase from SDR when looking at data in the 1970s and 1980s. Using data from the difference-in-difference design employed by Keele and Minozzi (2013), we replicate their difference-in-difference results on overall turnout and re-estimate for young people and find effects on the order of 11.4 ($p = 0.015$) to 17.9 ($p \approx 0.003$) percentage points.[13] Depending on years used, the observed turnout effects represent somewhere between 34 percent and 53 percent of the entire age gap between young and old voters. Put differently, estimates from various datasets and methods suggest that by implementing reforms that allow young people to register when they show up to the polls, states have the chance to cut their age gap by a third to a half, if not more.

Online Registration: Online registration may also increase youth turnout, but our level of uncertainty around this estimate is a bit higher relative to SDR. Figure 6.3 shows this visually. The point estimates vary from 2.1 (no controls; $p = 0.06$) to 3.3 (controls; $p = 0.019$) percentage points. Overall, these results are consistent with online registration

[13] Our estimates are also very similar to those reported in passing in Leighley and Nagler (2013, Ch. 4) in their examination of Presidential elections between 1972 and 2008 (12.1 percentage points among eighteen to twenty-four year olds).

maybe having an effect on youth voter turnout, but with a great deal of uncertainty around these estimates.

Preregistration: Like SDR, and to a lesser extent online registration, preregistration appears to be a viable means of increasing youth turnout. In the models with all other election laws, we find an effect somewhere on the order of 3.8–4.4 percentage points among eighteen to twenty-five year olds. These specifications are quite precise ($p < 0.005$ in both specifications). These model results are robust to alternative specifications. For example, across our difference-in-difference model specifications where we do not control for other election laws available in the state, the estimates range from about 3.9 to 5.7 percentage points. These are all statistically significant at high levels ($p \leq 0.01$ in all cases).[14] And these effects are substantively meaningful: representing about 12–23 percent of the overall gap in voter turnout between young and older voters. The difference-in-difference models specified with age differences in mind likewise show a meaningful positive effect. The coefficient estimates range from 4.0 to 4.3 percentage points (sixteen-year-old exposure) and 3.5–4.1 percentage points (sixteen- and seventeen-year-old exposure).[15] These model estimates are quite precise, with most of these easily clearing the 5 percent significance threshold.[16]

In addition, as a placebo test we run our preregistration models among older voters – individuals older than 60 – who should not see a turnout impact from having a preregistration law in place, being too old to preregister. As expected, we find no turnout effect in the placebo test: an estimate of −0.2 percentage points that is precisely estimated to not be different from 0 ($p = 0.87$).[17] In addition to helping validate our design, this test shows that preregistration is uniquely designed to narrow stubborn

14 If we collapse to the state-year level, the estimates range from 2.9 ($p = 0.046$) to 4.3 ($p = 0.001$) percentage points, depending on model specification.

15 As we mentioned earlier, another way to try and adjust for potential bias is to account for preregistration availability in previous periods. When we do so, the results do not change, with the estimates ranging from 4.5 to 6.0 percentage ($p < 0.04$ across all models).

16 Two specifications do not meet the 5 percent significance threshold, but do meet the 10 percent threshold ($p \approx 0.055$ and $p \approx 0.085$). Both of these are from the models using the smaller sample size (eighteen- to twenty-five-year-olds) that also does not have the added degree of precision that comes from including baseline controls. Once we add precision with controls, the estimates among eighteen- to twenty-five-year-olds become significant ($p \approx 0.007$ and $p \approx 0.020$); moreover, once we expand our age window a bit, the results become even more precise (being all less than $p = 0.01$).

17 Preregistration could indirectly affect older citizens' turnout if something similar to what Dahlgaard (2018) identifies (i.e. spillovers from child to parent) occurs. Unfortunately, the CPS is not well situated to test this proposition.

age-based turnout gaps. Whereas other election reforms could keep age gaps at similar levels – by raising the turnout of older voters – preregistration is unique in that it has a laser-like focus on young people.

One disadvantage of our approach to evaluating the effect of preregistration is our inability to precisely identify those targeted by the law. Ideally, we could add precision to our estimates if we could look exclusively at those who are just becoming able to vote, comparing those exposed to a preregistration law and those not. Unfortunately, the CPS has relatively few of these individuals; it has only about 12,000 eighteen-year-olds over the twelve years in our sample. Hence, if we wanted to isolate our sample down to those who are voting for the first time, the CPS is not the place to look. Our approach was to code individuals based on whether they had preregistration in their state when they were sixteen or seventeen and look at a wider age range that included those treated. As an alternative approach, we turn to an alternative data source: the Data Trust nationwide voter files that we used in Chapter 5 for our civic education estimates. Although it includes a short span of years, it has sufficient sample size to more precisely look at just eighteen-year-olds.[18] This provides us with a (weighted) sample of over 3 million eighteen-year-olds per election cycle (who are still nested in state-year treatment units) with whom we can calculate validated turnout rates. When we use this approach, the estimates for preregistration's contemporary effect range from 1.2 percentage points to 10.8 percentage points, depending on model specification.[19] Across all model specifications that we run, the median effect size is 6.0 percentage points and the median p-value is 0.006. If we pool our estimates together, the weighted average effect is 5.8 percentage points [95 percent confidence interval: 4.8 p.p., 6.8 p.p.]. Descriptively, most (79 percent) of estimates are in the 3–10 percentage point range.[20] If

[18] This panel includes turnout estimates accurate back to 2006 and up to 2014 (we only use up to 2012 because that is when our preregistration coding ends). As in Chapter 5, we collapse down to the state–year level (to improve computation time and avoid the possibility of differential registration bias) and weight based on the voting age population of eighteen-year-olds.

[19] To be thorough, we run twenty-four different difference-in-difference specifications that vary whether state time trends, lag and lead treatment variables, and whether other controls are included. These are all modifications recently recommended in the difference-in-difference literature.

[20] All estimates are positive. In total, 17/24 specifications are significant at the 5 percent level and 20/24 are significant at the 10 percent level. Qualitatively, the models with the weakest identification tend to show smaller, less precise effects.

we look at the effect of preregistration laws two years previous – an approach suggested by Garnett and Miller (2018), which among our eighteen-year-old sample is equivalent to having preregistration when one is sixteen years old (our preferred model), which includes the full set of other election laws we explore, along with their lagged and leaded values – provides an effect estimate of 12.9 percentage points ($p \approx 0.015$). This large estimate for preregistration's effect is consistent with an earlier implementation of the law exposing young people to a larger dosage of this reform.

Our estimates are also quite similar to others who have recently used various extensions to estimate the effect of preregistration. Our results are very similar to those provided by Garnett and Miller (2018), who extend the CPS time series to 1996–2016 and find a turnout effect of approximately 6 percentage points. Our results are also consistent with those provided by Bertocchi et al. (2017) who use CPS data from 1996–2014 and two identification strategies to estimate the effect of preregistration on turnout – a difference-in-difference design (analogous to ours) and a state geographic discontinuity approach. This approach augments the difference-in-difference by pairing it down to counties close to state borders between preregistration and non-preregistration states based on the assumption that these counties will be even more similar than a broader state-comparison. They find that preregistration increases youth turnout by 4.6–9.3 percentage points. We successfully replicate the Bertocchi et al. (2017) state boundary discontinuity analyses by using the Data Trust data at the county – year level from 2006 to 2012. Our effects estimated range from 7 to 12 percentage points ($p < 0.001$ in all specifications).[21] They show that this effect is robust and that preregistration's effect is centered on poor, young voters (a fact that we corroborate as well). Finally, they show that these gains result in a narrowed turnout gap between old and young voters; with their results indicating that when preregistration is introduced "the turnout gap between the 18–24 and 65–90 age groups decreases from 28.3% to 21.8%" (Bertocchi et al. 2017, 33). These studies provide an additional layer of confidence to the robustness of findings.

[21] Our base model includes state and year fixed effects. Our sample is eighteen-year-olds and treatment is preregistration when an individual was sixteen years old. We also account for whether preregistration is observed simultaneously and in the election afterwards and in some specifications the other election laws available in the state. We vary the distance around the state boundary from as wide as 150 to as narrow as 10 miles.

In short, the best evidence available suggests that preregistration is an effective electoral reform to increase low youth turnout. Where other electoral reforms like absentee or early voting fall short, preregistration makes a meaningful dent in the age-based gap in voter turnout. It doesn't close the age gap entirely, but it does work to get a nontrivial number of young people to the polls.

6.3.1 Why Do Some Electoral Reforms Work, but Others Fall Short?

To recap, our results suggest that among electoral reforms, those that make registration easier – same-day registration, online registration, and preregistration – are effective at increasing youth turnout. Preregistration and same-day registration offer particular promise at helping to close the age gap in turnout. While it is hard to know why exactly these reforms work, where others fall short, our results are consistent with other work that has begun to "distinguish between voting reforms that bring in new voters and therefore increase turnout from those reforms that simply provide alternative opportunities for voters who would cast a ballot under almost any set of rules" (Burden et al. 2014, 97). Put differently, whereas reforms like absentee and early voting may be primarily useful for individuals who are *already habitual voters*, reforms like preregistration and same-day registration are useful for those *unregistered individuals* for whom participation is unlikely sans intervention.

The observed pattern also fits with our theoretical framework. Same-day registration should reduce the need for noncognitive skills by allowing procrastination. When the time to vote arrives, young citizens who did not have the grit and self-control to register as much as thirty days in advance will only be able to do so in states where SDR is in place. While enhancing young people's noncognitive skills may help them follow through and vote, SDR helps bring in young people who might lack noncognitive skills.

Similarly, the patterns for preregistration would suggest a similar explanation for its effectiveness. By making it possible for those as young as sixteen to complete their registration form, it allows this potential barrier to participation to be removed at a time when there is greater institutional support and in contexts of increased political salience such as presidential elections. Removing the registration barrier to voting when young people are more likely to be paying attention or when they are assisted in the process means that they won't have to overcome this hurdle when they are eligible to vote. It also provides them with the experience of completing their registration forms, which should make it easier for them to repeat the process if they move between high school and college. While SDR and preregistration are distinct in terms of the timing of when they allow young people to register – with the first encouraging citizens to do so close to when an election is held and the other allowing individuals to do so long in advance – they are similar in that they remove the registration barrier when it is easier for the individual.

6.3.2 Who Do Electoral Reforms Help the Most?

An obvious follow-up question about electoral reforms is, who do they benefit the most? That is, do these laws help narrow the turnout gaps by race or socioeconomic status? With respect to heterogeneities among young people, we find that online registration ($\beta_{lowincome}$ = 3.5 p.p., $p_{lowincome}$ = 0.05; $\beta_{difference}$ = 1.9 p.p., $p_{difference}$ = 0.13), and preregistration ($\beta_{lowincome}$ = 8.4 p.p., $p_{lowincome}$ = 0.00; $\beta_{difference}$ = 1.2 p.p., $p_{difference}$ = 0.22) appear to perhaps be especially effective among low-income young people, thus helping to narrow stubborn socioeconomic gaps in voter turnout that appear among young people. We also find some evidence that while absentee voting has very little effect on young people overall, it may be especially effective among young minorities ($\beta_{minority}$ = 3.4 p.p., $p_{minority}$ = 0.04; $\beta_{difference}$ = 4.5 p.p., $p_{difference}$ = 0.01) – thus, it perhaps helps to narrow the racial gap in voting that manifests itself early in the life course.

6.3.3 Considering the Effect of Easing Registering/Voting Overall

Our final analysis considers the effect of making voting and registration easier overall. As we mentioned earlier in the chapter, this approach combines the electoral rules that we explore into scales (EOVS). The advantage of this approach is that it provides us with an idea of how the overall ease of registration and voting in a given state influences youth turnout. Especially as states consider new reforms and restrictions, this analysis offers a more general picture about the mobilizing effects of reducing the institutional hurdles to voting. Figure 6.4 shows the results from models that take this approach: providing coefficient plots for two scales – the first that combines all six electoral reforms together and the second that combines the three registration-based reforms together. As can be seen, the six-item scale produces an estimate somewhere on the order of 5.8 ($p \approx 0.050$) to 6.9 ($p \approx 0.024$) percentage points. The three-item registration-focused scale produces estimates that are between

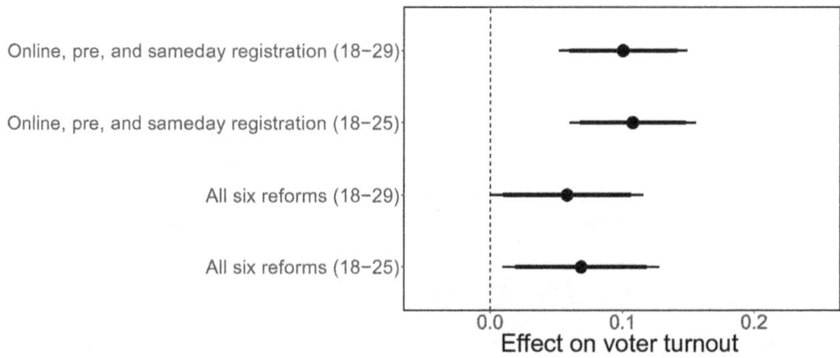

FIGURE 6.4 Effect of Ease of Voting Scale (EOVS) on youth turnout

The combined effect of our ease in registration and voting scale. Points reflect coefficient estimates and bars represent 90 percent and 95 percent confidence intervals. Models controls include age, marital status, gender, family income, educational attainment, whether an individual lives in a metropolitan center, race, Hispanic ethnicity, time living at current address, whether one is employed as a business or farm employee, whether the interview was done in person, and whether person registered in at the DMV. Numbers in parentheses next to the model description signify the age ranges used in estimation.

10.0 ($p < 0.001$) and 10.8 ($p < 0.001$) percentage points. That the three-item scale produces an estimate that is larger than the five item should make intuitive sense, given that the three-item scale contains only the registration-based reforms shown to be effective in the previous section.

These bundled effects are modest to large in size. As a substantive benchmark, the effect estimates for bundling all reforms together are equivalent to about a quarter of the entire age-based gap in voter turnout. The effect estimates for bundling the three registration-based reforms are even more sizable, being equivalent to as much as 40 percent of the age gap.[22]

Another way to gauge the substantive size of these effects is to compare them with the effect on older citizens. While the three registration reforms bundled together increase turnout among younger people (18–29) by 9.3 percentage points ($p < 0.001$), the same estimate for older citizens (ages 60 and older) is only about 3.3 percentage points ($p \approx 0.133$). This effect among older voters is nearly three times smaller than it is for young people ($p < 0.05$). This suggests that not only are

[22] The variation in estimate sizes depends entirely on how we define young and old voters and which effect estimate we use. If we define older voters as those over 50 and younger voters as those under 30, the gap in turnout is about 33 percentage points. If we simply break it by voters above and below 30, the gap is about 24 percentage points.

bundled registration reforms effective for simply raising turnout among young people but they also help to narrow the turnout gap between young and older citizens. While these registration-based reforms don't appear to be able to completely raise youth turnout to the levels that older citizens have long realized, they take a step in that direction.[23]

6.4 ELECTORAL REFORMS ON THE HORIZON

We have focused our attention on electoral rules that have been present, in at least some states, for a while. This is necessary because our identification strategy requires that we wait a while to see whether changes in electoral rules lead to changes in youth turnout. That said, there are a number of newer electoral reforms that, while not well-situated for evaluation at present, show potential for increasing youth turnout based on the patterns we have found in our analysis.

For example, a number of states have recently implemented automatic voter registration (AVR) – a reform that, just like its name implies, makes voter registration the default for eligible voters.[24] Unless citizens opt out, they are automatically added to voter registration rolls when they interact with other government agencies, such as the DMV. As of April 2018, twelve states – Alaska, California, Colorado, Georgia, Illinois, Maryland, New Jersey, Oregon, Rhode Island, Vermont, Washington, and West Virginia – plus the District of Columbia have approved AVR and at least twenty other states have considered doing so.[25] Some have speculated that "this policy boosts registration rates, cleans up the rolls, makes voting more convenient" (Brennan 2017). Indeed, there are some observational patterns that are promising, with Oregon's registration rate spiking in the months after AVR was implemented (Brater 2016).[26] Descriptive patterns of registration and voting in Oregon's AVR system have yielded promising results, especially among young people (Griffin et al. 2017). Consistent with this view, McGee et al. (2017) use a synthetic control approach to provide preliminary evidence that AVR may have played

[23] The data do not have enough common support to estimate models that interact all six electoral reforms together with their corresponding sub-interactions.

[24] It is also important to note that AVR requires some form of communication between election administrators and citizens.

[25] See "Automatic voter registration," Brennan Center for Justice Report, April 17, 2018.

[26] See, "Update: Oregon keeps adding new voters at torrid pace," Brennan Center for Justice Report, August 19, 2016.

a role in increasing turnout. (They do not explore the specific effect on young people because of inherent data limitations.) However, given that AVR has only been in place for a short time, there is still a high degree of uncertainty around these estimates. As such, formal program evaluations of AVR's effect on voter turnout are still to come. As more and more states implement AVR in the coming years, we will be able to better understand its impacts on voter turnout (and young people specifically). Given the results presented here, showing that reforms making registration easier increase youth turnout noticeably, there are strong reasons to suspect that this new reform might also increase youth turnout.

Similarly, in the United States some states have begun to experiment with lowering the voting age to sixteen or seventeen in municipal elections. The idea is that this change might allow young citizens to develop the habit for voting before they face the disruption of moving out of their home environment when they turn eighteen. As of June 2018, only four cities in the United States – Takoma Park, Maryland (in 2013); Hyattsville, Maryland (in 2015); Berkeley, California (in 2016); and Greenbelt, Maryland (in 2018) – have implemented this reform.[27,28] While these reforms are too new and small-scale to conduct a thorough evaluation of their effects, early results show that in these municipalities, very few young people take advantage of their right to vote. For example, Maryland state voter files reveal that in Takoma Park, there were only 230 young people registered to vote who were born within one year of the 2013 sixteen-year-old eligibility cutoff.[29] Once these citizens became eligible to vote in the next local elections (held in 2015), only eighteen (7.8 percent of registered voters) voted.[30] This low number suggests that lowering the voting age may not be enough on its own to bring in a host of new voters, unless it is supplemented by some interventions that encourage young people to exercise their right to vote. That said, given

[27] In June 2018, Washington DC also considered doing so; see "Should 16-year-olds be able to vote? A majority of the D.C. Council thinks so" *Washington Post*, June 28, 2018.

[28] In the United States, several states allow seventeen-year-olds to vote in primaries to nominate candidates for higher office if they will be eighteen by the general Election Day. Outside the United States, countries such as Austria, Argentina, Brazil, Germany, and the United Kingdom have all experimented with extending voting rights to citizens under eighteen.

[29] Population estimates for Takoma Park are only split by under/over eighteen. As of 2010, there were 3,749 citizens (22 percent of its population) under eighteen (see https://takomaparkmd.gov/about-takoma-park/facts-and-figures/).

[30] Six of these came from the pool of those marginally eligible to vote in 2013 and twelve came from the pool of those not quite old enough to do so.

that this reform is so new and has only been implemented in a few select localities, it is too early to know whether this approach can meaningfully increase youth voter turnout. Right now the data are too limited to produce reliable estimates. What we know theoretically suggests that lowering the voting age could work, but it is simply too early to tell.[31]

Finally, we note that some have gone so far as to argue that in order to increase turnout (especially among young people), voting should be made compulsory (e.g. Lijphart 1997). Although this reform appears to be especially effective at increasing youth voter turnout (Bechtel, Hangartner, and Schmid 2016; Blais 2006; Cepaluni and Hidalgo 2016; Jackman and Miller 1995; Jaitman 2013), it is not a very realistic reform. First, somewhat independent of the empirical effects of compulsory voting, there is a strong debate over whether making voting mandatory is ethical or politically feasible. While there are normative arguments for and against compulsory voting, this much is clear: Among reforms to increase participation, compulsory voting appears to be one of the (if not the) most controversial.[32] Second, there is at least some evidence that suggests that compulsory voting widens other types of participatory inequalities. For example, using an exact date-of-birth regression discontinuity design, Cepaluni and Hidalgo (2016) show that while compulsory voting in Brazil increases youth turnout, it does so unequally; increasing turnout 2.5 times more for educated youth than less educated youth (14.4 p.p. vs. 5.7 p.p.). While the debate over who compulsory voting affects most continues, this evidence provides some reason for pause. Third, there is some evidence that suggests that outside of increasing turnout, compulsory voting does little to affect other related civic attitudes and behaviors. Using an exact date-of-birth regression discontinuity design and large school administrative records from Brazil, Holbein and Rangel (Forthcoming) show that exposure to compulsory voting has no effect on political interest, political knowledge, belonging to associational memberships, or overall social awareness. If part of our goal in increasing youth turnout is to also increase other forms of civic participation, compulsory voting may fall short. Put differently, contrary to what some

[31] On this point, observational research from Denmark suggests that citizens whose first voting experience is earlier in their lives (i.e. eighteen as opposed to nineteen) are more likely to continue to vote later on in life (Bhatti and Hansen 2012). While this alone does not prove the effectiveness of lowering the voting age, it suggests that lowering the voting age might be quite effective.

[32] For an overview of the normative and political arguments for and against compulsory voting, see Lijphart (1997, 10–11), Hill (2000, 2006, or 2015), or Lacroix (2007).

have asserted, compulsory voting may actually not "be able to serve as an equivalent, but much less expensive, form of civic education and political stimulation" (Lijphart 1997, 10). These limitations alone should not rule out compulsory voting, but they should provide enough reason to not make us completely rely on this approach. Compulsory voting is no panacea.

6.5 THE POLITICAL DYNAMICS OF ELECTORAL LAWS

In this chapter, we have shown that some – but not all – electoral reforms work to increase youth turnout. On the one hand, reforms like early voting and no-excuse absentee voting appear to have little effect on youth turnout. However, reforms like SDR and preregistration appear effective at increasing youth voting. Moreover, our analysis of bundled reforms confirms that making registration and voting less costly will help to meaningfully increase youth turnout. These results suggest that in order to increase youth participation, policymakers should focus on passing reforms that work to minimize the obstacles, burdens, and costs that young people face with a prioritization on reforms that make registration easier.

Of course, we have to recognize that electoral reforms have been politicized in recent years, reducing the likelihood of nationwide adoption. Republican-controlled state legislatures have shown ambivalence – or outright hostility – to electoral reforms that make voting easier.[33] The dynamics of election reform in North Carolina, for instance, are illustrative. In 2009, a preregistration law passed the North Carolina State Legislature and was signed into law with wide bipartisan support. In July 2013, however, a new Republican majority abruptly repealed preregistration as part of legislation instituting a number of voting restrictions. Federal courts would ultimately strike down the repeal in July 2016 after it was determined the law was motivated to reduce turnout among young people and minorities.

The partisan dynamics of electoral reform are shown in Figure 6.5. As can be seen, states with Democratic-controlled legislatures and governors are much more likely to put easier electoral reforms in place than Republican controlled bodies – with the difference being about 7–7.5 percentage points, or equivalent to somewhere between 0.3 and 0.5 standard deviations. This makes the adoption of election laws that make register-

33 For a recent example of this, see "Republicans limiting early voting in Marion County, letting it bloom in suburbs," Indy Star, August 10, 2017.

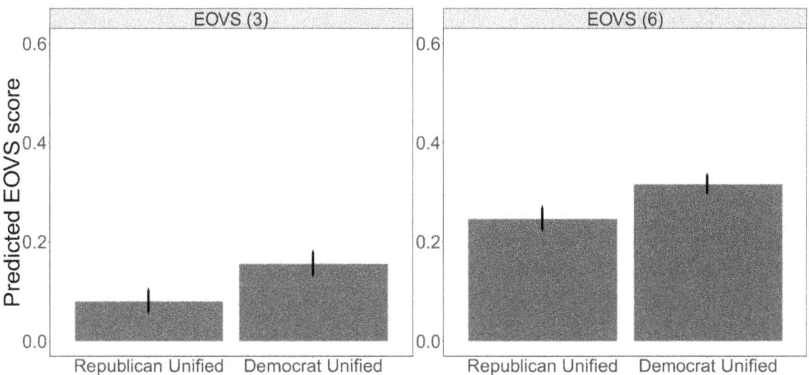

FIGURE 6.5 Who implements electoral reforms?

Predicted levels of our ease of voting scale broken by party control of the two legislative bodies and governorship. Bars reflect mean levels, with corresponding 90 percent and 95 percent confidence intervals also shown. Dependent variables are the ease of voting (3) and the ease of voting (6) scales (n+2). Models include state and year fixed effects, the full set of interactions between control of the two legislative chambers and the governorship, and the state electoral reforms at baseline (n-1). Data on state legislative/gubernatorial control are drawn from Jordan and Grossmann (2016).

ing and voting easier unlikely in many states. Republican-led legislatures have been hesitant to make voting easier for young people because of the perceived partisan implications of increased youth turnout.

Although perceptions about the partisan advantage associated with electoral reform are widespread, they are not actually rooted in the empirical evidence. For example, in earlier work, we showed that the adoption of preregistration laws in Florida helped to narrow the Democratic advantage among young voters (Holbein and Hillygus 2016). Likewise, we find that the adoption of preregistration in North Carolina increased unaffiliated registration more than either Democratic or Republican registration. Other work similarly finds that electoral reforms tend to have the effect of registering more Democrats, but mobilizing more Republicans (Neiheisel and Burden 2012).[34]

6.6 CONSIDERATIONS IN DESIGNING TOMORROW'S ELECTORAL REFORMS

Before concluding, we make one general note about the methods used in this chapter. The difference-in-difference models that we have used

[34] See also Herron and Smith (2012) and Cain and McCue (1985).

here come with the distinct advantage of allowing us to further approach causality than models that simply control for observable features. That said, the difference-in-difference approach is not without its detractors. To some, we will never truly know whether these estimates are really causal until electoral reforms can be randomly assigned. At present, random or plausibly random variation in electoral reforms does sometimes exist. However, exogenous variation is often not perfect – sometimes giving us causal estimates that have little substantive meaning (see the Appendix for an example). Moreover, truly exogenous variation in electoral rules is incredibly rare; it is the exception, rather than the rule.

The need for evaluating electoral reforms is widespread. Until policymakers implement electoral reforms in a way that is more conducive to evaluation, there will be inherent uncertainty in whether the results are truly causal. Policymakers and advocates of election law reforms who desire to know how to design laws to increase youth turnout should also make it part of their agenda to push for reforms that are designed with evaluation in mind. Not all electoral reforms work, and indeed some may even backfire. Given it is typically not possible to truly experiment with electoral laws (by randomly assigning exposure to one law or another), scholars will always face difficulty in evaluating the impact of electoral reforms, increasing the importance of a clear theoretical frameworks and multifaceted empirical approaches.

6.7 THE BIG PICTURE

We have shown that reducing the external voting costs will help to promote youth turnout, but we also recognize that this is only part of the policy solution. Unfortunately, electoral laws remain politically charged; in many states the trend is toward more restrictive voter registration and turnout requirements, not less. Moreover, we have to recognize that electoral reforms are inherently constrained in their capacity to increase youth turnout. Our most optimistic estimates in this chapter still leave a significant portion of the age gap unresolved. Even if we remove a large portion of external barriers to voting, many young people will still not vote because not all barriers to voting are external: Individual-level distractions and obstacles can still interfere. Given the interaction of personal and contextual barriers to participation, we next step back to consider a broader set of lessons about how we might help turn their civic attitudes into civic action.

7

Looking Ahead

On February 14, 2018, an armed gunman entered Marjory Stoneman Douglas High School in Parkland, Florida, and brutally murdered seventeen students, faculty, and staff members. The tragedy triggered a youth-driven political movement demanding policy action on gun violence. Led by a handful of Parkland students, youth activism rapidly spread through the country. Young people staged school walkouts, sparked a viral social media campaign, and organized a widely televised demonstration attended by more than a million people nationwide.[1] In the aftermath of the Parkland shooting, young people in the United States seemed poised for unprecedented levels of civic and political engagement; by many indications, young Americans appeared to (finally) be finding their political voice. And, yet, nearly 70 percent of young citizens stayed home in the 2018 election.

We've seen this story unfold many times before. Young people lead a movement for social change – rallying in the streets and (more recently) on social media – but fail to mobilize at the ballot box. As a part of the Civil Rights Movement in the 1960s and 1970s, for instance, young people showed signs of breaking through to higher levels of political participation: engaging in protests, boycotts, marches, and other forms of democratic engagement. However, *even then* – amid the high water mark of youth engagement – levels of youth turnout lagged far behind their older Americans (Leighley and Nagler 2013; Wolfinger and

[1] For protest counts see Crowd Counting Consortium, March 2018 Report, sites.google .com/view/crowdcountingconsortium

Rosenstone 1980).[2] More recently, young people voted at their highest rate in decades in the 2008 presidential election, but turnout levels plummeted by the next election and reached a historical low point in 2014 when fewer than 20 percent of those aged 18–29 cast a ballot.

Why is turnout so low among young Americans? And what exactly can be done to increase youth turnout? It is widely recognized that voter turnout is fundamental to democratic citizenship because those who participate are more likely to have their voices represented. And the enduring problem of low youth voter turnout has long captured the attention of policy-makers, youth advocacy groups, and scholars; yet, despite the considerable hand-wringing about this civic malaise, these questions have remained largely unanswered. In this book, we have examined the contextual and personal barriers that stand in the way of higher youth participation. In exploring this question, we conducted qualitative interviews with young people and civics teachers and we examined quantitative data from large-scale surveys, school administrative records, and voter files using observational, quasi-experimental, and experimental methods. Our findings offer a new perspective on the barriers to higher youth turnout and provide a promising path forward for scholarly research and policy reform.

In contrast to popular wisdom, we show that a lack of political motivation is not the primary deterrent to higher levels of youth turnout. Abysmally low youth turnout occurs despite the fact that the vast majority of young people in the United States report they are interested in politics and intend to vote before the election. The 2016 American National Election Study, for example, found that 75 percent of eighteen to twenty-nine year olds interviewed before the election reported that they intended to vote, but less than half were found to have actually voted when administrative election records were checked after the election. Too often, young people intend to be politically engaged, but ultimately fail to *follow through* on their intentions to vote. Any policy solutions to increasing youth turnout must start by understanding this gap between turnout intention and behavior.

Challenging previous models of voting behavior, we argue that cognitive capacities, such as political knowledge and verbal abilities, do not account for the gap between civic attitudes and civic action. It has long

[2] Eighteen-year-olds received the right to vote in 1972.

been assumed that teaching more facts about government and politics – the current approach to civic education in the United States – would reap dividends in the form of higher turnout at the ballot box. Our analysis shows that is not the case. Rather, we find that a set of noncognitive skills – a constellation of capacities related to self-regulation, effortfulness, and interpersonal interactions – helps to explain who votes and who does not. Beyond simply knowing more, individuals require the ability to control their thoughts, motivations, emotions, and behaviors in order to overcome the institutional and personal obstacles and distractions that can otherwise prevent acting on a participatory intention. Importantly, we show that noncognitive and cognitive skills do not overlap; many individuals with high degrees of cognitive aptitude fail to participate in politics because they lack the ability to follow through on their behavioral intentions.

In recent years, these noncognitive skills have received a great deal of attention in economics, education, and child development research – with scholars in these fields showing that noncognitive skills are not rigid across the life course, but are, instead, teachable, and appear to be important for a variety of school and career outcomes (e.g. Heckman, Stixrud, and Urzua 2006). Although political science research has emphasized cognitive abilities, our analysis shows, across multiple datasets and methodological approaches, that those with well-honed noncognitive skills are more likely to vote.

To be sure, there remains much to be learned about the nature and role of noncognitive skills for political participation. Are noncognitive skills relevant for other forms of civic participation, such as attending political meetings, discussing politics online, or participating in a campaign? Which specific skills matter? More generally, there remain fundamental questions about the conceptualization and measurement of these competencies. There is also still much to learn about how the education system can be designed to promote noncognitive skills. A rich, but nascent, body of research in economics, developmental psychology, and education policy has started to evaluate the ways that formal and informal learning environments can develop noncognitive skills, and we hope that this book encourages political scientists to join in this research agenda.

In this final chapter, we consider the implications of our results for theory and policy. We outline these contributions in this chapter, with the goal of speaking both to future researchers seeking to understand what sets people on a path toward participating in politics and to reformers seeking to improve youth civic engagement.

7.1 THEORETICAL IMPLICATIONS

The first contribution of our work is the development of a more complete theoretical framework for voter turnout. Whereas previous work focused on the decision to turn out, we focus on the gap between individuals' motivations and intentions to participate and the actual behavior of voting. Most models of voter turnout recognize that voting can be costly, but we call attention to the way that unanticipated obstacles and distractions can derail turnout intentions. In drawing attention to the importance of follow-through, the relevance of noncognitive skills becomes evident.

Noncognitive skills are an individual resource that help with the execution of participatory aspirations. Whereas cognitive abilities – especially political knowledge and verbal capabilities – have traditionally been considered the key resources needed for voter turnout (Verba, Schlozman, and Brady 1995), we show that skills not captured by standardized tests of cognitive ability help determine who turns out and who stays home. This finding also highlights the importance of distinguishing political motivation from *general* motivation – both are needed to understand political behavior. In focusing on the predictive power of markers of political motivation, such as feelings of civic duty and political interest, the field of political behavior has overlooked the nonpolitical attributes that help individuals to persevere in pursuing their political goals.

In addition to reshaping models of voter turnout, our analysis contributes to the ongoing debate over the importance of education for political participation (Campbell 2006b; Nie, Junn, and Stehlik-Barry 1996; Sondheimer and Green 2010; Verba, Schlozman, and Brady 1995; Wolfinger and Rosenstone 1980). Political science research has long emphasized the importance of education, which is thought to promote voter turnout primarily through the development of cognitive skills, especially verbal proficiency and political knowledge (Luskin 1990; Nie, Junn, and Stehlik-Barry 1996; Verba, Schlozman, and Brady 1995). Our analyses in Chapter 4 offer a provocative conclusion that noncognitive skills are part of the reason education contributes to political engagement. That is, education develops and reinforces an ability to self-regulate emotions, thoughts, and behaviors in working on academic tasks and interacting with others. Beyond identifying a plausible new channel linking education and voting, the results outlined in this book suggest a reorientation of this literature. Rather than focusing exclusively on the number of years a citizen spends in school, we argue that it is important to consider what content young people were exposed to while in school. Specifically, our analysis shows that a civics curriculum focused solely on teaching knowledge and facts of government and politics will not increase voter turnout. Our results suggest that schools can better promote civic engagement by helping young citizens overcome the costs of voting, offering a new perspective for rethinking the curricular goals of civic education. Based on existing large-scale interventions, we make specific recommendations in Chapter 5 and we urge new lines of research.

More generally, our findings also speak to the importance of childhood development for adult political participation. Our results show that the skills and experiences one has before they becoming eligible to vote shape later-life participation decisions. Most voting research is focused on identifying the correlates of participation *among adults*. Political surveys tend to include only those already old enough to vote, making it difficult to explore the path to civic engagement. Moreover, most research in this area has focused on the role of stable individual-level attributes. Whereas most of the standard predictors of civic participation (e.g. age, race, income, genes) are difficult to change, noncognitive skills appear to be malleable, especially in childhood and adolescence. The Fast Track intervention results discussed in Chapter 4 (combined with the other evidence we have from previous work on the causal effects of childhood interventions) indicate that experiences that long predate voting do matter, with childhood and adolescence acting as critical periods in determining whether young people will or will not start on the path toward becoming an active voter. Thus, our findings highlight the value of studying pre-voting aged young people, building on the political socialization literature.

By focusing on childhood, we hope to revive the body of political socialization research that, according to many, has lain dormant in recent years (Jennings, Stoker, and Bowers 2009; Niemi and Hepburn 1995; Sapiro 2004). We note that this contribution is separate from that made by those studying the habituation or persistence in voting patterns (Coppock and Green 2016; Fujiwara, Meng, and Vogl 2016; Gerber, Green, and Shachar 2003; Meredith 2009). While work in that area focuses on how voting in one period affects whether one votes in the future, our work focuses on how to get young people started voting *in the first place*. By exploring the childhood and early adolescent experiences, attributes, and contexts that affect youth voting, we help to identify the way that childhood development can shape future civic engagement. Our work implies that many studies of political behavior start too late in the life course. Scholars in this area should work to expand research on the experiences and attributes of children and early adolescents and how those shape turnout in adulthood. Of course, this requires new data collections that will require significant resources and careful planning. However, our results suggest that such a deep dive into the early life roots of political attitudes and behaviors are a worthwhile investment for the field.

7.2 POLICY IMPLICATIONS

Recognizing that some individuals have an orientation to participate but lack the skills to overcome the obstacles and distractions that get in the way offers a new perspective for thinking about potential solutions to help address low and unequal rates of civic participation. This perspective highlights two complementary paths toward promoting youth turnout: educational reforms and electoral reforms. In short, we argue that in order to narrow the age gap in voting young people need both electoral reforms that make voting easier *and* education reforms that increase young citizens' capacity to overcome the obstacles, barriers, costs, and distractions that get in the way of voting. Future public policies should not only focus on promoting the development of young peoples' noncognitive skills – a worthy goal in its own right – but should also help structure the voting process to minimize voters' need for noncognitive skills. Recognition of the factors that often stand in the way of political participation helps to inform more effective mobilization efforts.

7.3 WHAT ELECTORAL REFORMERS CAN DO

Our work underscores one institutional change that will increase youth engagement: electoral reforms that reduce the costs of voting. In showing that individuals require a set of noncognitive abilities to overcome the obstacles that can stand in their way of participating in politics, our analysis brings focus to the voting obstacles themselves. After all, if voting is so difficult that it requires a great deal of self-control, perhaps there are ways to reduce those difficulties.

Our analysis speaks to how we should structure the electoral rules that determine how, when, and where young people can vote. In Chapter 6, we showed that the most effective electoral reforms are those that lower the obstacles for new voters by reducing the costs of voter registration when citizens are most politically attentive. Rules like same day registration (SDR) and preregistration appear to be the most effective because they work to bring in young voters at critical points: allowing young people who have procrastinated registering, perhaps as a result of a lack of self-control (as SDR does) or pre-committing young people well in advance of the election, when one's eligible peers are excited and being mobilized (as preregistration does). These reforms help remove the obstacles to voting when individuals are most attentive to politics, making it easier to then follow through on voting. This second piece of evidence helps us build out our broader framework of what makes young voters.

Still, our work implies that reducing voting costs, on its own, may not be enough to substantially increase voter participation. Our results suggest that in trying to understand how to increase youth voting, it is important not only to focus on the obstacles that these citizens face – as proponents of electoral reform often do – but also to promote their capacity to overcome those obstacles. Given that making voting completely and totally costless is an unachievable task, developing individuals' ability to overcomes the voting barriers that they face is also important. Previous work has under-emphasized the importance of developing individuals' capacity to overcome voting obstacles. These two approaches need not be substitutes; they can fit together nicely in the two-pronged strategy. Simply put, to increase youth participation, voting should be made easier *and* citizens' capacity to overcome lingering obstacles, costs, barriers, and distractions should be amplified.

7.4 WHAT SCHOOLS CAN DO

We discussed what education reformers can do in Chapter 5 as a part of our broader discussion about civic education in America. There we highlighted the need for policymakers to fundamentally rethink civic education. Civics is broken. It has failed to live up to the lofty ideals that the founding fathers, education reformers, and modern-day politicians envisioned. Despite laudably increasing political knowledge, civics has little to no effect on whether young people become civically engaged. This has been true for *decades*. It is beyond time for American educators to experiment with new modes of promoting active citizenship. In so doing, policymakers should consider that the timing of civics instruction matters (high school is too late); the quantity of civic education needs to be increased (requiring one civics class for graduation is insufficient); and the content of civic education is crucial (plying students with facts is not enough).

On a more basic level, there are many things that schools can do to help young citizens navigate the complex set of institutional rules governing the voting process. These things include – but are not limited to –

holding registration and preregistration drives in schools, conducting mock elections, incorporating service learning requirements, and implementing applied learning environments where students hone their noncognitive abilities and gain hands-on experience in the political domain. To get a better sense of what schools are doing to help encourage young citizens, in 2018 we conducted a short online survey of North Carolina schools. In these interviews, we asked school administrators about the activities in their schools that could promote civic engagement. Overall, 245 officials responded, representing 42 percent of invited schools. In our sample, only 39 percent reported holding registration drives in the school (despite the fact that it is a legislative mandate in the state) and among this minority, only about 1 in 3 (12.6 percent of the entire sample) do so every year. Given the state now allows preregistration, this is a significant lost opportunity to bring young people into the electorate when they have supportive institutions available to them in high schools. Some schools are doing better than others and certain programs are implemented more than others.[3] However, this much is clear – at present there is quite a bit of variation in terms of what schools actually do and most schools do fewer than half of the activities listed in this section. Many public schools for which engaging students in democracy is an *explicit* goal are not doing enough to help individuals overcome the obstacles that stand in the way of their engagement in politics.

7.5 WHAT CAMPAIGNS AND YOUTH ADVOCACY GROUPS CAN DO

Although we have not focused on get-out-the-vote (GOTV) efforts, our work also sheds light on some ways political campaigns and youth advocacy groups might reconsider their mobilization efforts to increase youth turnout. At present, many get-out-the-vote initiatives focus on drumming up political motivation (i.e. one's levels of interest or civic duty). As meta-analyses have shown, these approaches generally have very modest effects

[3] Here are the numbers for various activities related to encouraging active student participation: conducting mock elections (56 percent), serving as a voting site on Election Day (14 percent), incorporating service learning or volunteer requirements (47 percent), and implementing applied learning environments where students learn to hone their noncognitive abilities (51 percent).

on voter turnout, with some notable exceptions (Green, McGrath, and Aronow 2013). Our work suggests a slightly different strategy. Given that young people have an especially large gap between vote intentions and voting campaigners would do well to recognize citizens' levels of general motivation rather than soley trying to move political motivation. Rather than asking "how can we get more young people interested in politics?" vested parties would do well to ask "how can we help young people follow through on their interest in politics?"

Although research is clearly needed in this area, our findings and existing research point to some potential ideas to consider. First, GOTV efforts could implement, within the political domain, strategies that have been used to reinforce follow through in other areas. These strategies include goal-setting, task planning, and anticipation of obstacles. For voting, this might entail activities like voting pledge cards, helping individuals to set a concrete plan for how, when, and where they will vote, and providing them with an easy way to set a calendar reminder. It might also include retroactively diagnosing what went wrong and assessing how to improve when they fail to vote in a given election – a technique commonly used in interventions designed to increase individuals' self-regulatory capacities. Recognizing that people are less likely to vote when they are tired and lose their general motivation (Holbein, Schafer, and Dickinson 2019; Schafer and Holbein Forthcoming), advocacy groups might provide pizza and coffee for voters waiting in long lines at the polling location. While none of these interventions are likely to fundamentally change individuals' noncognitive abilities in a lasting, meaningful way, they structure the voting decision to make it easier to follow through. While there is still much to learn about specific GOTV initiatives that could promote follow through, such studies would be worthwhile. The limited research available has shown that these approaches hold promise (Costa, Schaffner, and Prevost 2018; Dale and Strauss 2009; Malhotra et al. 2011; Nickerson and Rogers 2010).

7.6 DIRECTIONS FOR FUTURE RESEARCH

We want to acknowledge that, in some ways, our examination of the influence of noncognitive skills for political participation should be viewed as a first pass. The opportunities for future research are many. Future work would do well to expand the exploration of whether and why noncognitive skills matter in other aspects of the civic and political domain. One could easily envision noncognitive attributes are vital for even costlier political acts, such as volunteering, donating, protesting, contacting public officials, canvassing, or engaging in campaign activities. We have restricted our focus on voting intentionally, given its fundamental role in democracy. Likewise, considerable work is needed to understand the nature of noncognitive skills – how they should be measured and if different constructs matter for different types of activities or through different mechanisms.

Our view is that a more thorough understanding of the political relevance of noncognitive skills will require multiple modes of inquiry. Given the relative nascency of research in this area, observational research in this area is highly valuable. More research linking noncognitive abilities and voting should use models that leverage the best possible controls, along with various fixed effects strategies and panel techniques. These observational studies will help build a broader foundation for research in this area. From this foundation, natural experiments, short-run randomized control experiments, and larger (more expensive) longer-term randomized control experiments can be built. The results from the Fast Track, Democracy Prep, Citizenship Foundation, Envision, VAWK/IMAGO, and other interventions described in this text are promising, but more experiments are needed to fully understand which noncognitive programs will work best. New experiments are needed to answer questions about the particular points during the life course that noncognitive attributes are most malleable. Experimental research across a variety of disciplines has only begun to scratch the surface in this area.

Such research inherently comes with its own challenges. Large-scale interventions are costly and complex, requiring cooperation with education administrators and interdisciplinary collaborations. There are also challenges to making use of existing interventions that might be evaluated with respect to political outcomes. Many early childhood interventions focused on developing noncognitive skills do not follow their participants through adulthood. Among those that do, study investigators might not be willing or able to match their participants to voter files, especially if such a process involves handing their data over to partisan third party vendors for matching. Another challenge is that many early childhood programs see voting as a secondary outcome, despite its importance in establishing a well-functioning democracy and its *explicit* role as an outcome desired of the education system. In collecting data for this book, we sometimes found that study designers were reluctant to evaluate political outcomes. More generally, large-scale childhood interventions are typically multifacted and broad in scope so any effects can spillover through multiple pathways beyond the development of noncognitive skills. Though they make theoretical inferences about noncognitive ability more difficult, we consider the evaluation of such programs with respect to political outcomes to be a critical step toward better policy design.

In sum, it is not our intention to provide the last word on the importance of noncognitive skills for political behavior; rather, we hope to provoke a broader discussion in political science – similar to that which is currently being had in economics, psychology, and education research – as to when, where, and how noncognitive abilities matter. We believe noncognitive skills should become part of the political science lexicon, data collections, and basic theories. Our initial work suggests that noncognitive skills are a critical factor to determining who does and does not vote.

7.7 THE BIG PICTURE: MAKING YOUNG VOTERS

Young citizens' track record of participation in American elections is dismal. But, we should not accept this as an inevitable reality. Much is at stake – with turnout patterns being persistent, inequalities being stubborn, and resultant gaps in democratic representation bringing about serious consequences. While other social concerns – such as reducing income inequality, closing achievement gaps, and increasing access to quality healthcare – often take priority in the public eye, we contend that low and unequal patterns of voter participation should receive just as much attention. Voting is a barometer of societal well-being. Voting determines who has power and, as such, plays a key role in determining how these other social problems get addressed in the political arena. Increasing youth turnout is valuable in and of itself but also has the potential to fundamentally shape who gets elected, the policies they implement, and the overall health of our democracy.

Making young voters, then, is an important goal. This book has not provided all of the answers, but it has illuminated key considerations and critical next steps for scholars, education stakeholders, and policymakers.

Appendix

A.1 CHAPTER 1 APPENDIX

Figure A.1 shows where the United States stands in overall rates of voter turnout relative to other voting countries.

There is at least some evidence that levels of youth turnout might be getting worse over time. Figure A.2 shows levels of midterm voter turnout by age groups, broken by the generation in which one is born.[1] Young voters are turning out at rates noticeably lower than previous generations at the same age. For instance, baby boomers' turnout when they were eighteen to twenty-four was nearly 6 percentage points higher than millennials at the same point in their lives: a 30 percent difference. Young people today are less likely than older generations to become voters as they age.

Figure A.3 shows disparities in turnout by income, education, and race.[2] As we mentioned in Chapter 1, we see that even among young people, large disparities in voter turnout already exist: with the poorer (13 percentage points less likely to vote), less educated (23 percentage points less likely to vote), and minorities (14 percentage points less likely to vote) much less likely to vote than their more advantaged counterparts. These other stubborn inequalities in voter participation have their roots in the experiences that predate adulthood.

[1] The figure follows Pew's coding of generations. We present only midterm congressional elections for clarity, but a similar pattern can be seen in presidential elections.

[2] These come from simple probit models among eighteen to twenty-nine year olds. These gaps persist if we include all of these demographics in a single model and/or look just among eighteen-year-olds.

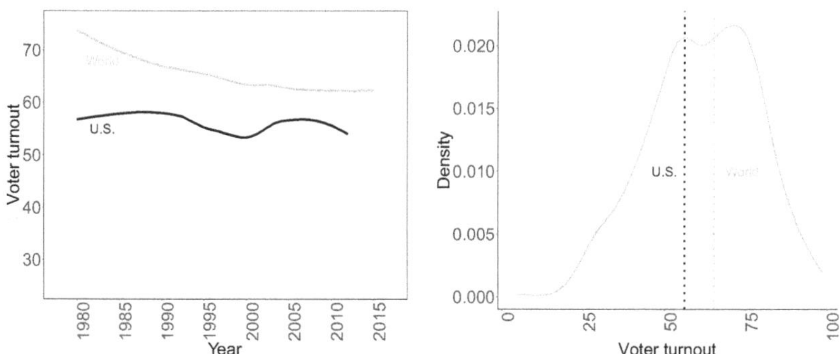

FIGURE A.1 Voter turnout in the United States relative to other countries

This figure provides two comparisons to illustrate the rate of voter turnout in the United States relative to other countries. The figure on the left plots voter turnout in the United States (black line) to that in the non-compulsory voting countries (grey line). Voter turnout rates reported with lines presenting a smoothed non-parametric function to allow for the flexibility given that elections are held in different years. The figure on the right places the mean level of voter turnout in the United States in the distribution of turnout across other countries in the world. This is plotted with a vertical dashed black line. Other countries' turnout mean level is shown with a vertical dashed grey line. Source: Voter Turnout Database, International Institute for Democracy and Electoral Assistance (IDEA).

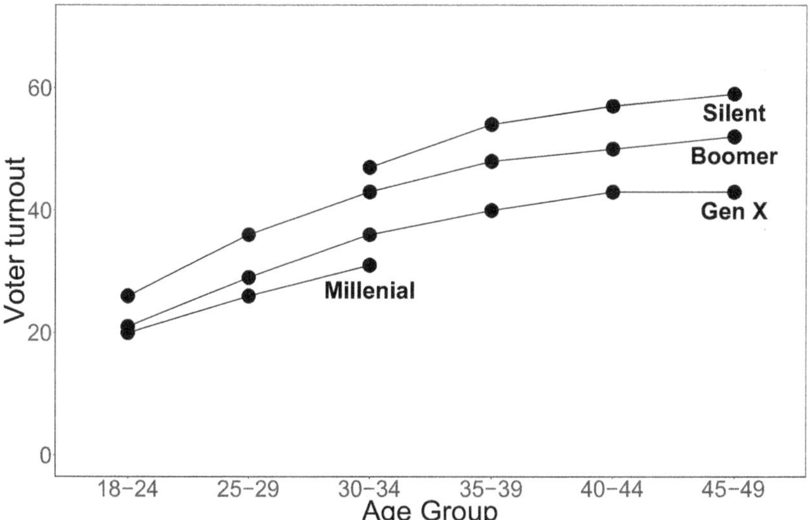

FIGURE A.2 Voter turnout by age and generation

Voter turnout (1978–2014 midterms) by age, broken by generation. Source: Current Population Survey November Supplement (recreated as reported by Pew Research Center). Following Pew's coding, millennials are those born between 1981 and 1996, Generation X as those born between 1965 and 1980, baby boomers as those born between 1946 and 1964, and the silent generation as those born between 1928 and 1945.

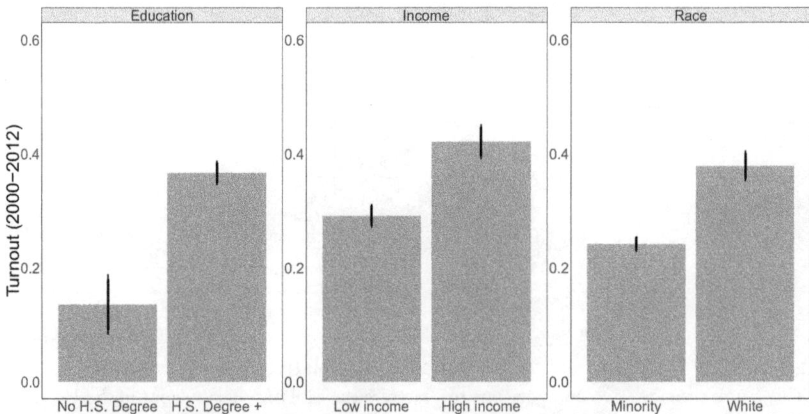

FIGURE A.3 Inequality in voter turnout among young people

Voter turnout (2000–2012) of young people (18–29). High income defined as those above the median. Source: Current Population Survey November Supplement. The bars plot mean levels, the brackets plot the corresponding 95 percent (narrower line) and 90 percent (wider line) confidence intervals. Results from a probit specification with each of these items with standard errors clustered by age.

A.2 CHAPTER 2 APPENDIX

Qualitative Interviews were conducted by trained interviewers and audio-recorded and transcribed. Interviews with young adults conducted by undergraduate and graduate research assistants in a Education and Human Development Bass Connections Team. Interviews with civics teachers were conducted by Dr. Noelle Roth and Dr. Jack Zhou, post-doctoral fellows with the Social Science Research Institute at Duke University. Interviewers were blinded to the research hypotheses. Teachers received a $20 Amazon gift card for participating and the young people received a $5 Amazon gift card. Teachers were solicited through a system-wide email invitation to all civics teachers in the Wake County Public School System. Young people were recruited through the high school social networks of Duke and UNC students affiliated with the Duke Initiative on Survey Methodology. Political Science majors were excluded from the pool.

A.2.1 Interview Guide for Qualitative Interviews with Civics Teachers

1. Tell me a little bit about yourself. How long have you been teaching social studies?

   (a) How long have you been teaching at this school?
   (b) What course or courses do you teach?

2. Let's talk about your students. Are your students engaged in politics?
   (a) If so: generally speaking, how are they politically active? If no: why not?

3. Do you feel it is important for your students to be engaged in politics?
   (a) If so: why?
   (b) If no: why not?

4. In the course(s) you teach, do you currently engage your students in politics?
   (a) If so: what are some methods you use?
   (b) If so: what do you think students need to learn to become actively engaged in politics?
   (c) If so: let's think specifically about voting. What role do you think your course plays in encouraging young people to vote?
   (d) If so: what do you think students need to learn to become voters?
   (e) If no: why not?

5. Do you use a standardized civics curricula in your class?
   (a) If so: how well do you think it prepares students to know how to vote?

6. Is there anything preventing you from making your students more engaged in politics?
   (a) If so: what?
   (b) (If no: move to next question.)

7. Does your school hold any voter registration drives?
   (a) If so: what was behind the decision to do so? Who or what organization puts them together?
   (b) Are any of your students old enough to vote? Do they? If no: why do you think that is?

8. Do you think that young people are interested in voting?
   (a) If so: why?
   (b) If no: why not?

9. Do you have the sense that young people know how to vote, procedurally? (ex: where the polling location is, how to register, etc.)
   (a) If so: how do you think they learn this information?
   (b) (If no: move to next question.)

10. From your perspective, is there anything preventing young people from voting?
    (a) If yes, what? [Ask about institutional barriers, such as free time, polling location, registration.]
    (b) (If no: move to next question.)

11. What can schools do to encourage young people to vote?
    (a) What can teachers do to encourage young people to vote?
    (b) What can or do you do in your class(es) to encourage young people to vote?

12. Do you feel that standardized testing has an impact on your ability to engage your students in politics?
    (a) If so: how?
    (b) If no: why not?

13. Have you ever experienced parental backlash due to engaging your students in discussions about politics or political engagement?
    (a) If so: how did you respond to that backlash?
    (b) If no: why do you think that is?

14. The Supreme Court recently declined to hear the North Carolina voter ID law, so students as young as 16 can now preregister to vote. Have you heard about this?
    (a) What impact, if any, do you think this should have on your school? (Ask about voter registration drives, if their school holds them.) Why?
    (b) Do you think preregistration has any impact on whether students vote?
    (c) What impact, if any, do you think this will have on how you discuss voting and voter registration in class? Why?

15. Is there anything else you'd like to tell us?

A.2.2 Interview Guide for Qualitative Interviews with Young People

1. Just to get us started. Thinking about your friends and peers, do you consider them interested in and engaged in politics? How are they engaged? Can you share any specific examples? Perhaps something they talked about or shared on social media?

2. What do you think motivates young people, in general, to participate in politics? What about you specifically?

3. What do you think are some of the barriers or hurdles to getting young people to participate in politics – whether it's voting or attending a protest or even just talking with friends and family about politics?

4. I next want to think about voting specifically. Have you ever talked with anyone about voting or voter registration? Who was that?

5. Do you plan to vote in 2020? Do you know how you will vote? In-person? Early?
   (a) What could prevent you from voting? (transportation issues)
   (b) What do you think would be most likely to interfere with your plans to vote?

6. Are you registered to vote?
   (a) If so: walk me through the steps that you took to get registered? Did you have any mis-steps? Is there a different way that you would have preferred to have registered? At what age did you register? Which state did you initially register to vote? Have you moved since then? If so: have you re-registered? Or changed your address?
   (b) If no: what are some of the main reasons you are not registered?
   (c) Were you prompted or urged to register?
   (d) Have you had people ask you to register?

7. Explain to me your voting history? Where/how did you vote? Which election?

8. Were there some offices that you couldn't decide which candidate to support? Did you skip those offices – like county

commissioner – on which you didn't have very much information or did you have a strategy about how to vote?

9. Do you think it's a problem for people to just vote for the same party on the entire ballot rather than researching the issues and candidates? How important do you think it is for people to research the candidates and issues before voting?
10. In talking to young people, we find that some people worry they do not have enough information about some individual candidates? Is that something you've thought about? Or worry about?
11. What do you think are some of the biggest challenges to getting young people to vote?
12. What do you think might help increase turnout among young people?

A.3 CHAPTER 3 APPENDIX

Here we outline the specifics of the various data sources we use in linking noncognitive abilities with voting. Table A.2 at the end of this appendix provides additional detail about the skill measures, definitions, measurement source, measurement details, and citations to work using these items/scales.

Figure A.4 plots the distributions of noncognitive ability across our datasets. As can be seen, at a very basic level, there is considerable variation in terms of noncognitive ability across the samples used. And in most cases the distributions of noncognitive ability appear to be close to normal (the WLS data has slightly heavier tails and the NLSY97 is skewed towards the high end). That is, relatively few young people show signs of having very high or very low levels of noncognitive ability and most show signs of being somewhere in between.

The Mturk sample for the benchmarking of the Add Health and Duckworth grit scales was drawn on May 13, 2015. This national online nonprobability sample included 400 US residents over the age of 18 who were paid $0.60 for completion of the survey. We restricted eligibility to those with at least a 90 percent HIT approval rate. This sample was separate from the experiment discussed in Chapter 4. The survey included the 12-item Duckworth and Quinn (2009) grit battery along with the battery of Add Health items. To allow direct comparison of the constructs, the same response options were provided for both sets of questions. We standardized the two scales to have equivalent response categories on a

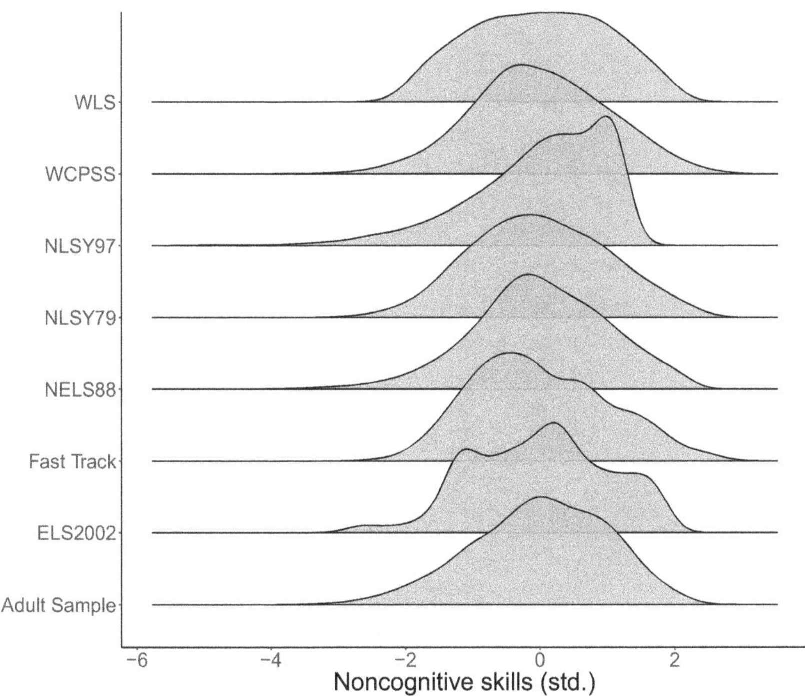

FIGURE A.4 Noncognitive skill distributions

The distribution of our combined measures of noncognitive skills across our datasets. Add Health is withheld because it is on a separate server which we cannot place data on or remove data from. All scales are standardized.

five-point scale ranging from "very much like me" to "not like me at all." These create a single scale that is highly reliable (Cronbach's $\alpha = 0.9$). Subjects were also asked whether they voted in 2014.

A.3.1 WLS

The Wisconsin Longitudinal Study (WLS) is a survey of a random sample of 10,317 men and women who graduated from Wisconsin high schools in 1957 (most respondents were born in 1939). Follow-up waves were conducted in 1964, 1975, 1992, 2004, and 2011, and selected siblings were interviewed in 1977, 1994, 2005, and 2011 (a fact we leverage in some of our models below). In the most recent follow up, 70 percent of eligible, living individuals responded.[3] The survey data has been matched to external measures of cognitive ability and school performance (from

3 For more information on the survey sample, sample eligibility, and various measures used, see www.ssc.wisc.edu/wlsresearch/about/description.php.

school records), as well as to characteristics of communities of residence, employers, and, most recently, to public voting records. Housed at the University of Wisconsin-Madison, the survey has been used in a number of contexts to study various aspects of the life course, including intergenerational transfers and relationships, family functioning, academic performance, physical and mental health and well-being, morbidity, and even one study on political behavior (Burden et al. 2017).

The WLS contains measures that can be used to infer individuals' noncognitive ability. These are drawn from the WLS battery on psychological well-being.[4] Our scale is a composite of eight noncognitive characteristics that capture individual autonomy,[5] environmental mastery,[6] personal growth,[7] positive relations to others,[8] purpose in

[4] Of all our data sources, this scale is measured latest in the life-course – in 1992–1993, when individuals were in their fifties.

[5] The questions for autonomy all start with the stem "to what extent do you agree that" and include the items "your decisions are not usually influenced by what everyone else is doing," "you have confidence in your opinions even if they are contrary to the general consensus," "you tend to worry about what other people think of you," "you are not afraid to voice your opinions, even when they are in opposition to the opinions of most people," "being happy with yourself is more important to you than having others approve of you," and "it's difficult for you to voice your opinions on controversial matters."

[6] The environmental mastery items all start with the stem "to what extent do you agree that" and ask about whether "you are good at juggling your time so that you can fit everything in that needs to be done," "you often feel overwhelmed by your responsibilities," "you are quite good at managing the many responsibilities of your daily life," "you do not fit very well with the people and community around you," "you have difficulty arranging your life in a way that is satisfying to you," "you have been able to create a lifestyle for yourself that is much to your liking," and "you generally do a good job of taking care of your personal finances and affairs."

[7] The personal growth items all start with the stem "to what extent do you agree that" and ask about whether "you are not interested in activities that will expand your horizons," "you have the sense that you have developed a lot as a person over time," "when you think about it, you haven't really improved much as a person over the years," "you think it is important to have new experiences that challenge how you think about yourself and the world," "you don't want to try new ways of doing things, i.e. your life is fine the way it is," "you do not enjoy being in new situations that require you to change your old familiar ways of doing things," and "there is truth to the saying you can't teach an old dog new tricks."

[8] The positive relations to others items all start with the stem "to what extent do you agree that" and ask about whether "you don't have many people who want to listen when you need to talk," "you enjoy personal and mutual conversations with family members and friends," "you often feel lonely because you have few close friends with whom to share your concerns," "it seems to you that most other people have more friends than you do," "people would describe you as a giving person, willing to share your time with others," "most people see you as loving and affectionate," and "you know you can trust your friends, and they know they can trust you."

life,[9] self-acceptance,[10] flexible goal adjustment,[11] and tenacious goal pursuit.[12] While each of these has been used in separate scales in the past, on closer examination we find that these measures all belong to a single scale or construct. Together, these combine to give us a good composite proxy of individuals' self-regulation and social skills. These combine together to make a factor-weighted scale that is highly reliable ($\alpha = 0.87$), loads on a single common factor (Factor 1 Eigenvalue = 3.75, Factor 2 Eigenvalue = 0.22), and is separate from cognitive ability and family income. Given this, we use the weights from the first factor to predict a scale that captures noncognitive ability.[13]

The WLS also contains several measures of individuals' voting. These include both self-reported voting (in 1974 and 2008) and validated voting (in 2000, 2002, 2004, 2006, 2008, 2010, and 2012). The validated voting was obtained by matching WLS participants (and siblings) to Catalist (a nationwide voter file vendor with a 280 million person voter file). The data from this match were used in Burden et al. (2017) and further details

9 The purpose in life items all start with the stem "to what extent do you agree that" and ask about whether "you enjoy making plans for the future and working to make them a reality," " your daily activities often seem trivial and unimportant to you," "you are an active person in carrying out the plans you set for yourself," "you tend to focus on the present, because the future nearly always brings you problems," "you don't have a good sense of what it is you are trying to accomplish in life," "you sometimes feel as if you've done all there is to do in life," and "you used to set goals for yourself, but that now seems like a waste of time."

10 The self acceptance items all start with the stem "to what extent do you agree that" and ask about whether "in general, you feel confident and positive about yourself," "when you compare yourself to friends and acquaintances, it makes you feel good about who you are," "your attitude about yourself is probably not as positive as most people feel about themselves," "the past had its ups and downs, but in general, you wouldn't want to change it," and "in many ways you feel disappointed about your achievements in life."

11 The flexible goal adjustment items all start with the stem "to what extent do you agree that" and ask about whether "if you don't get something you want, you take it with patience," "it is very difficult for you to accept a setback or defeat," "you find it easy to see something positive even in a serious mishap," "when everything seems to be going wrong, you can usually find a bright side to a situation," and "in general, you are not upset very long about an opportunity passed up."

12 The tenacious goal pursuit items all start with the stem "to what extent do you agree that" and ask about whether "even when things seem hopeless, you keep on fighting to reach your goals," "you stick to your goals and projects even in the face of great difficulties," "the harder a goal is to achieve, the more appeal it has to you," "you can be very stubborn in pursuing your goals," and "to avoid disappointments, you don't set your goals too high."

13 In our main results, we construct a factor-weighted scale from the scales. This is justified as previous research and our validation confirm that each of these scales when considered individually is unidimensional. Our results remain very similar and even get stronger if we construct a scale based on all the individual items.

about the specifics of the match can be found therein. In our analyses using the WLS data, we primarily use validated voting; however, our results are unchanged if we use the self-reported measures. This suggests that our results are not driven by the respondents' desire to give the socially desirable response. In addition to voting, the WLS files contain information on respondents' number of civics courses taken in high school, cognitive ability, gender, race, age, parents' education, family income, and the Big Five personality traits, which we include as controls in our statistical models. The WLS also contains information from matched sibling pairs, which we use in our models.

A.3.2 NLSY79

The National Longitudinal Survey of Youth of 1979 (NLSY79) is a nationally representative sample of 12,686 young men (50 percent) and women (50 percent) in 1979 who were fourteen to twenty-two years old (born between 1957 and 1964). After the original survey wave in 1979, individuals were interviewed annually through 1994 and then biennial thereafter. The most recent follow up (round 25) was conducted in 2012 – at which time, about 58 percent of respondents remained part of the panel.[14] Housed in the Bureau of Labor Statistics, this dataset has primarily been used as a tool to assess individuals' progression into the labor force from adolescence to adulthood. It contains information on education, training, and academic achievement; employment; parents, families, and childhood; marriage and sexual patterns; income and assets; health; crime and substance abuse; and a host of other household, geographic, and contextual factors. This dataset has been widely used in a number of contexts, including in a few studies of political behavior (e.g. Healy and Malhotra 2013). Importantly for our purposes, there are measures of our two key constructs of interest imbedded in this survey: noncognitive ability in adolescence and voter turnout in adulthood.

The NLSY79 contains two scales that can be used to measure noncognitive ability: the Rotter Locus of Control scale and the Rosenberg Self-Efficacy Scale. Both of these were measured in the initial wave of the survey in 1979. Both of these have been used in the past to measure noncognitive ability (e.g. Deming 2017; Heckman, Stixrud, and Urzua 2006). With the four Rotter Locus of Control items, students were

[14] For more information on the sample design, screening process, interview methods, and attrition from the sample, see www.nlsinfo.org/content/cohorts/nlsy79/intro-to-the-sample.

asked to chose between one of the two statements that best describes them.[15] For the ten Rosenberg Self-Esteem scale, students were asked to respond with how strongly they agreed or disagreed (4-point scale) with statements about themselves.[16] Heckman, Stixrud, and Urzua (2006) show that these two scales capture a single latent dimension separate from cognitive ability and socioeconomic status that is highly reliable ($\alpha = 0.81$) and loads on a common factor (Factor 1 Eigenvalue = 3.59, Factor 2 Eigenvalue = 0.60). We are able to successfully replicate this result. Given this, we use the weights from the first factor to predict a scale that captures noncognitive ability. The resultant combined scale captures an individuals' ability to control their thoughts and behaviors, a key noncognitive skill.

The only measure of voting available in the NLSY79 is a self-reported item for whether an individual voted in the 2006 midterm elections, measured in the 2008 follow up. In addition to our core outcomes, the NLSY79 contains information on the number of civics courses that students took in high school, cognitive ability, family income, mother's education, father's education, race, ethnicity, number of siblings, gender, and age. We include these as controls in the models we run.

A.3.3 NELS:88

The National Education Longitudinal Study of 1988 (NELS:88) is a longitudinal, nationally representative sample of 12,144 eighth-graders first surveyed in the spring of 1988. These were re-surveyed in four follow-ups in 1990, 1992, 1994, and 2000, with 82 percent of original survey respondents remaining in the sample at the last wave. The first (eighth grade), second (tenth grade), and third (twelfth grade) waves were

[15] Item 1: "what happens to me is my own doing" v.s. "sometimes I feel that I don't have enough control over the direction my life is taking"; Item 2: "when I make plans, I am almost certain that I can make them work" v.s. "it is not always wise to plan too far ahead, because many things turn out to be a matter of good or bad fortune anyhow"; Item 3: "Getting what I want has little or nothing to do with luck" v.s. "Many times we might just as well decide what to do by flipping a coin"; and Item 4: "Many times I feel that I have little influence over the things that happen to me" v.s. "It is impossible for me to believe that chance or luck plays an important role in my life."

[16] The ten statements are "I feel that I'm a person of worth, at least on an equal basis with others," "I feel that I have a number of good qualities," "All in all, I am inclined to feel that I am a failure (reverse coded)," "I am able to do things as well as most other people," "I feel I do not have much to be proud of (reverse coded)," "I take a positive attitude toward myself," "On the whole, I am satisfied with myself," "I wish I could have more respect for myself," "I certainly feel useless at times," and "At times I think I am no good at all."

conducted when respondents were in school.[17] Housed at the National Center for Education Statistics (US Department of Education), the survey contains information on a variety of topics, including: school, work, and home experiences; cognitive ability; educational resources; parents and peers; health; extracurricular activities; neighborhood characteristics; educational and occupational aspirations; and several civic behaviors including voting, to name a few. The study has been used to study a variety of topics, including a number of studies of political behavior (e.g. Sandell and Plutzer 2005).

The NELS:88 contains several measures that can be used to infer respondents' noncognitive abilities. Following the approach of Dee and West (2011), we use both a set of teacher-ratings and a set of self-ratings. The teacher-rated measures of students' noncognitive skills capture components of student self-control. Specifically, teachers were asked to categorize students' behavior according to a number of statements, with response options being yes or no. The specific items include: "Student rarely completes homework," "Student is frequently tardy," "Student is frequently absent," "Student is exceptionally passive/withdrawn," "Student is inattentive in class," and "Student is frequently disruptive." All of these are reverse coded, so that higher scores indicate higher levels of self-control. Together, these make a factor-weighted scale that is reliable ($\alpha = 0.65$), loads on a common factor (Factor 1 Eigenvalue = 1.54, Factor 2 Eigenvalue = 0.26), and is separate from cognitive ability and family income. Given this, we use the weights from the first factor to predict a scale that captures noncognitive ability.

The self-rated measures of students' noncognitive ability most closely align with conceptualizations of general self-efficacy and grit. Students were asked to respond to how well a set of statements describe them, with response options being on a 4-point scale ranging from "strongly agree" to "strongly disagree."[18] Together, these make a factor-weighted

[17] For a more comprehensive overview of the survey and sample design, questionnaires, and other features, see https://nces.ed.gov/surveys/nels88/ or the user's manual, here https://nces.ed.gov/pubs2002/2002323.pdf.

[18] The specific items include "I feel good about myself," "I don't have enough control over the direction my life is taking (reverse coded)," "In my life, good luck is more important than hard work for success (reverse coded)," "I feel I am a person of worth, the equal of other people," "I am able to do things as well as most other people," "Every time I try to get ahead, something or somebody stops me (reverse coded)," "My plans hardly ever work out, so planning only makes me unhappy (reverse coded)," "On the whole, I am satisfied with myself," "I certainly feel useless at times (reverse coded)," "At times I think I am no good at all (reverse coded)," "When I make plans, I am almost certain I can make them work," "I feel I do not have much to be proud of (reverse coded)," and "Chance and luck are very important for what happens in my life (reverse coded)."

scale that is reliable ($\alpha = 0.82$), loads on a common factor (Factor 1 Eigenvalue = 3.59, Factor 2 Eigenvalue = 0.76), and is separate from cognitive ability and family income.

NELS:88 contains several self-reported measures of voting in both federal and local elections in 1992 and 1996. These are combined together to make a scale that measures the proportion of elections when a person voted. Also available in the NELS:88 are the number of civics courses respondents took in high school, cognitive ability, race, gender, age, parents' education, family income, number of siblings, and whether the child reported discussing school with their parents. We include these as controls in our models.

A.3.4 Fast Track

We use the Fast Track data to make two types of comparisons: one that is observational and one that is experimental. Regarding the first, Fast Track contains a host of information relevant to students' noncognitive ability, which we use here to construct a composite scale that measures students' ability to self-regulate and work well with others. In the Fast Track files there are self, teacher, peer, and parent evaluations of students' noncognitive ability. Here we rely primarily on the teacher evaluations as these produce scales that have been well-studied and are highly reliable. The composite scale that we employ here is measured using teacher evaluations of students' ability to finish tasks; to persevere when they face obstacles; control their thoughts, emotions, and behaviors; and work together in small groups. These evaluations come from years 1–10 of the Fast Track study and combine to make a scale that is reliable ($\alpha = 0.62$) and that is distinct from cognitive ability and socioeconomic status. Also included in the files are measures of subjects' cognitive ability, gender, race, age, socioeconomic status, family dynamics, and geographic location, which we include as controls in our observational models. With this approach we are able to see whether students' noncognitive abilities are predictive of who votes in adulthood.

The second comparison looks at the rates of voter turnout across the treatment and control groups. This provides us with direct insights into the effect of school programs that seek to develop noncognitive abilities on voter turnout. While this approach provides us with the added benefit of causality, eliciting the mechanisms behind any treatment effect is difficult because of the bundled, multifaceted nature of the program.

In addition to having a rich array of measures of noncognitive ability, the Fast Track sample – like the WLS data – contains information on validated voting. These come from a match conducted by the Fast Track organization of participants to statewide voter records. These come from work done by Holbein (2017), who matched Fast Track participants to public voter files. This was done by searching for participants by their name, birthday, current address, and in some instances social security number. Subjects were also searched in original intervention states. This match produced validated voting in 2004, 2006, 2008, 2010, and 2012. Here, we average these to create a mean scale measuring the proportion of elections subjects voted. Numerous specification checks suggest that the quality of the match was the same across the treatment and the control groups; however, Holbein (2017) also uses a survey measure of voting and finds the same result, lending credence to the estimates' validity. More details on the match to voter files can be found in Holbein (2017).

A.3.5 Add Health

The National Longitudinal Study of Adolescent to Adult Health (Add Health) is a nationally representative panel study of 20,745 students aged 11–19 (grades 7–12) in the 1994–1995 school year. Housed at the University of North Carolina, the survey contains information on a rich array of individual characteristics including cognitive and noncognitive ability, health, school experiences, family relationships, crime, and civic behavior, to name a few. The survey has been used in publications in a number of prestigious outlets, including a handful of political behavior topics (e.g. Fowler, Baker, and Dawes 2008). The survey consisted of an in-school questionnaire and an in-home interview. Since the first wave in 1994–1995, there have been three follow ups: in 1996, 2001–2002, and 2008–2009 (with a fifth wave planned for 2016–2018). In the most recent follow-up, 79 percent of the remaining eligible panelists were re-interviewed.[19]

The Add Health data allow us to elicit a measure of noncognitive ability that captures grit, perseverance, hard work, determination, and systematic thinking. We elicit this measure from nine survey items (some reverse-coded), which include subjects' response to statements such as "When you get what you want, it's usually because you worked hard for it;" "You can pretty much determine what will happen in your life;" and "You usually go out of your way to avoid having to deal with

[19] For more information on the survey design and implementation, see www.cpc.unc.edu/projects/addhealth/documentation/guides.

TABLE A.1 *Correlates of Add Health Noncognitive Skill Scale*

	Scale	#1	#2	#3	#4	#5	#6	#7	#8	#9
Cognitive skill (0–1)	0.114	0.027	0.173	−0.007	0.045	−0.003	−0.033	0.083	−0.042	0.161
Mother ed. (1–9)	0.067	0.009	0.091	0.003	0.016	0.013	−0.019	0.061	−0.001	0.084
Family income (1–11)	0.022	−0.010	0.077	−0.026	−0.002	−0.021	−0.042	0.025	−0.040	0.086
Ideology (0–4)	0.022	0.033	−0.029	0.031	0.012	0.021	0.025	−0.014	0.042	−0.014
Ideo. strength (0–2)	0.083	0.024	0.055	0.042	0.053	0.039	0.028	0.057	0.028	0.031
Non-white (0/1)	0.020	0.005	−0.028	0.060	0.041	0.062	0.079	−0.027	0.065	−0.113
Age (10–19)	0.103	0.063	0.066	0.056	0.069	0.048	0.063	−0.007	−0.015	0.053
Female (0/1)	0.013	−0.036	0.070	−0.003	0.000	−0.018	−0.009	0.003	−0.023	0.041
Religiosity (1–4)	0.124	0.080	0.035	0.097	0.093	0.090	0.088	0.042	0.074	−0.032
Conscientious (0–1)	0.122	0.089	0.057	0.068	0.077	0.076	0.054	0.051	0.040	0.018
Extravert (0–1)	0.063	0.014	−0.010	0.020	0.025	0.016	0.025	0.158	0.039	0.034
Agreeable (0–1)	0.132	0.049	0.125	0.054	0.080	0.050	0.068	0.058	0.020	0.044
Open (0–1)	0.127	0.034	0.109	0.044	0.077	0.044	0.049	0.087	0.015	0.066
Neurotic (0–1)	−0.109	−0.067	−0.106	−0.045	−0.057	−0.047	−0.004	−0.046	−0.031	−0.041
Pearlin scale (0–4)	0.134	0.051	0.126	0.039	0.073	0.029	0.035	0.089	0.039	0.066

Simple Pearson's r correlation coefficients with the overall noncognitive scale, and individual components. Variables are coded as in the text. The scaling of individual items is included in parentheses next to the variable name in the first column.

problems in your life (reverse coded)."[20] These combine to a scale that is reliable ($\alpha = 0.65$), compares favorably with the more-commonly used Duckworth et al. (2007) grit scale (Cronbach's $\alpha = 0.88; \beta = 0.8$ ($p < 0.01$); $R = 0.63 (p < 0.01)$), and loads on a common factor (Eigen 1: 1.77, Eigen 2: 0.25) separate from cognitive ability and socioeconomic status.

Add Health also contains two measures of individual voting indicating whether subjects voted in 2000 or in local elections in 2008 or 2009. As in our other data sources, we average these together to create a scale measuring the proportion of elections one voted in. This information is combined with controls such as cognitive ability, political motivation, mother's education, educational attainment, parents' income, gender, church attendance, and the Big Five personality traits. Add Health also includes information from sibling pairs, which allows us to run models that purge out observed and unobserved characteristics shared among family members.

A.3.6 NLSY97

The National Longitudinal Survey of Youth 1997 (NLSY97) is a nationally representative sample of 8,984 twelve- to sixteen-year-olds (born between 1980 and 1984). After the initial survey wave in 1997, respondents have been interviewed on an annual basis, with the most recent interviews (round 16) being fielded in 2013–2014. Presently, 80 percent of the sample remain active participants in the follow-up surveys.[21] Housed in the US Bureau of Labor Statistics, the survey covers a number of topics, including employment, income, education, cognitive and noncognitive ability, household and social context, family, individual relationships, health, crime, and civic participation.

In the NLSY97, subjects provide self-reported measures of noncognitive ability that are closely aligned with conceptualizations of individual

[20] The other items in the index include, "When you have a problem to solve, one of the first things you do is get as many facts about the problem as possible," "When you are attempting to find a solution to a problem, you usually try to think of as many different ways to approach the problem as possible," "When making decisions, you generally use a systematic method for judging and comparing alternatives," "After carrying out a solution to a problem, you usually try to analyze what went right and what went wrong," "You are assertive," and "When making decisions, you usually go with your 'gut feeling' without thinking too much about the consequences of each alternative (reverse coded)."

[21] For more information on survey sampling, composition, interview methods, and attrition from the survey, see www.nlsinfo.org/content/cohorts/nlsy97/intro-to-the-sample.

effortful control. Students are asked to indicate how much they agree or disagree the following statements: "I make every effort to do more than what is expected of me," "I do what is required, but rarely anything more (reverse coded)," "I do not work as hard as the majority of people around me (reverse coded)," and "I have high standards and work toward them." These have been used to measure noncognitive skills previously (e.g. Deming 2017). Together, these make a factor-weighted scale that is reliable ($\alpha = 0.68$), loads on a common factor (Factor 1 Eigenvalue = 1.37, Factor 2 Eigenvalue = 0.15), and is separate from cognitive ability and family income. Given this, we use the weights from the first factor to predict a scale that captures noncognitive ability.

Voting in the NLSY97 is measured through self-reported behavior in the 2004, 2006, and 2008, and 2010 elections, which we combine into a mean scale below (as we do in our other samples). In addition to our two outcomes of interest, the NLSY97 also contains information on the number of civics courses one took in high school, cognitive ability, the Big Five Personality Traits, gender, age, parents' education, and family income, which we use as controls below.

A.3.7 ELS:2002

The Education Longitudinal Study of 2002 (ELS:2002) is a nationally representative, longitudinal study of just over 16,000 10th graders (from 750 schools) in 2002. Housed in the National Center for Education Statistics (US Department of Education), the survey was designed to understand students' trajectories from the beginning of high school into postsecondary education and beyond. Administered as an in-school survey during the spring term of that year, the survey contains information on cognitive and noncognitive ability, performance in secondary and postsecondary education, family experiences, and a few civic items, to name a few. The survey contained follow ups in 2004, 2006, 2007, and 2012, with the response rate in the last follow-up being over 80 percent.[22]

In the ELS:2002, individuals' noncognitive ability can be elicited in two ways: through teacher evaluations and through self-evaluations. Teacher evaluations provide a reasonable proxy for individuals' overall levels of self-control. In the initial wave of the survey, math teachers were

[22] For more information on the survey design and implementation of the ELS:2002, see https://nces.ed.gov/pubs2014/2014364.pdf.

asked how often students exhibited the five behaviors, with response options on a 5-point scale ranging from "never" to "all of the time." These items included: "How often student is attentive in class," "How often student completes homework," "How often student is absent (reverse coded)," "How often student is tardy (reverse coded)," and "How often student is disruptive in class (reverse coded)." In addition, teachers were asked whether a set of three statements described students (response options: yes/no), which included: "Student usually works hard for good grades," "Student is exceptionally passive (reverse coded)," and "Student talks with teacher outside of class." These combine to make a factor-weighted scale that is highly reliable ($\alpha = 0.68$) and loads on a common factor (Factor 1 Eigenvalue = 2.73, Factor 2 Eigenvalue = 0.40) that is separate from cognitive ability and family income. Given this, we use the weights from the first factor to predict a scale that captures noncognitive ability.

In addition, in the initial wave, subjects evaluated their own noncognitive abilities. Students responded to nine items that align with theoretical conceptualizations of self-control, instrumental motivation, effort and persistence. Students were asked to identify how often a set of items applied to themselves, with response options being on a 4-point scale ranging from "strongly agree" to "strongly disagree." The specific items include whether the subject "Can learn something really hard," "Can get no bad grades if decides to," "Can get no problems wrong if decides to," "Can learn something well if wants to," "Remembers most important things when studies," "Works as hard as possible when studies," "Keeps studying even if material is difficult," "Does best to learn what studies," and "Puts forth best effort when studying." These combine to a single factor-weighted scale that is highly reliable ($\alpha = 0.91$) and loads on a common factor (Factor 1 Eigenvalue = 5.00, Factor 2 Eigenvalue = 0.69) that is separate from cognitive ability and family income.

Also included in the ELS:2002 is whether subjects voted in adulthood in federal elections in 2004 and 2008 and whether they voted in local elections between 2004 and 2006 or 2009 and 2011. We combine these together into a mean scale measuring the proportion of elections one voted in. In addition to measures of noncognitive ability and voting, the ELS:2002 contains information on the number of civics courses taken in high school, cognitive ability, gender, race, age, parents' education, and family income, which we can employ as controls in our model below.

A.3.8 CCES Module, 2014

Our adult sample comes from the 2014 Cooperative Congressional Election Study (CCES), administered by YouGov. The CCES is a nonprobability national sample that is stratified by both state and congressional district and weighted to look similar to the US population on a set of political and demographic characteristics. Respondents first filled out the CCES common content portion before being filtered into team modules ($n = 1,000$). The Duke module was an omnibus questionnaire and included a battery of noncognitive skill items. These noncognitive skill items measured the Duckworth grit scale, (Duckworth et al. 2007) emotional control,[23] and sociability.[24] These combine to make a scale that is highly reliable ($\alpha = 0.83$) and appears to load on a factor separate from cognitive ability and socioeconomic status. The CCES contains measures of political interest and validated voting from a match to Catalist, among a host of other variables.

While the CCES module is useful for several reasons, there are distinct drawbacks to this dataset. First and foremost, the CCES module is small, nonprobability, sample – hence, not surprisingly we find that this dataset's estimates are the most sensitive and least precise among all datasets in our exploration. Moreover, the CCES is unique in that it is not a sample of young people but rather all adults. This limits our ability to make direct comparisons across the other samples that focus primarily on young people. Further, the CCES has well-noted issues with accurately measuring voter turnout (especially among young people) even though this sample matches to Catalist's voter files (Fraga and Holbein 2018; Grimmer et al. 2018; Hillygus, Jackson, and Young 2014). Finally, unlike the other datasets we use the CCES is an *explicitly* political survey that may have priming effects that influence all of our measures of interest. All of these reasons should lead us to pause before we rely too heavily on this sample alone.

[23] This consists of five items that ask people the extent to which they control their temper, whether they get so frustrated that they could explode (reverse coded), whether they get upset easily (reverse coded), whether they lose control over their feelings (reverse coded), and whether they slam doors when they are mad (reverse coded).

[24] There are five sociability items that ask the extent to which the respondent likes to have many people around, likes to talk with others, does things alone (reverse coded), finds people stimulating, and works well with others.

A.3.9 WCPSS

Finally, we employ an original data source from the Wake County Public Schools System Longitudinal Student Engagement Survey (WCPSS). For those unfamiliar, the WCPSS is the largest school district in North Carolina and the fifteenth largest in the United States; the system has 171 schools serving a diverse mix of 160,000 students in both urban and rural areas. In collaboration with WCPSS, we fielded an in-school student survey of all students in grades 5, 8, and 9, beginning in Spring term of 2015. Wave two of the survey was fielded in Spring of 2016. The student response rate in 2015 was 72.9 percent and the 2016 response rate was 82.5 percent. All survey respondents in both years were linked to school administrative records, resulting in a dataset that is exceptional not only in its size, but also in its scope and richness. For more details on the WCPSS sample, see Holbein et al. (Forthcoming).

Imbedded in the WCPSS survey, we measured noncognitive ability using the Duckworth et al. (2007) 8-item grit scale for children. This battery of questions asks students to identify how well the following statements describe them: "New ideas and projects sometimes distract me from previous ones," "Setbacks don't discourage me," "I have been obsessed with a certain idea or project for a short time but later lost interest," "I am a hard worker," "I often set a goal but later choose to pursue a different one," "I have difficulty maintaining my focus on projects that take more than a few months to complete," "I finish whatever I begin," and "I am diligent." These combine to create a scale that is reliable ($\alpha = 0.7$) and loads on a common factor (Eigen $1 = 2.13$, Eigen $2 = 0.76$) that is separate from cognitive ability and socioeconomic status.

As the WCPSS subjects were too young to vote legally in North Carolina, we measured students' vote intentions. This measure provides us with the distinct advantage of being able to explore whether noncognitive ability sets students on a path toward becoming active voters in adulthood. Eventually, student records will be matched to public-use vote records. But, in the meantime, the panel of vote intentions will suffice. In addition to this outcome measure, the WCPSS data also contains information on cognitive ability, political interest, gender, age, limited English proficiency, attendance, and geographic location, which we can include in our models as controls. This dataset also contains information that allows us to link siblings, twin pairs, and individuals to themselves over time. We leverage this information in some of our model specifications below.

TABLE A.2 *Noncognitive skill scales used in this book*

Noncognitive Skill	Short Definition	Reporter	Measurement	Citations
WLS				
Individual Autonomy	self-determination, independence, & internal locus of control	Self	6-item scale e.g. "your decisions are not usually influenced by what everyone else is doing"	Ryff (1989)
Environmental Mastery	ability to choose environments suitable for well-being	Self	7-item scale e.g. "you are quite good at managing the many responsibilities of your daily life"	Ryff (1989)
Personal Growth	ability to continue to grow/ develop as a person	Self	7-item scale e.g. "you are not interested in activities that will expand your horizons" (reverse)	Ryff (1989)
Positive Relations	ability to have warm, trusting interpersonal relations	Self	7-item scale e.g. "most people see you as loving and affectionate"	Ryff (1989)
Purpose in Life	ability to act with drive, directedness, & intentionality	Self	7-item scale e.g. "you are an active person in carrying out the plans you set for yourself"	Ryff (1989)
Self Acceptance	ability to self-actualize and optimally function	Self	5-item scale e.g. "you feel confident and positive about yourself"	Ryff (1989)
Flexible Goal Adjustment	ability to choose environments suitable for well-being	Self	5-item scale e.g. "if you don?t get something you want, you take it with patience"	Brandtstädter and Renner (1990)
Tenacious Goal Pursuit	ability to pursue goals in the face of obstacles	Self	5-item scale e.g. "you can be very stubborn in pursuing your goals"	Brandtstädter and Renner (1990)

(continued)

TABLE A.2 *continued*

Noncognitive Skill	Short Definition	Reporter	Measurement	Citations
NLSY79				
Locus of Control	ability to pursue goals in the face of obstacles	Self	4-item scale e.g. "what happens to me is my own doing"	Rotter (1966)
Self-Efficacy Scale	belief in a capacity to operate well across domains	Self	10-item scale e.g. "I am able to do things as well as most other people"	Rosenberg (1965)
NELS88				
Teacher-Rated Self-Control	ability to finish what they start, work with other students, and not be disruptive	Teacher	6-item scale e.g. "Student rarely completes homework" (reverse)	Dee and West (2011)
Self-Rated Self-Control	perseverance, self-efficacy, implementation intentions	Self	13-item scale e.g. "Every time I try to get ahead, something or somebody stops me" (reverse)	Dee and West (2011)
Add Health				
Self-Rated Self-Control	perseverance, self-efficacy, implementation intentions	Self	9-item scale e.g. "You can pretty much determine, what will happen in your life"	Paternoster and Pogarsky (2009)
NLSY97				
Self-Rated Self-Control	effortful control	Self	4-item scale e.g. "I have high standards and, work toward them"	Deming (2017)

Noncognitive Skill	Short Definition	Reporter	Measurement	Citations
ELS:2002				
Teacher-Rated Self-Control	ability to finish what they start, work with other students, and not be disruptive	Teacher	5-item scale e.g. "How often student completes homework"	Fredricks (2012)
Self-Rated Self-Control	perseverance, self-efficacy, implementation intentions	Self	9-item scale e.g. "Keeps studying even if material is difficult"	Fredricks (2012)
CCES				
Grit Emotional Control Sociability	persever., efficacy, implementation intentions ability to control one's temper/emotions affinity for and ability to work with others	Self	8, 5, and 5 item scales e.g. "setbacks don't discourage me"	Duckworth et al. (2007)
WCPSS				
Grit	perseverance, self-efficacy, implementation intentions	Self	8-item scale e.g. "setbacks don't discourage me"	Duckworth et al. (2007)
Fast Track (Reproduced from Holbein (2017))				
Grit	Persistence toward long-term goals	Teacher (TRF)	TRF Items: 4, 8, 78, 100 (e.g., "Fails to finish things")	Achenbach (1991) Duckworth et al. (2007)
Emotion Recognition	Ability to identify others' emotions	Subject/Rater (ERQ)	Subject identifies emotions in pictures	Ribordy et al. (1988)

(continued)

TABLE A.2 *continued*

Noncognitive Skill	Short Definition	Reporter	Measurement	Citations
Self Efficacy	Belief that actions will yield results	Subject/Rater	Subject answers questions about belief in ability	CPPRG (2010)
Emotion Regulation	Ability to control emotions (avoid negative, approach positive)	Teacher (TSC)	TSC Items: 1a, 3a, 4aR, 5aR (e.g., "copes well with failure", "calms down")	CPPRG (1999a)
Attentiveness	Ability to focus on task at hand	Teacher (TRF)	TRF Items: 1, 4, 8, 13, 17, 22, 49, 60, 61, 62, 72, 78, 80, 92, 100 (e.g., "Stares blankly")	Achenbach (1991)
Behavioral control	Engaging in delinquent behavior	Subject	Public crime records & self-reports	CPPRG (2010)
Hostility control	Ability to avoid hostile behavior towards others	Subject/Rater (HIC)	Subject shown drawings of individuals being harmed. They were then asked why these negative events occurred and how they would respond. FT workers coded hostile responses.	CPPRG (1999a) Dodge et al. (1990)
Aggression control	Control over outbursts	Subject/Rater (HIC)	Subject shown drawings of individuals being harmed. Asked how they would respond.	CPPRG (1999a) Dodge et al. (1990)
self-control	Ability to control impulses	Subject/Rater (IEE)	Raters interviews child about experiences	CPPRG(1999a)

Noncognitive Skill	Short Definition	Reporter	Measurement	Citations
Social Problem Solving	Acting appropriately in groups	Subject/Rater (SPS)	Subject responds to social situations. Coders rate responses as competent if subject offers a direct, socially appropriate way of handling the situation.	Dodge et al. (1990) CPPRG (1999a)
Withdrawn	Distant in social groups	Teacher (TRF)	TRF Items: 42, 65, 69, 75, 102, 103, 111 (e.g., "Would rather be alone than with others")	Achenbach (1991)
Internalizing	Negative social behaviors	Teacher (TRF)	TRF Items: 11, 31, 32, 35, 42, 47, 50, 52, 60, 65, 69,71, 75, 80, 81, 99, 102, 103, 106, 108, 111, 112 (e.g., "Clings to adults or too dependent")	Achenbach (1991)
Anti Social	Behaving inappropriately in social settings	Teacher (TRF)	TRF Items: 20, 21, 43, 82, 90 (e.g., "Swearing or obscene language")	Achenbach (1991)
Social Skills	Overall social skills	Teacher (TSA)	Teachers asked to evaluate subjects' overall social skills	
Social Problems	Inability to get along with others	Teacher (TRF)	TRF Items: 1, 11, 25, 38, 48, 62, 64 (e.g., "Doesn't get along with other pupils")	Achenbach (1991)

TRF = teacher report form, TSC = teacher social competence questionnaire, IEE = third-party raters interview on emotional experiences, TSA = teacher rating of social adjustment, HIC = self-rated general interview in homes, SPS = self-rated social problem solving questionnaire

A.3.10 Who Has Noncognitive Skills?

We have shown in the book that noncognitive skills are capturing an individual-level characteristic that is distinct from cognitive ability, socioeconomic status, and personality. Previous analyses have shown these skills to be predictive of various education and labor force outcomes and has shown them to be malleable, especially in childhood. Here we consider how noncognitive skills vary across the population. That is, who currently has these skills? Such descriptive analysis can shed light on possible unobserved covariates that need to be accounted for in our analyses, but also provide a bigger picture about possible disparities that needs to be addressed by public policy.

Figure A.5 displays the underlying variation in noncognitive abilities – in this case, proxied by a measure of grit (Duckworth et al. 2007) – by social context. It does so by showing variation across schools within the Wake County Public School System (WCPSS). As can be seen, there is a considerable amount of variation across (as can be seen comparing plotted coefficients) and within schools (as can be seen by looking at the size of the confidence interval).[25] The least gritty school scores about 0.93 standard deviations below the highest performing school – a considerable gap. However, this slightly overstates the school-level variation in our estimates. The standard deviation in this collapsed dataset is 0.21 standard deviations – suggesting that most schools are actually fairly close to the mean. That being said, there is considerable variation across schools. This variation is not totally explained by the most likely culprit in school-level variation in student test scores: socioeconomic status. While the percent of students on free-reduced price lunch (a common measure of SES in education policy research) is a significant predictor of school-level mean grit levels ($p < 0.001$), it only explains about 27 percent of the gap between high and low grit schools. By comparison, the percent of free-reduced price lunch students explains 63 percent of the school performance gap in student test scores. This suggests that something else about schools – perhaps their underlying quality – explains why some students develop higher noncognitive abilities, while others fail to do so. This could be about the learning environment, classroom experiences, or other aspects of the geographic location/social nework. This is not conclusive proof that noncognitive skills are influenced by school inputs,

[25] A third component – the size of the school – can be seen with the variation in the size of the point estimates.

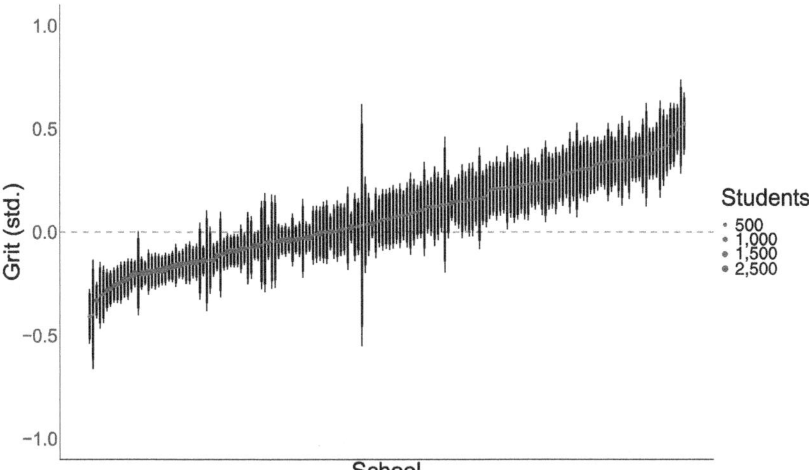

FIGURE A.5 Noncognitive skills by school context (WCPSS)

Figure A.5 plots mean levels (and corresponding standard errors) of noncognitive skills across schools in the Wake County Public School System in the 2015 (i.e. Wave 1) and 2016 (i.e. Wave 2) school years. The measure of noncognitive ability here is the Duckworth et al. (2007) grit scale. Red line shows the student-level mean. Points are sized by the number of students in the school ($N_{surveyed} = 53{,}451$). Schools are ordered by mean levels of noncognitive ability.

but it is consistent with the evaluations already cited that provide experimental (and quasi-experimental) evidence from localized contexts that this is the case. Given the contextual variation in noncognitive abilities, in our models we include school or contextual fixed effects when we can to pick up underlying unobserved levels of heterogeneity that might be biasing our estimates.[26]

Figure A.6 displays levels of noncognitive ability by various demographic characteristics – including race, family income, and mother's education (all at survey baseline). As can be seen, there are gaps along these dimensions, reflecting common population disparities. High education families have noncognitive abilities 0.12 (NLSY97) to 0.42 (NLSY79) standard deviations above low education families. While these are not so closely correlated that we might worry that we are capturing the same thing, the socioeconomic gap is larger in these other datasets than in

[26] By forcing comparisons within schools, school fixed effects accounts for possible reference bias if students were to benchmark their level of grit relative to their social surroundings (West et al. 2016).

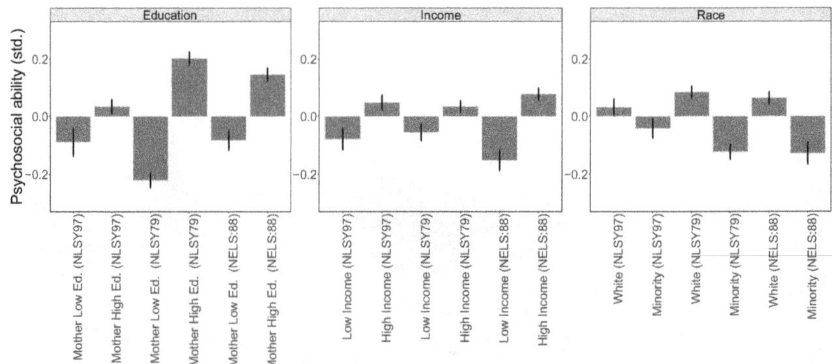

FIGURE A.6 Inequalities in noncognitive skill development

Figure A.6 plots the mean levels of noncognitive skills across several relevant demographic factors. These come from the National Longitudinal Survey of Youth of 1997 (NLSY97), the National Longitudinal Survey of Youth of 1979 (NLSY79), and the National Education Longitudinal Study of 1988 (NELS:88) (the Wisconsin Longitudinal Study (WLS) is not included because race is only available in the restricted files).

the Add Health data. We can see a similar pattern with income – 0.09 (NLSY79) to 0.23 (NELS:88) standard deviations – and race – with white adolescents scoring 0.073 (NLSY97) to 0.207 (NLSY79) standard deviations ahead of minorities. All of these gaps are highly significant ($p < 0.002$ in all cases). More advantaged children appear to develop noncognitive abilities at a higher rate than disadvantaged. However, consistent with our conclusion just outlined, these gaps are not nearly as large as for cognitive ability.

A.4 CHAPTER 4 APPENDIX

As a robustness check we made tweaks to the noncognitive skills measure to make sure our results are not a product of scale composition. Given the relative nascency of the study of noncognitive abilities (especially in studies of political behavior), we think this exercise is important. As we discussed in the last chapter, there are many ways to measure noncognitive ability. To evaluate if our results are sensitive to the particular items we included in the scale, we re-estimated our models with two different scale construction techniques: one driven by theory and one driven by scale diagnostics. The first takes the items that we think are most explicitly related to self-control – one of the core theorized mechanisms linking noncognitive ability and voting. These items include "When you get what you want, it's usually because you worked hard for it," "You can pretty

TABLE A.3 *Noncognitive skills and turnout*

	Presidential Vote (W3, 2001–2002)			Vote in Local Elections (W4, 2008–2009)		
	(1)	(2)	(3)	(4)	(5)	(6)
Grit (0–1)	0.207*	0.189*	0.209*	0.207*	0.134*	0.112*
	(0.053)	(0.053)	(0.053)	(0.056)	(0.055)	(0.056)
Cognitive ability (0–1)	0.446*	0.412*	0.430*	0.437*	0.357*	0.372*
	(0.074)	(0.077)	(0.073)	(0.073)	(0.072)	(0.074)
Political motivation (0–1)	0.207*	0.202*	0.194*	0.182*	0.173*	0.163*
	(0.022)	(0.022)	(0.022)	(0.019)	(0.019)	(0.020)
Mother's education (1–9)	0.018*	0.017*	0.012*	0.017*	0.016*	0.012*
	(0.003)	(0.003)	(0.003)	(0.003)	(0.004)	(0.004)
College education	0.132*	0.129*	0.137*	0.126*	0.113*	0.120*
	(0.012)	(0.012)	(0.013)	(0.012)	(0.012)	(0.013)
Parents' income (1–11)	0.013*	0.013*	0.015*	0.005	0.004	0.007*
	(0.003)	(0.003)	(0.003)	(0.003)	(0.003)	(0.003)
Female	−0.002	0.006	0.005	0.038*	0.047*	0.051*
	(0.011)	(0.013)	(0.013)	(0.010)	(0.013)	(0.013)
Church attendance (0–5)	0.026*	0.027*	0.022*	0.035*	0.034*	0.029*
	(0.004)	(0.004)	(0.004)	(0.004)	(0.004)	(0.004)
Big 5: Conscientiousness (0–1)		0.008	0.042		0.046	0.083*
		(0.043)	(0.043)		(0.040)	(0.039)
Big 5: Extraversion (0–1)		0.082*	0.092*		0.167*	0.186*
		(0.036)	(0.040)		(0.041)	(0.043)
Big 5: Agreeableness (0–1)		−0.052	−0.040		0.065	0.067
		(0.057)	(0.062)		(0.059)	(0.062)
Big 5: Openness (0–1)		0.139*	0.126*		0.217*	0.238*
		(0.049)	(0.051)		(0.058)	(0.061)
Big 5: Neuroticism (0–1)		−0.022	−0.047		−0.161*	−0.170*
		(0.045)	(0.048)		(0.049)	(0.051)
Other Demographic controls	Yes	Yes	Yes	Yes	Yes	Yes
Data Quality controls	Yes	Yes	Yes	Yes	Yes	Yes
Geographic controls	No	No	Yes	No	No	Yes
Observations	12,262	12,252	11,289	12,259	12,249	11,286

$+p < 0.10$, $^{*}p < 0.05$. Table plots the average marginal effects for all coefficients; results for the grit coefficient do not change if controls held constant at mean levels. DV is whether an individual reported voting in the 2000 presidential election (W3) and at least "often" in local elections (W4). The individual controls displayed in the table are measured during the following waves: cognitive ability (W1), whether subjects were at college in Wave 3 (W3), mother's education (W1), parents' income (W1), political motivation (W3; folded ideology), race (W1), age (W1), gender (W1), church attendance (W4), and grade in school (W1), and Big Five personality traits (W4). Other demographic controls include grade in school (W1) and race (W1). We imputed missing cognitive ability (mean), family income (mean), mother's education (median), initial grade in school (median) and included an indicator for imputed observations. Census tract controls include population, urban/rural, race/ethnicity, age, marriage rates, socioeconomic status, health, ideology, religiosity, among others (for a full list, see the Online Appendix).

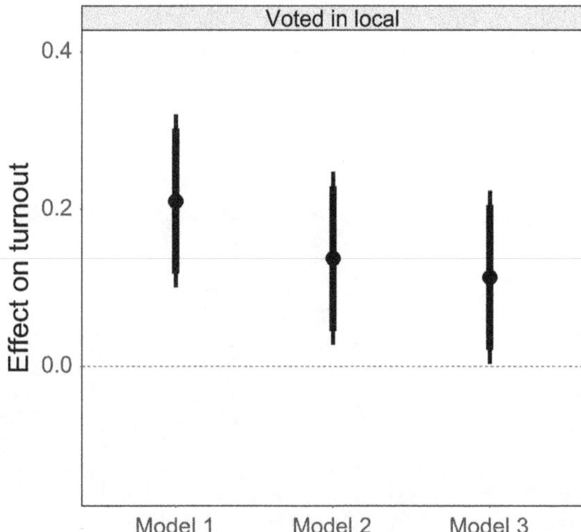

FIGURE A.7 Noncognitive ability and voter turnout (Add Health, models with controls: local elections)

Figure A.7 plots the average marginal effects for the noncognitive ability coefficient across models with several groups of controls. The dependent variable is whether an individual marked at least "often" in local elections voting question (W4).
The individual controls in *Model 1* are cognitive ability, political motivation, mother's education, education, parents' income, gender, and church attendance. The controls in *Model 2* are those in Model 1 plus measures of the Big Five: conscientiousness, extraversion, agreeableness, openness to experience, and neuroticism. The controls in *Model 3* are those in Model 2 plus census-tract controls for population, urban/rural, race/ethnicity, age, marriage rates, socioeconomic status, health, ideology, religiosity.

much determine what will happen in your life," and "You usually go out of your way to avoid having to deal with problems in your life" (reverse coded). Whether we use these items individually or as a reduced scale, our conclusions do not change – noncognitive ability remains a strong predictor of voting.[27] The second takes an agnostic approach by trimming scale items to try to maximize the reliability of our scale. Doing so leaves five items. Again, with this slightly different measure our conclusions are the same – noncognitive ability remains a strong predictor of voting.[28]

[27] This reduced 3-item scale predicts a 8.0 percentage point increase in the probability of voting in the 2000 presidential election ($p < 0.01$) (5th to 95th comparison). This is statistically and substantively indistinguishable from the corresponding estimate from the full scale. The positive estimate for the reduced scale holds among models with siblings (results comparing the 5th with the 95th percentile – 10.1 p.p., $p < 0.01$).

[28] The items in this scale include: 1, 4, 5, 6, and 7. This reduced 5-item scale predicts a 7.3 percentage point increase in the probability of voting in the 2000 presidential

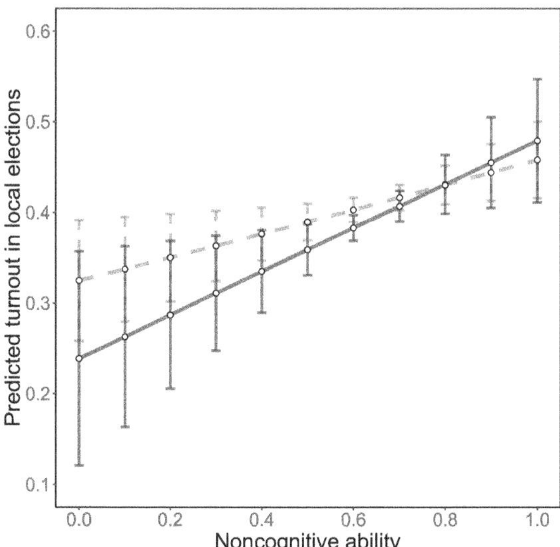

FIGURE A.8 Family fixed effect vs. controls (local elections, Add Health)

Compares predicted turnout values in local elections from our models with controls to those produced from a sibling subsample and a family fixed effect model. Solid black lines correspond to the family fixed effect model predictions; dashed lines correspond to the model with controls. Bars represent 95 percent confidence intervals. As can be seen, thes two slopes are statistically indistinguishable.

In Add Health, we are able to take advantage of the Add Health oversample of siblings to leverage intra-familial differences in levels of noncognitive ability, which offers a stringent robustness check because it accounts unobservable family factors such as parents' background, political interest, noncognitive skills, etc.[29]

The results from the family fixed effects models show the same strong and positive relationship between noncognitive ability and turnout. Figure A.10 shows this visually. As in Figure 4.1, Figure A.10 plots predicted probabilities of turnout (the circles in the figure) as well as 95 percent confidence intervals (bars) from this model. It benchmarks the family fixed effect models (solid line) with those that come from observable controls (dashed line). As can be seen, the estimates for both

election ($p < 0.01$) (5th to 95th comparison). This is statistically and substantively indistinguishable from the corresponding estimate from the full scale. The positive estimate for the reduced scale holds among models with siblings (results comparing the 5th with the 95th percentile – 5.0 p.p., $p = 0.052$).

[29] Our measure of noncognitive ability has an intra-cluster correlation among siblings of 0.13 ($p < 0.01$) – somewhat lower than sibling ICC estimates of the Big Five, which tend to range around 0.2–0.4 (Hettema and Deary 2013).

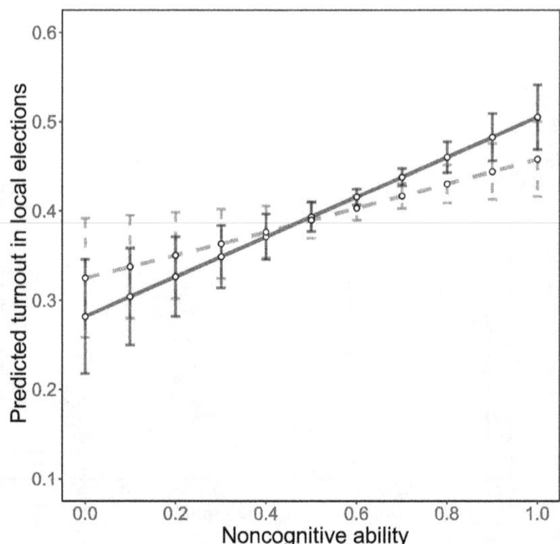

FIGURE A.9 School fixed effects vs. controls (local elections, Add Health)

Compares predicted turnout values to those produced with no geographic controls and instead a school fixed effect. Solid, black lines correspond to the school fixed effect; dashed lines correspond to the model with controls. Bars represent 95 percent confidence intervals. As can be seen, these two slopes are statistically indistinguishable.

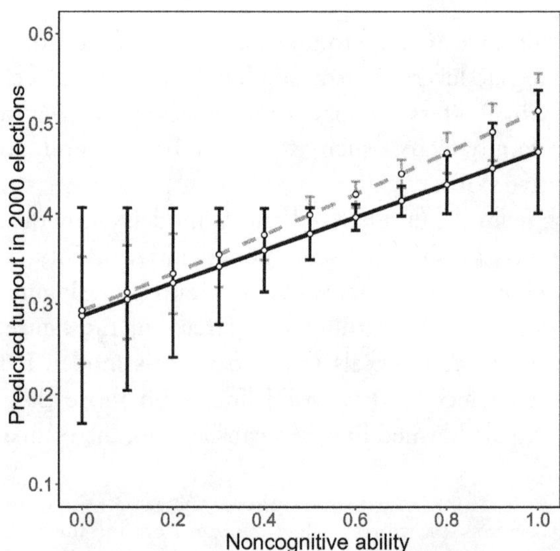

FIGURE A.10 Family fixed effect vs. controls (Add Health)

Compares predicted turnout values in the 2000 election from our models with controls to those produced from a sibling subsample and a family fixed effect model. Solid, black lines correspond to the family fixed effect model predictions; dashed lines correspond to the model with controls. Bars represent 95 percent confidence intervals. As can be seen, the two slopes are statistically indistinguishable.

approaches are overlapping and nearly identical. The family fixed effect model indicates an 18.2 percentage point increase in the probability of voting in 2000 for those at the top of the noncognitive ability scale relative to the bottom ($p = 0.056$). The estimates for voting in local elections (measured in 2008/2009) are larger and even more precise; individuals at the top of the distribution are predicted to vote a rate 24.0 percentage points higher than those at the bottom ($p = 0.011$; see Figure A.7). While this difference between electoral context is not statistically distinct, the coefficient for noncognitive skills is about 33 percent larger in local elections. This is consistent with noncognitive skills, perhaps, being more useful in electoral contexts where more obstacles stand in the way of voting. A combined scale that measures the fraction of elections in which someone votes predicts an increase of about 21.9 percentage points ($p = 0.002$).[30,31]

A.5 CHAPTER 5 APPENDIX

The evaluation of the VAWK/IMAGO used the following measures. Cooperation was measured by agree/disagree (1–10) scales in response to the items: "I can work with someone who has different opinions to me" and "I enjoy working together with other students my age." Empathy is measured by agree/disagree (1–10) scales in response to the items: "I feel bad when somebody gets their feelings hurt" and "I try to understand what people go through"; Grit is measured by agree/disagree (1–10) scales in response to the items "I often figure out different ways of doing things," "If something goes wrong I am able to bounce back and carry on," and "Once I have started a task, I like to finish it." Problem-solving is measured by agree/disagree (1–10) scales in response to the items "I know where to go for help with a problem," "I am confident about having a

30 The estimate that uses a mean scale may be the preferred approach when working with the sibling subsample. Part of the difficulty of using a sibling subsample is only about 1/4 of the Add Health sample has sibling pairs. The mean voting scale gives us some precision back by reducing measurement error in our dependent variable. Given this fact, in our models we mostly use scales of the fraction of elections one votes, if that is available.

31 Here we display results from sibling pair models without additional controls. However, if we control for factors that vary within families – like age, gender, and cognitive ability – our results remain the same ($\beta = 14.2$ percentage points; $p = 0.042$). When we control for things like our proxy for political motivation and the Big Five, our coefficient remains in the same ballpark, but we lose a lot of power because these controls are missing for roughly 1/4 members of the sibling subsample. The coefficient for noncognitive skills is virtually unchanged, but no longer significant ($p = 0.13$).

go at things that are new to me"; Sense of community is measured by agree/disagree (1–10) scales in response to the items "I feel able to have an impact on the world around me," "I feel motivated to take action on issues in my community." Willingness to volunteer time in the future was measured as a response to the prompt "I would like to learn more about how I can spend my own time helping people in my community in the future."

A.6 CHAPTER 6 APPENDIX

As anyone who works with coding election laws knows, coding of electoral rules takes great care given variation in statutes across states. We code electoral rules based on information from a thorough review of several sources, including the National Conference on State Legislatures (NCSL), the Pew Trust, the Correlates of State Policy Project (Jordan and Grossmann 2016), data from Biggers and Hanmer (2015), data from Keele and Minozzi (2013), and our own review of state-level statues on election laws. We coded preregistration status based on our own extensive review of historical state statutes and, in some instances, contact with state elections boards. We did this because the NCSL – the predominant source of election laws – includes states that did not meet our criteria as having preregistration. For example, they sometimes include states that allow young people to register before they turn 18 as long as they will be 18 by Election Day (something already allowed in most states). For instance, they include Alaska as having preregistration, when this state's law only permits those under 18 to register anytime 90 days before their 18th birthday, making this a relatively exclusionary treatment. Alaska is not alone. Texas (which requires young voters to be seventeen years and ten months of age to register) and Georgia, Iowa, and Missouri (which require the person to be 17.5 *and* turning 18 before the next election to register) are all included as having preregistration. We draw a distinction between states that allow sixteen/seventeen-year-olds to register *regardless of whether they turn 18 by the next election* and the many other states that place restrictions on that rule. All states – excepting North Dakota, which does not have a registration requirement – allow someone to register if they are 17 turning 18 by the next election. There is also some evidence that the NCSL and others have not fully traced the historical dynamics of preregistration implementation over time. For example, Fowler (2017) and NCLS miscode California as not having preregistration until 2014; however, Governor Schwarzenegger signed AB30 – which "authorize[d] a person who [was] at least seventeen years of age and otherwise meets all voter eligibility requirements to submit his or her affidavit of registration" – into law on October 11, 2009. Preregistration was expanded in 2014 with S113, which modified the state's preregistration law such that anyone who was "16 years of age and otherwise meets all voter eligibility requirements" could register.

Because there can be ambiguity in how to code election laws, reasonable people may thus disagree on which states get coded in particular ways. While we have been extremely careful and thorough in coding preregistration laws, we want to be absolutely sure that small coding decisions do not influence our results. We run four types of permutation tests that iteratively change how we measure preregistration in order to see how sensitive our coding decisions are to alternative and reasonable specifications. The first permutation test drops one treatment unit (state-year) iteratively across the dataset and then re-estimates the effect of preregistration each time. The logic behind this test is that if people were unable to come to a consensus about whether a treatment unit does or does not have preregistration, we could drop it to see if this point influences our end results. This is a relatively modest change to the coding. The second approach iteratively codes one treated unit as being untreated and, again, re-estimates the effect of preregistration with this change. This is a slightly stronger conceptual approach – one that switches the direction of our coding decisions. This again gives us another way of seeing if there are any influential units. The third does the reverse of the second: coding one untreated unit as being treated. The fourth follows a more classic permutation-based approach: randomly assigning preregistration status to twenty-four state-years that we observe in our Data Trust panel to having preregistration. This is a relatively harsh check: providing an estimate that compares our preregistration coding decisions to random draws. Across all four checks, our results hold. In the first, across the 204 regressions run (fifty-one states by four election years), all of the estimates are positive and in the neighborhood of our estimates from the original coding, ranging from 3.0 to 9.1 percentage points (most are between 7.2 and 8.2 percentage points). Only 2/204 (0.98 percent) of the regressions run are not significant at the 5 percent level. In the second check, 23/24 estimates (one test for each of the treated units) are positive. The median effect size across these checks is 6.9 percentage points, with the median p-value being 0.017. In the third, 180/181 estimates (one test for each of the untreated units) are positive. The median effect size across these checks is 6.8 percentage points, with the median p-value being 0.023.

In the fourth, all of our estimates are substantially larger than the estimated placebo treatment effects. The largest simulated effect is about 4.8 percentage points (the median effect is 0.0 percentage points), much smaller than the estimate from the same model specification (7.7 percentage points). While we are confident that our coding decisions for preregistration are accurate, these results show that our results are highly robust to various coding changes.

In our previous work on preregistration (Holbein and Hillygus 2016), we sometimes included a control for registration status in the difference-in-difference specifications. This was intended to provide a stringent test for whether our preregistration estimates were biased by one's motivation to participate in politics (for which registration was the best available proxy). The rationale was that if there still was a significant effect when this powerful control was included, we could be reasonably confident that our results were not being driven by individual selection of this variety. In our models, we do not include registration as this may actually remove some (perhaps even a large portion) of preregistration's actual effect (Garnett and Miller 2018; Nyhan, Skovron, and Titiunik 2017). This allows us to get a better view of the likely substantive size of preregistration's effect, rather than just its statistical significance alone.

Across our various electoral reforms, as best we can tell parallel trends hold. Looking at pre-treatment trends in a pooled cross-sectional dataset is challenging, as individuals are not surveyed repeatedly. To do so, we collapse the youth turnout data from the CPS to the state-year level and explore the gap between states that ever implement the various laws and those that do not. The raw pre-treatment gap in youth turnout (i.e. 18–25) between states that implemented nonexcuse absentee voting in the period of study and nonabsentee voting states appears to be parallel, with the raw turnout gap being substantively similar and not statistically distinguishable over time (lag 1 gap: −0.006 [−0.035, 0.024], lag 2 gap: −0.008 [−0.041, 0.024], lag 3 gap: −0.0006 [−0.036, 0.033], lag 4 gap: −0.004 [−0.044, 0.036]). Preregistration shows no pre-treatment differences of substantive or statistical meaning (lag 1 gap: −0.002 [−0.038, 0.033], lag 2 gap: −0.009 [−0.050, 0.032], lag 3 gap: −0.015 [−0.056, 0.025], lag 4 gap: −0.019 [−0.069, 0.030]). The same holds true for online registration (lag 1 gap: −0.030 [−0.061, 0.001], lag 2 gap: −0.039 [−0.074, −0.005], lag 3 gap: −0.038 [−0.074, −0.002], lag 4 gap: −0.032 [−0.074, 0.010]). Early voting shows a significant (negative) pre-treatment gap between treatment and control units, but one that is consistent over time (lag 1 gap: −0.035 [−0.065, −0.005], lag 2 gap: −0.035 [−0.068, −0.002], lag 3 gap: −0.027 [−0.062, 0.007], lag 4 gap: −0.029 [−0.070, 0.012]). The same holds true for same-day registration (lag 1 gap: 0.071 [0.033, 0.108], lag 2 gap: 0.079 [0.039, 0.120], lag 3 gap: 0.076 [0.033, 0.119], lag 4 gap: 0.082 [0.032, 0.133]).

On EDR specifically, while Keele and Minozzi are able to go one step beyond the difference-in-difference and utilize a unique natural experiment in their paper, this option is not available for our research question about young voters. Their natural experiment leverages county-level population-based thresholds for EDR (vs. no registration) in Wisconsin and Minnesota that were present in the 1970s, but were later discontinued. In this part of their analysis, Keele and Minozzi use administrative data from the Wisconsin Bluebook. While this data source contains raw turnout counts, it does not break turnout by age, and we are unaware of any data sources representative at the county-level that provide this information in the 1970s. Hence, our best available methodological approach remains the difference-in-difference. In our view, this is not as large of a loss in terms of internal validity as it might seem. Keele and Minozzi (2013, 201) argue that this difference-in-difference design is "clearly superior" to observational comparisons conditional-on-observables, but may still suffer from bias from time-variant unobservables and, as such, is inferior to natural experimental/Regression Discontinuity (RD) models. We completely agree. However, we note (as they do) that pre-treatment trends over the period of study provide assuring evidence of the validity of the parallel trends assumption (see their Figure 1). Further, even if we had the data to replicate their RD analysis among young voters, these natural experimental results would provide a substantively different effect estimate than what we are interested in exploring. With their RD approach, they can only estimate the effect of EDR vs. *no registration requirement*. They simply cannot estimate the effect of EDR vs. standard registration systems (a point Keele and Minozzi readily acknowledge). To us, it seems that this somewhat unique comparison point is likely muting the effect estimate of EDR in their RD analysis. The logic here is that EDR may represent a significant cost reduction from standard registration systems, but likely does *not* represent a significant cost reduction from no registration at all. (EDR may be even be *more* costly than no registration.) Viewed from this light, it is perhaps not surprising that they find that EDR does not increase turnout in the aggregate. Their results simply show that compared to no registration, EDR is no different. Given that only one state (North Dakota) has no registration, this comparison is less meaningful, though better causally identified.

Bibliography

Abelson, Robert P., Elizabeth F. Loftus, and Anthony G. Greenwald. 1992. "Attempts to improve the accuracy of self-reports of voting."

Achen, Christopher H. and André Blais. 2015. "Intention to vote, reported vote and validated vote." In *The Act of Voting: Identities, Institutions and Locale*, ed. Johan A. Elkink and David M. Farrell. London: Routledge, pp. 195–209.

Adams, John. 1788. *A Defence of the Constitutions of Government of the United States of America*. Vol. 3. Philadelphia: Printed by Budd and Bartram, for William Cobbett, opposite Christ Church. https://archive.org/details/defenceofconstit03adamrich/page/n6

Addonizio, Elizabeth M. 2011. "The Fourth of July Vote: A social approach to voter mobilization and election day." PhD thesis, Yale University.

Ahn, Tom and Jacob Vigdor. 2014. "The impact of NCLB's accountability sanctions on school performance: Regression discontinuity evidence from North Carolina." *NBER Working Paper* 20511.

Ajzen, Icek and Martin Fishbein. 1977. "Attitude-behavior relations: A theoretical analysis and review of empirical research." *Psychological Bulletin* 84(5):888.

Akee, Randall, William Copeland, E. Jane Costello, and Emilia Simeonova. 2018a. "How does household income affect child personality traits and behaviors?" *American Economic Review* 108(3):775–827.

Akee, Randall, William Copeland, E. Jane Costello, John B. Holbein, and Emilia Simeonova. 2018b. "Family income and the intergenerational transmission of voting behavior: Evidence from an income intervention." (w24770).

Alan, Sule, and Seda Ertac. 2016. "Good things come to those who (are taught how to) wait: An educational intervention on time preference." *Working Paper*.

Alan, Sule, Teodora Boneva, and Seda Ertac. 2019. "Ever failed, try again, succeed better: Results from a randomized educational intervention on grit." *Quarterly Journal of Economics*. Vol. 134.

Almond, Gabriel Abraham and Sidney Verba. 2015. *The Civic Culture: Political Attitudes and Democracy in Five Nations*. Princeton, NJ: Princeton University Press.

Angrist, Joshua D. and Jörn-Steffen Pischke. 2008. *Mostly Harmless Econometrics: An Empiricist's Companion.* Princeton, NJ: Princeton University Press.

Ansolabehere, Stephen and Eitan Hersh. 2012. "Validation: What big data reveal about survey misreporting and the real electorate." *Political Analysis* 20(4):437–459.

Ansolabehere, Stephen, Eitan Hersh, and Kenneth Shepsle. 2012. "Movers, stayers, and registration: Why age is correlated with registration in the US." *Quarterly Journal of Political Science* 7(4):333–363.

Anzia, Sarah F. 2013. *Timing and Turnout: How Off-Cycle Elections Favor Organized Groups.* Chicago: University of Chicago Press.

Ashenfelter, Orley and David Card. 1985. "Using the longitudinal structure of earnings to estimate the effect of training programs." *The Review of Economics and Statistics* 67(4):648–660.

Ashenfelter, Orley and David J. Zimmerman. 1997. "Estimates of the returns to schooling from sibling data: Fathers, sons, and brothers." *Review of Economics and Statistics* 79(1):1–9.

Atkeson, Lonna R., Lisa A. Bryant, Thad E. Hall, Kyle Saunders, and Michael Alvarez. 2010. "A new barrier to participation: Heterogeneous application of voter identification policies." *Electoral Studies* 29(1):66–73.

Bachner, Jennifer. 2010. "From classroom to voting booth: The effect of high school civic education on turnout." *Working Paper. www.gov.harvard.edu/files/Bachner%20Civic%20Education%20Article.pdf*

Bandura, Albert, Claudio Barbaranelli, Gian Vittorio Caprara, and Concetta Pastorelli. 2001. "Self-efficacy beliefs as shapers of children's aspirations and career trajectories." *Child Development* 72(1):187–206.

Baron, Reuben M. and David A. Kenny. 1986. "The moderator–mediator variable distinction in social psychological research: Conceptual, strategic, and statistical considerations." *Journal of Personality and Social Psychology* 51(6):1173.

Baron-Cohen, Simon, Sally Wheelwright, Jacqueline Hill, Yogini Raste, and Ian Plumb. 2001. "The 'Reading the Mind in the Eyes' Test revised version: A study with normal adults, and adults with Asperger syndrome or high-functioning autism." *The Journal of Child Psychology and Psychiatry and Allied Disciplines* 42(2):241–251.

Bechtel, Michael M., Dominik Hangartner, and Lukas Schmid. 2016. "Does compulsory voting increase support for leftist policy?" *American Journal of Political Science* 60(3):752–767.

Belli, Robert F., Santa Traugott, and Steven J. Rosenstone. 1994. "Reducing over-reporting of voter turnout: An experiment using a source monitoring framework." NES Technical Reports Number 35 (1994). http://anesold.isr.umich.edu/Library/papers/documents/neso10153.pdf

Bennett, Stephen Earl. 1998. "Young Americans' indifference to media coverage of public affairs." *PS: Political Science & Politics* 31(3):535–541.

Bennett, W. Lance. 2007. "Civic learning in changing democracies: Challenges for citizenship and civic education." *Young Citizens and New Media.* London: Routledge.

Bennion, Elizabeth A. 2006. "Civic education and citizen engagement: Mobilizing voters as a required field experiment." *Journal of Political Science Education* 2(2):205–227.

2009a. "Advice for raising registration and turnout rates: Field experiments on 37 college campuses." In APSA 2009 Toronto Meeting Paper. 2009.

2009b. "I'll register to vote if you teach me how: Results of a classroom-based field experiment." *Indiana Journal of Political Science* 11:20–27.

Bennion, Elizabeth A. and David W. Nickerson. 2011. "The cost of convenience: An experiment showing e-mail outreach decreases voter registration." *Political Research Quarterly* 64(4):858–869.

Berinsky, Adam J. and Gabriel S. Lenz. 2011. "Education and political participation: Exploring the causal link." *Political Behavior* 33(3):357–373.

Berry, Christopher R. and Jacob E. Gersen. 2011. "Election timing and public policy." *Quarterly Journal of Political Science* 6(2):103–135.

Bertocchi, Graziella, Arcangelo Dimico, Francesco Lancia, and Alessia Russo. 2017. "Youth enfranchisement, political responsiveness, and education expenditure: Evidence from the U.S." *DEMB Working Paper* 118.

Bettinger, Eric, Sten Ludvigsen, Mari Rege, Ingeborg F. Solli, and David Yeager. 2018. "Increasing perseverance in math: Evidence from a field experiment in Norway." *Journal of Economic Behavior & Organization* 146:1–15.

Bhatti, Yosef and Kasper M. Hansen. 2012. "Leaving the nest and the social act of voting: Turnout among first-time voters." *Journal of Elections, Public Opinion & Parties* 22(4):380–406.

Bierman, Karen, John Coie, Kenneth Dodge, Mark Greenberg, John Lochman, Robert McMahon, and Ellen Pinderhughes. 1999a. "Initial impact of the Fast Track prevention trial for conduct problems: I. The high-risk sample." *Journal of Consulting and Clinical Psychology* 67(5):631–647.

1999b. "Initial impact of the Fast Track prevention trial for conduct problems: II. Classroom effects." *Journal of Consulting and Clinical Psychology* 67(5):648–657.

2002. "Evaluation of the first 3 years of the Fast Track prevention trial with children at high risk for adolescent conduct problems." *Journal of Abnormal Child Psychology* 30(1):19–35.

2004. "The effects of the Fast Track program on serious problem outcomes at the end of elementary school." *Journal of Clinical Child and Adolescent Psychology* 33(4):650–661.

2007. "Fast track randomized controlled trial to prevent externalizing psychiatric disorders: Findings from grades 3 to 9." *Journal of the American Academy of Child & Adolescent Psychiatry* 46(10):1250–1262.

2010. "Fast Track intervention effects on youth arrests and delinquency." *Journal of Experimental Criminology* 6(2):131–157.

2011. "The effects of the Fast Track preventive intervention on the development of conduct disorder across childhood." *Child Development* 82(1):331–345.

Biggers, Daniel R. and Michael J. Hanmer. 2015. "Who makes voting convenient? Explaining the adoption of early and no-excuse absentee voting in the American states." *State Politics & Policy Quarterly* 15(2):192–210.

Blais, André. 2000. *To Vote or Not to Vote?: The Merits and Limits of Rational Choice Theory*. University of Pittsburgh Press.

2006. "What affects voter turnout?" *Annual Review of Political Science* 9:111–125.

2007. "Turnout in elections." In *The Oxford Handbook of Political Behavior*, ed. Russell J. Dalton and Hans Dieter Klingemann. New York: Oxford University Press pp. 621–635.

Blais, André and Christopher H. Achen. 2018. "Civic duty and voter turnout." *Political Behavior* 1–25.

Blais, André and Robert Young. 1999. "Why do people vote? An experiment in rationality." *Public Choice* 99(1-2):39–55.

Blais, André and Simon Labbé St-Vincent. 2011. "Personality traits, political attitudes and the propensity to vote." *European Journal of Political Research* 50(3):395–417.

Blanden, Jo, Paul Gregg, and Lindsey Macmillan. 2007. "Accounting for intergenerational income persistence: Non-cognitive skills, ability and education." *The Economic Journal* 117(519).

Blattman, Christopher, Julian C. Jamison, and Margaret Sheridan. 2017. "Reducing crime and violence: Experimental evidence from Cognitive Behavioral Therapy in Liberia." *American Economic Review* 107(4):1165–1206.

Borghans, Lex, Angela Lee Duckworth, James J. Heckman, and Bas Ter Weel. 2008. "The economics and psychology of personality traits." *Journal of Human Resources* 43(4):972–1059.

Boudreau, Cheryl. 2009. "Closing the gap: When do cues eliminate differences between sophisticated and unsophisticated citizens?" *The Journal of Politics* 71(3):964–976.

Bowen, Daniel H. and Brian Kisida. 2019. "Investigating causal effects of arts education experiences: Experimental evidence from Houston's Arts Access Initiative." *Working Paper*.

Bowman, Carole H. and Martin Fishbein. 1978. "Understanding public reaction to energy proposals: An application of the Fishbein Model 1." *Journal of Applied Social Psychology* 8(4):319–340.

Braconnier, Céline, Jean-Yves Dormagen, and Vincent Pons. 2017. "Voter registration costs and disenfranchisement: Experimental evidence from France." *American Political Science Review* 111(3):1–21.

Brady, Henry E. and John E. McNulty. 2011. "Turning out to vote: The costs of finding and getting to the polling place." *American Political Science Review* 105(01):115–134.

Brady, Henry E., Sidney Verba, and Kay Lehman Schlozman. 1995. "Beyond SES: A resource model of political participation." *American Political Science Review* 89(02):271–294.

Brandtstädter, Jochen and Gerolf Renner. 1990. "Tenacious goal pursuit and flexible goal adjustment: Explication and age-related analysis of assimilative and accommodative strategies of coping." *Psychology and Aging* 5(1):58.

Brians, Craig Leonard and Bernard Grofman. 2001. "Election day registration's effect on U.S. voter turnout." *Social Science Quarterly* 82(1):170–183.

Brighouse, Harry, Helen F Ladd, Susanna Loeb, and Adam Swift. 2016. "Educational goods and values: A framework for decision makers." *Theory and Research in Education* 14(1):3–25.

Burden, Barry C. 2009. "The dynamic effects of education on voter turnout." *Electoral Studies* 28(4):540–549.

Burden, Barry C., David T. Canon, Kenneth R. Mayer, and Donald P. Moynihan. 2014. "Election laws, mobilization, and turnout: The unanticipated consequences of election reform." *American Journal of Political Science* 58(1): 95–109.

Burden, Barry C. and Jacob R. Neiheisel. 2013. "Election administration and the pure effect of voter registration on turnout." *Political Research Quarterly* 66(1):77–90.

Burden, Barry C., Jason M. Fletcher, Pamela Herd, Donald P. Moynihan, and Bradley M. Jones. 2017. "How different forms of health matter to political participation." *The Journal of Politics* 79(1):166–178.

Cahan, Sorel and Alon Noyman. 2001. "The Kaufman Ability Battery for Children mental processing scale: A valid measure of 'pure' intelligence?" *Educational and Psychological Measurement* 61(5):827–840.

Camilli, Gregory, Sadako Vargas, Sharon Ryan and W Steven Barnett. 2010. "Meta-analysis of the effects of early education interventions on cognitive and social development." *Teachers College Record* 112(3):579–620.

Campbell, Andrea Louise. 2003. *How Policies Make Citizens: Senior Political Activism and the American Welfare State*. Princeton University Press.

Campbell, David E. 2006a. "What is education's impact on civic and social engagement." In *Measuring the effects of education on health and civic engagement: Proceedings of the Copenhagen symposium*, ed. Richard Desjardins and Tom Schuller. pp. 25–126.

2006b. *Why We Vote: How Schools and Communities Shape Our Civic Life*. Princeton, NJ: Princeton University Press.

Campbell, David E. and Richard G. Niemi. 2016. "Testing civics: State-level civic education requirements and political knowledge." *American Political Science Review* 110(3):495–511.

Cantoni, Enrico and Vincent Pons. 2019. Strict ID Laws Don't Stop Voters: Evidence from a US Nationwide Panel, 2008–2016. Technical Report w25522 National Bureau of Economic Research.

Caprara, Gian Vittorio, Guido Alessandri, and Nancy Eisenberg. 2012. "Prosociality: The contribution of traits, values, and self-efficacy beliefs." *Journal of Personality and Social Psychology* 102(6):1289–1303.

Carmines, Edward G. 1978. "Psychological origins of adolescent political attitudes: Self-esteem, political salience, and political involvement." *American Politics Quarterly* 6(2):167–186.

Carpini, Michael X. Delli and Scott Keeter. 1996. *What Americans Know about Politics and Why It Matters*. Yale University Press.

Cepaluni, Gabriel and F. Daniel Hidalgo. 2016. "Compulsory voting can increase political inequality: Evidence from Brazil." *Political Analysis* 24(2):273–280.

Charney, Evan and William English. 2012. "Candidate genes and political behavior." *American Political Science Review* 106(01):1–34.

Chetty, Raj, John N. Friedman, Nathaniel Hilger, Emmanuel Saez, Diane Whitmore Schanzenbach, and Danny Yagan. 2011. "How does your kindergarten classroom affect your earnings? Evidence from Project STAR." *The Quarterly Journal of Economics* 126(4):1593–1660.

Cobb-Clark, Deborah A. and Stefanie Schurer. 2012. "The stability of big-five personality traits." *Economics Letters* 115(1):11–15.

Collins, Kevin, Joshua L. Kalla and Laura Keane. 2018. "Youth voter mobilization through online advertising: Evidence from two GOTV field experiments." *Working Paper*.

Condon, Meghan and Matthew Holleque. 2013. "Entering politics: General self-efficacy and voting behavior among young people." *Political Psychology* 34(2):167–181.

Conner, Mark. 2015. "Extending not retiring the theory of planned behaviour: A commentary on Sniehotta, Presseau and Araújo-Soares." *Health Psychology Review* 9(2):141–145.

Converse, Philip E. 1972. "Change in the American electorate." In *The Human Meaning of Social Change*. New York: Russell Sage Foundation, pp. 263–337.

Coppock, Alexander and Donald P Green. 2016. "Is voting habit forming? New evidence from experiments and regression discontinuities." *American Journal of Political Science* 60(4):1044–1062.

Cornelissen, Thomas and Christian Dustmann. 2019. "Early school exposure, test scores, and non-cognitive outcomes." *American Economic Journal: Economic Policy*.

Corvalan, Alejandro and Paulo Cox. 2018. "The impact of procedural information costs on voting: Evidence from a natural experiment in Chile." *Political Behavior* 40:3–19.

Costa, Mia, Brian F. Schaffner, and Alicia Prevost. 2018. "Walking the walk? Experiments on the effect of pledging to vote on youth turnout." *PLoS ONE* 13(5):e0197066.

Cramer, Katherine J. and Benjamin Toff. 2017. "The fact of experience: Rethinking political knowledge and civic competence." *Perspectives on Politics* 15(3):754–770.

Cunha, Flavio and James Heckman. 2007. "The technology of skill formation." *American Economic Review* 97(2):31–47.

Cunha, Flavio, James J. Heckman, Lance Lochner, and Dimitriy V. Masterov. 2006. "Interpreting the evidence on life cycle skill formation." *Handbook of the Economics of Education* 1:697–812.

Cunha, Flavio, James J. Heckman, and Susanne M. Schennach. 2010. "Estimating the technology of cognitive and non-cognitive skill formation." *Econometrica* 78(3):883–931.

Currie, Janet and Duncan Thomas. 1995. "Does head start make a difference?" *The American Economic Review* 85(3):341.

Dahlgaard, Jens Olav. 2018. "Trickle-up political socialization: The causal effect on turnout of parenting a newly enfranchised voter." *American Political Science Review* 112(3):698–705.

Dale, Allison and Aaron Strauss. 2009. "Don't forget to vote: Text message reminders as a mobilization tool." *American Journal of Political Science* 53(4):787–804.

Davis, Mark H. 1994. *Empathy: A Social Psychological Approach.* Westview Press.

Dawes, Christopher and Aaron Weinschenk. 2019. "Civic coursework in high school and voter turnout in adulthood." *Working Paper.*

Dawes, Christopher, David Cesarini, James H. Fowler, Magnus Johannesson, Patrik K. E. Magnusson, and Sven Oskarsson. 2014. "The relationship between genes, psychological traits, and political participation." *American Journal of Political Science* 58(4):888–903.

De Tocqueville, Alexis. 2003. *Democracy in America.* Vol. 10 Regnery Publishing.

Deary, Ian J., Wendy Johnson, and Lorna M. Houlihan. 2009. "Genetic foundations of human intelligence." *Human Genetics* 126(1):215–232.

Dee, Thomas S. 2004. "Are there civic returns to education?" *Journal of Public Economics* 88(9):1697–1720.

Dee, Thomas S. and Brian Jacob. 2011. "The impact of No Child Left Behind on student achievement." *Journal of Policy Analysis and Management* 30(3):418–446.

Dee, Thomas S. and Martin R. West. 2011. "The non-cognitive returns to class size." *Educational Evaluation and Policy Analysis* 33(1):23–46.

Deming, David J. 2017. "The growing importance of social skills in the labor market." *The Quarterly Journal of Economics* 132(4):1593–1640.

Denny, Kevin and Orla Doyle. 2008. "Political interest, cognitive ability and personality: Determinants of voter turnout in Britain." *British Journal of Political Science* 38(02):291–310.

Duckworth, Angela. 2016. *Grit: The Power of Passion and Perseverance.* Scribner.

Duckworth, Angela L., Christopher Peterson, Michael D. Matthews, and Dennis R. Kelly. 2007. "Grit perseverance and passion for long-term goals." *Journal of Personality and Social Psychology* 92(6):1087–1101.

Dunn, Lloyd M. and Douglas M. Dunn. 2007. *PPVT-4: Peabody Picture Vocabulary Test.* Circle Pines, MN: American Guidance Service.

Dunn, Lloyd M., Leota M. Dunn, Stephan Bulheller, and Hartmut Häcker. 1965. *Peabody Picture Vocabulary Test.* American Guidance Service Circle Pines, MN.

Dweck, Carol. 2006. *Mindset: The New Psychology of Success.* New York: Random House, Inc.

Dweck, Carol S. 2000. *Self-Theories: Their Role in Motivation, Personality, and Development.* Psychology Press.

Dweck, Carol S. and Ellen L. Leggett. 1988. "A social-cognitive approach to motivation and personality." *Psychological Review* 95(2):256.

Elder, Laurel, Andrew Seligsohn, and Daniel Hofrenning. 2007. "Experiencing New Hampshire: The effects of an experiential learning course on civic engagement." *Journal of Political Science Education* 3(2):191–216.

Elliott, Colin D. 1979. *British Ability Scales.* Nfer-Nelson.

Erikson, Robert S. and Lorraine C. Minnite. 2009. "Modeling problems in the voter identification-voter turnout debate." *Election Law Journal* 8(2): 85–101.

Farrington, Camille A., Melissa Roderick, Elaine Allensworth, Jenny Nagaoka, Tasha Seneca Keyes, David W Johnson, and Nicole O. Beechum. 2012. Teaching Adolescents to Become Learners: The Role of Non-cognitive Factors in Shaping School Performance–A Critical Literature Review. Technical report University of Chicago CCSR.

Feldman, Lauren, Josh Pasek, Daniel Romer, and Kathleen Hall Jamieson. 2007. "Identifying best practices in civic education: Lessons from the student voices program." *American Journal of Education* 114(1):75–100.

Ferejohn, John A. and Morris P. Fiorina. 1974. "The paradox of not voting: A decision theoretic analysis." *American Political Science Review* 68(2): 525–536.

Finkel, Steven E. 2002. "Civic education and the mobilization of political participation in developing democracies." *Journal of Politics* 64(4):994–1020.

Fiorina, Morris P. 1990. "Information and rationality in elections." *Information and Democratic Processes* pp. 329–342.

Fishbein, Martin, James Jaccard, Andrew R. Davidson, Icek Ajzen, and Barbara Loken. 1980. "Predicting and understanding family planning behaviors." In *Understanding Attitudes and Predicting Social Behavior*. Prentice Hall.

Fitzgerald, Mary. 2005. "Greater convenience but not greater turnout: the impact of alternative voting methods on electoral participation in the United States." *American Politics Research* 33(6):842–867.

Fowler, Anthony. 2013. "Electoral and policy consequences of voter turnout: Evidence from compulsory voting in Australia." *Quarterly Journal of Political Science* 8(2):159–182.

2017. "Does voter preregistration increase youth participation?" *Election Law Journal: Rules, Politics, and Policy* 16(4):485–494.

Fowler, James H. and Cindy D. Kam. 2006. "Patience as a political virtue: Delayed gratification and turnout." *Political Behavior* 28(2):113–128.

2007. "Beyond the self: Social identity, altruism, and political participation." *Journal of Politics* 69(3):813–827.

Fowler, James H., Laura A. Baker, and Christopher T. Dawes. 2008. "Genetic variation in political participation." *American Political Science Review* 102(2):232–248.

Fraga, Bernard L. 2018. *The Turnout Gap: Race, Ethnicity, and Political Inequality in a Diversifying America*. Cambridge University Press.

Fraga, Bernard L. and John B. Holbein. 2018. "Measuring youth and college student voter turnout." *Working Paper*.

Frankel, Laura Lazarus and D. Sunshine Hillygus. 2013. "Looking beyond demographics: Panel attrition in the ANES and GSS." *Political Analysis* 22(3):336–353.

Franklin, Mark N. 2004. *Voter Turnout and the Dynamics of Electoral Competition in Established Democracies since 1945*. Cambridge University Press.

Fredricks, Jennifer A. 2012. "Extracurricular participation and academic outcomes: Testing the over-scheduling hypothesis." *Journal of Youth and Adolescence* 41(3):295–306.

Freedman, David A., David Collier, and Jasjeet S. Sekhon. 2010. *Statistical Models and Causal Inference: A Dialogue with the Social Sciences*. New York, NY: Cambridge University Press.

Fryer Jr, Roland G., Steven D. Levitt, and John A. List. 2015. "Parental incentives and early childhood achievement: a field experiment in Chicago heights." *National Bureau of Economic Research* (21477).

Fryer, Roland G. 2017. "The production of human capital in developed countries: Evidence from 196 randomized field experiments." In *Handbook of Economic Field Experiments*, ed. Abhijit V. Banerjee and Esther Duflo. Vol. 2 Elsevier pp. 95–322.

Fujiwara, Thomas, Kyle C. Meng, and Tom Vogl. 2016. "Habit formation in voting: Evidence from rainy elections." *American Economic Journal: Applied Economics* 8(4):160–188.

Galston, William A. 2004. "Civic education and political participation." *PS: Political Science and Politics* 37(2):263–266.

Garnett, Holly Ann and Peter Miller. 2018. "Registration Innovation: The Impact of American Registration Regimes, 1996–2016." *Presented at the 2018 Election Sciences, Reform, and Administration Conference.*

Gerber, Alan S. and Donald P. Green. 2012. *Field Experiments: Design, Analysis, and Interpretation*. WW Norton.

Gerber, Alan S., Donald P. Green, and Ron Shachar. 2003. "Voting may be habit-forming: Evidence from a randomized field experiment." *American Journal of Political Science* 47(3):540–550.

Gerber, Alan S., Gregory A. Huber, David Doherty, and Conor M. Dowling. 2011. "The Big Five personality traits in the political arena." *Annual Review of Political Science* 14:265–287.

Gerber, Alan S., Gregory A. Huber, and Seth J. Hill. 2013. "Identifying the effect of all-mail elections on turnout: Staggered reform in the evergreen state." *Political Science Research and Methods* 1(01):91–116.

Gershtenson, Joseph, Dennis L. Plane, Joshua M. Scacco, and Jerry Thomas. 2013. "Registering to vote is easy, right? Active learning and attitudes about voter registration." *Journal of Political Science Education* 9(4):379–402.

Gershtenson, Joseph, Glenn W. Rainey Jr, and Jane G. Rainey. 2010. "Creating better citizens? Effects of a model citizens' assembly on student political attitudes and behavior." *Journal of Political Science Education* 6(2):95–116.

Gibson, Cynthia and Peter Levine. 2003. "The civic mission of schools." *Report for Carnegie Corporation of New York and the Center for Information and Research on Civic Learning and Engagement.*

Gill, Brian, Charles Tilley, Emilyn Whitesell, Mariel Finucane, Liz Potamites and Sean Corcoran. 2018. "The impact of democracy prep public schools on civic participation." *Mathematica Policy Research Policy Report.*

Gomez, Brad T., Thomas G. Hansford, and George A. Krause. 2007. "The Republicans should pray for rain: Weather, turnout, and voting in US presidential elections." *Journal of Politics* 69(3):649–663.

Gottlieb, Jessica. 2016. "Greater expectations: A field experiment to improve accountability in Mali." *American Journal of Political Science* 60(1): 143–157.

Green, Donald P., Mary C. McGrath, and Peter M. Aronow. 2013. "Field experiments and the study of voter turnout." *Journal of Elections, Public Opinion & Parties* 23(1):27–48.

Green, Donald P., Peter M. Aronow, Daniel E. Bergan, Pamela Greene, Celia Paris, and Beth I. Weinberger. 2011. "Does knowledge of constitutional principles increase support for civil liberties? Results from a randomized field experiment." *The Journal of Politics* 73(2):463–476.

Green, Donald P., Shang E. Ha, and John G. Bullock. 2010. "Enough already about "black box" experiments: Studying mediation is more difficult than most scholars suppose." *The Annals of the American Academy of Political and Social Science* 628(1):200–208.

Griffin, Rob, Paul Gronke, Tova Wang, and Liz Kennedy. 2017. Who Votes With Automatic Voter Registration? Technical report.

Grimmer, Justin, Eitan Hersh, Marc Meredith, Jonathan Mummolo, and Clayton Nall. 2018. "Obstacles to estimating voter ID laws' effect on turnout." *The Journal of Politics* 80(3):1045–1051.

Grofman, Bernard. 2018. "A Reasonable Choice Approach to Turnout." *Málaga Serie de seminarios de teoría e historia económica* (March 22).

Gross, Jana, Simone Balestra and Uschi Backes-Gellner. 2017. "Does class size affect student 'Grit': Evidence from a randomised experiment in early grades." *University of Zurich Working Paper* (129).

Grumbach, Jacob M. and Charlotte Hill. 2019. "Rock the registration: Same day registration increases turnout of young voters." *Working Paper*.

Hajnal, Zoltan and Jessica Trounstine. 2016. "Race and class inequality in local politics." In *The Double Bind: The Politics of Racial and Class Inequalities in the Americas*, ed. Juliet Hooker and Alvin B. Tillery. APSA Task Force on Racial and Class Inequalities in the Americas pp. 1–17.

Hanmer, Michael J. 2009. *Discount Voting: Voter Registration Reforms and Their Effects*. Cambridge University Press.

Hanmer, Michael J., Won-Ho Park, Michael W. Traugott, Richard G. Niemi, Paul S. Herrnson, Benjamin B. Bederson, and Frederick C. Conrad. 2010. "Losing fewer votes: The impact of changing voting systems on residual votes." *Political Research Quarterly* 63(1):129–142.

Hanushek, Eric A., John F. Kain, and Steven G. Rivkin. 2004. "Disruption versus Tiebout improvement: The costs and benefits of switching schools." *Journal of public Economics* 88(9):1721–1746.

Hart, Sara A., Stephen A. Petrill, Lee A. Thompson, and Robert Plomin. 2009. "The ABCs of math: A genetic analysis of mathematics and its links with reading ability and general cognitive ability." *Journal of Educational Psychology* 101(2):388.

Healy, Andrew and Neil Malhotra. 2013. "Childhood socialization and political attitudes: Evidence from a natural experiment." *The Journal of Politics* 75(4):1023–1037.

Heckman, James J. 2000. "Policies to foster human capital." *Research in Economics* 54(1):3–56.

Heckman, James J. and Dimitriy V Masterov. 2007. "The productivity argument for investing in young children." *Applied Economic Perspectives and Policy* 29(3):446–493.

Heckman, James J., John Eric Humphries, and Gregory Veramendi. 2018. "The nonmarket benefits of education and ability." *Journal of Human Capital* 12(2):282–304.

Heckman, James J., Jora Stixrud, and Sergio Urzua. 2006. "The effects of cognitive and non-cognitive abilities on labor market outcomes and social behavior." *Journal of Labor Economics* 24(3):411–482.

Heckman, James J., Lena Malofeeva, Rodrigo Pinto, and Peter A. Savelyev. 2007. "The effect of the Perry Preschool Program on the cognitive and non-cognitive skills of its participants." *Working Paper, University of Chicago, Department of Economics.*

Heckman, James J., Seong Hyeok Moon, Rodrigo Pinto, Peter A. Savelyev, and Adam Yavitz. 2010. "The rate of return to the HighScope Perry Preschool Program." *Journal of public Economics* 94(1-2):114–128.

Heckman, James J. and Tim Kautz. 2013. "Fostering and measuring skills: Interventions that improve character and cognition." *NBER Working Paper* (w19656). www.nber.org/papers/w19656

Heckman, James J. and Yona Rubinstein. 2001. "The importance of non-cognitive skills: Lessons from the GED testing program." *The American Economic Review* 91(2):145–149.

Heckman, James, Rodrigo Pinto, and Peter Savelyev. 2013. "Understanding the mechanisms through which an influential early childhood program boosted adult outcomes." *American Economic Review* 103(6):2052–2086.

Heller, Sara B., Anuj K. Shah, Jonathan Guryan, Jens Ludwig, Sendhil Mullainathan, and Harold A. Pollack. 2017. "Thinking, fast and slow? Some field experiments to reduce crime and dropout in Chicago." *The Quarterly Journal of Economics* 132(1):1–54.

Henderson, John A. 2018. "Hookworm eradication as a natural experiment for schooling and voting in the American South." *Political Behavior* 40(2): 467–494.

Henderson, John and John Brooks. 2016. "Mediating the electoral connection: The information effects of voter signals on legislative behavior." *The Journal of Politics* 78(3):653–669.

Henselmans, Inge, Joke Fleer, Eric van Sonderen, Ans Smink, Robbert Sanderman, and Adelita V. Ranchor. 2011. "The tenacious goal pursuit and flexible goal adjustment scales: A validation study." *Psychology and Aging* 26(1):174.

Hernstein, R. J. and Charles Murray. 1994. *The Bell Curve: The Reshaping of American Life by Difference in Intelligence*. New York: Free Press.

Herrnson, Paul S., Richard G. Niemi, Michael J. Hanmer, Peter L. Francia, Benjamin B. Bederson, Frederick G. Conrad, and Michael W. Traugott. 2008. "Voters' evaluations of electronic voting systems results from a usability field study." *American Politics Research* 36(4):580–611.

Hersh, E. 2017. "Political hobbyism: a theory of mass behavior." *Working Paper*.

Hettema, P. Joop and Ian J. Deary. 2013. *Foundations of Personality*. Vol. 72 Springer Science & Business Media.

Hibbing, John R. and Elizabeth Theiss-Morse. 2002. *Stealth Democracy: Americans' Beliefs about How Government Should Work*. Cambridge University Press.

Highton, Benjamin. 2005. "Self-reported versus proxy-reported voter turnout in the current population survey." *Public Opinion Quarterly* 69(1):113–123.

Hill, Lisa. 2000. "Compulsory voting, political shyness and welfare outcomes." *Journal of Sociology* 36(1):30–49.

2006. "Low voter turnout in the United States: Is compulsory voting a viable solution?" *Journal of Theoretical Politics* 18(2):207–232.

2015. "Republican democracy and compulsory voting." *Critical Review of International Social and Political Philosophy* 18(6):652–660.

Hill, Seth J. 2018. "Following through on an intention to vote: Present bias and turnout." *Political Science Research and Methods*.

Hillygus, D. Sunshine. 2005. "The missing link: Exploring the relationship between higher education and political engagement." *Political Behavior* 27(1):25–47.

Hillygus, D. Sunshine, Natalie Jackson and M Young. 2014. "Professional respondents in non-probability online panels." *Online panel research: A data quality perspective* 1:219–237.

Hirsch Jr., Eric D., Joseph F. Kett, and James S. Trefil. 1988. *Cultural Literacy: What Every American Needs to Know*. Vintage.

Hitt, Collin, Julie Trivitt, and Albert Cheng. 2016. "When you say nothing at all: The predictive power of student effort on surveys." *Economics of Education Review* 52:105–119.

Holbein, John. 2016. "Left behind? Citizen responsiveness to government performance information." *American Political Science Review* 110(2):353–368.

Holbein, John B. 2017. "Childhood skill development and adult political participation." *American Political Science Review* 111(3):572–583.

Holbein, John B. and D. Sunshine Hillygus. 2016. "Making young voters: The impact of preregistration on youth turnout." *American Journal of Political Science* 60(2):364–382.

Holbein, John B., D. Sunshine Hillygus, Christina M. Gibson-Davis, Darryl V. Hill, and Matthew A. Lenard. Forthcoming. "The development of students' engagement in school, community, and democracy." *British Journal of Political Science*.

Holbein, John B. and Helen F. Ladd. 2017. "Accountability pressure: Regression discontinuity estimates of how No Child Left Behind influenced student behavior." *Economics of Education Review* 58:55–67.

Holbein, John B., Jerome P. Schafer, and David L. Dickinson. 2019. "Insufficient sleep reduces voting and other prosocial behaviors." *Nature Human Behavior*.

Holbein, John B. and Marcos A. Rangel. Forthcoming. "Does voting have upstream and downstream consequences? Regression discontinuity tests of the transformative voting hypothesis." *Journal of Politics*.

Holbrook, Allyson L. and Jon A. Krosnick. 2009. "Social desirability bias in voter turnout reports: Tests using the item count technique." *Public Opinion Quarterly* 74(1):37–67.

Hoover, Michael and Susan Orr. 2007. The fountain of youth: Strategies and tactics for mobilizing America's young voters. In *Youth Political Engagement: Why Rock the Vote Hits the Wrong Note*, ed. Daniel M. Shea and John C. Green. New York: Roman and Littlefield Publishers, Inc.

Howe, Paul. 2011. *Citizens Adrift: The Democratic Disengagement of Young Canadians*. Vancouver: UBC press.

Huerta, Juan Carlos and Joseph Jozwiak. 2008. "Developing civic engagement in general education political science." *Journal of Political Science Education* 4(1):42–60.

Imai, Kosuke, Luke Keele and Dustin Tingley. 2010. "A general approach to causal mediation analysis." *Psychological Methods* 15(4):309.

Imai, Kosuke, Luke Keele, Dustin Tingley, and Teppei Yamamoto. 2011. "Unpacking the black box of causality: Learning about causal mechanisms from experimental and observational studies." *American Political Science Review* 105(04):765–789.

Ivcevic, Zorana and Marc Brackett. 2014. "Predicting school success: Comparing conscientiousness, grit, and emotion regulation ability." *Journal of Research in Personality* 52:29–36.

Jackman, Robert W. and Ross A. Miller. 1995. "Voter turnout in the industrial democracies during the 1980s." *Comparative Political Studies* 27(4): 467–492.

Jackson, C. Kirabo. 2018. "What do test scores miss? The importance of teacher effects on non–test score outcomes." *Journal of Political Economy* 126(5):2072–2107.

Jacob, Brian A. 2002. "Where the boys aren't: Non-cognitive skills, returns to school and the gender gap in higher education." *Economics of Education Review* 21(6):589–598.

Jacobson, Gary C. 1983. *The Politics of Congressional Elections*. London: Pearson Longman.

Jaitman, Laura. 2013. "The causal effect of compulsory voting laws on turnout: Does skill matter?" *Journal of Economic Behavior & Organization* 92: 79–93.

Jennings, M. Kent, Laura Stoker, and Jake Bowers. 2009. "Politics across generations: Family transmission reexamined." *The Journal of Politics* 71(3): 782–799.

Jones, Edward E. and Richard E. Nisbett. 1987. The actor and the observer: Divergent perceptions of the causes of behavior. In *Preparation of This Paper Grew Out of a Workshop on Attribution Theory Held at University of California, Los Angeles, Aug 1969*. Lawrence Erlbaum Associates, Inc.

Jordan, Marty P. and Matt Grossmann. 2016. "The Correlates of State Policy Project v.1.0." www.ippsr.msu.edu/public-policy/correlates-state-policy

Kalla, Joshua. 2018a. "Results from 2016 Illinois Text Message Experiment." *Working Paper*.

2018b. "Results from 2016 Online Ad Voter Turnout Experiment." *Working Paper.*

2018c. "Results from 2017 Virginia Text Message Experiment." *Working Paper.*

Kaufman, Alan S., Susan Engi Raiford, and Diane L. Coalson. 2015. *Intelligent Testing with the WISC-V.* John Wiley & Sons.

Kautz, Tim, James J. Heckman, Ron Diris, Bas Ter Weel, and Lex Borghans. 2014. Fostering and measuring skills: Improving cognitive and non-cognitive skills to promote lifetime success. Technical report National Bureau of Economic Research.

Keele, Luke and William Minozzi. 2013. "How much is Minnesota like Wisconsin? Assumptions and counterfactuals in causal inference with observational data." *Political Analysis* 21(2):193–216.

Kelley, Truman Lee. 1927. *Interpretation of Educational Measurements.* Yonkers, NY: World Book Co.

Kiousis, Spiro and Michael McDevitt. 2008. "Agenda setting in civic development: Effects of curricula and issue importance on youth voter turnout." *Communication Research* 35(4):481–502.

Kirkman, Elspeth, Michael Sanders, Natalia Emanuel and Chris Larkin. 2016. "Does Participating in Social Action Boost the Skills Young People Need to Succeed in Adult Life." *Behavioral Insights Team Report.* www.behaviouralinsights.co.uk/education-and-skills/does-social-action-help-develop-the-skills-young-people-need-to-succeed-in-adult-life/

Kleiman, Evan M., Leah M. Adams, Todd B. Kashdan, and John H. Riskind. 2013. "Gratitude and grit indirectly reduce risk of suicidal ideations by enhancing meaning in life: Evidence for a mediated moderation model." *Journal of Research in Personality* 47(5):539–546.

Knack, Stephen. 1995. "Does 'motor voter' work? Evidence from state-level data." *The Journal of Politics* 57(3):796–811.

Kohler, Ulrich, Kristian Bernt Karlson, and Anders Holm. 2011. "Comparing coefficients of nested nonlinear probability models." *Stata Journal* 11(3):420–438.

Kraft, Matthew A. 2019. "Teacher effects on complex cognitive skills and social-emotional competencies." *Journal of Human Resources* 54(1):1–36.

Lacroix, Justine. 2007. "A liberal defence of compulsory voting." *Politics* 27(3):190–195.

Ladd, Helen F., Charles T. Clotfelter, and John B. Holbein. 2017. "The growing segmentation of the charter school sector in North Carolina." *Education Finance and Policy* 12(4):536–563.

Langton, Kenneth P. and M. Kent Jennings. 1968. "Political socialization and the high school civics curriculum in the United States." *American Political Science Review* 62(03):852–867.

Lee, David S., Enrico Moretti, and Matthew J. Butler. 2004. "Do voters affect or elect policies? Evidence from the US House." *The Quarterly Journal of Economics* 119(3):807–859.

Leighley, Jan E. and Jonathan Nagler. 2013. *Who Votes Now?: Demographics, Issues, Inequality, and Turnout in the United States*. Princeton University Press.

Lieberman, Evan S. 2016. "Can the biomedical research cycle be a model for political science?" *Perspectives on Politics* 14(4):1054–1066.

Lijphart, Arend. 1997. "Unequal participation: Democracy's unresolved dilemma." *American Political Science Review* 91(1):1–14.

Litt, Edgar. 1963. "Civic education, community norms, and political indoctrination." *American Sociological Review* 28(1):69–75.

Littvay, Levente, Paul T. Weith, and Christopher T. Dawes. 2011. "Sense of control and voting: A genetically-driven relationship." *Social Science Quarterly* 92(5):1236–1252.

Loewen, Peter John, Henry Milner, and Bruce M. Hicks. 2008. "Does compulsory voting lead to more informed and engaged citizens? An experimental test." *Canadian Journal of Political Science/Revue canadienne de science politique* 41(3):655–672.

Longo, Nicholas V., Christopher Drury, and Richard M. Battistoni. 2006. "Catalyzing political engagement: Lessons for civic educators from the voices of students." *Journal of Political Science Education* 2(3):313–329.

Luders, Eileen, Katherine L. Narr, Paul M. Thompson, and Arthur W. Toga. 2009. "Neuroanatomical correlates of intelligence." *Intelligence* 37(2):156–163.

Lupia, Arthur. 1994. "Shortcuts versus encyclopedias: Information and voting behavior in California insurance reform elections." *American Political Science Review* 88(1):63–76.

2016. *Uninformed: Why People Know So Little about Politics and What We Can Do about It*. Oxford University Press.

Luskin, Robert C. 1990. "Explaining political sophistication." *Political Behavior* 12(4):331–361.

MacMullen, Ian. 2015. *Civics beyond Critics: Character Education in a Liberal Democracy*. Oxford University Press.

Madestam, Andreas, Daniel Shoag, Stan Veuger, and David Yanagizawa-Drott. 2013. "Do political protests matter? Evidence from the Tea Party movement." *The Quarterly Journal of Economics* 128(4):1633–1685.

Maki, Ruth H. 1998. "Test predictions over text material." *Metacognition in Educational Theory and Practice* 14:117–144.

Malhotra, Neil, Melissa R. Michelson, Todd Rogers, and Ali Adam Valenzuela. 2011. "Text messages as mobilization tools: The conditional effect of habitual voting and election salience." *American Politics Research* 39(4):664–681.

Martins, Pedro S. 2017a. Can non-cognitive skills programs improve achievement? Quasi-experimental evidence from EPIS. Technical Report 105 GLO Discussion Paper.

2017b. (How) Do non-cognitive skills programs improve adolescent school achievement? Experimental evidence. Technical Report 614 INOVA Working Paper.

McCarthy, J. Patrick and Liam Anderson. 2000. "Active learning techniques versus traditional teaching styles: Two experiments from history and political science." *Innovative higher education* 24(4):279–294.

McClearn, Gerald E., Boo Johansson, Stig Berg, Nancy L. Pedersen, Frank Ahern, Stephen A. Petrill, and Robert Plomin. 1997. "Substantial genetic influence on cognitive abilities in twins 80 or more years old." *Science* 276(5318):1560–1563.

McCrae, Robert R. and Paul T. Costa. 1989. "Reinterpreting the Myers-Briggs type indicator from the perspective of the five-factor model of personality." *Journal of Personality* 57(1):17–40.

McDevitt, Michael and Spiro Kiousis. 2004. "Education for deliberative democracy: The long-term influence of kids voting USA. CIRCLE Working Paper 22." *Center for Information and Research on Civic Learning and Engagement (CIRCLE).*

McDevitt, Michael and Steven Chaffee. 2000. "Closing gaps in political communication and knowledge: Effects of a school intervention." *Communication Research* 27(3):259–292.

McGee, Eric, Paul Gronke, Mindy Romero, and Rob Griffin. 2017. "Voter registration and turnout under Oregon Motor Voter: A second look." *Working Paper.*

McGuire, Margit and John Waldman. 2008. "Get real: Teaching about the presidential election." *Phi Delta Kappan* 90(2):99–102.

McLuhan, Marshall and Lewis H. Lapham. 1994. *Understanding Media: The Extensions of Man.* MIT press.

Medland, Sarah E. and Peter K. Hatemi. 2009. "Political science, biometric theory, and twin studies: A methodological introduction." *Political Analysis* pp. 191–214.

Meirick, Patrick C. and Daniel B. Wackman. 2004. "Kids voting and political knowledge: Narrowing gaps, informing votes." *Social Science Quarterly* 85(5):1161–1177.

Mendelberg, Tali. 2002. "The deliberative citizen: Theory and evidence." In *Research in Micropolitics: Political Decisionmaking, Deliberation and Participation*, ed. Michael X Delli Carpini, Leonie Huddy, and Robert Y. Shapiro. Greenwich, CT: JAI Press pp. 151–193.

Meredith, Marc. 2009. "Persistence in political participation." *Quarterly Journal of Political Science* 4(3):187–209.

Meyers, Raymond, Anne Pignault, and Claude Houssemand. 2013. "The role of motivation and self-regulation in dropping out of school." *Procedia-Social and Behavioral Sciences* 89:270–275.

Michelson, Melissa R. 2006. "Mobilizing the Latino youth vote: Some experimental results." *Social Science Quarterly* 87(5):1188–1206.

Miller, Peter, Rebecca Reynolds, and Matthew Singer. 2017. "Mobilizing the young vote: Direct mail voter guides in the 2015 Chicago mayoral election." *Research & Politics* 4(4):2053168017738410.

Milligan, Kevin, Enrico Moretti, and Philip Oreopoulos. 2004. "Does education improve citizenship? Evidence from the United States and the United Kingdom." *Journal of Public Economics* 88(9):1667–1695.

Mondak, Jeffery J., Matthew V. Hibbing, Damarys Canache, Mitchell A. Seligson, and Mary R. Anderson. 2010. "Personality and civic engagement: An

integrative framework for the study of trait effects on political behavior." *American Political Science Review* 104(01):85–110.
Mondak, Jeffrey J. 2010. *Personality and the Foundations of Political Behavior*. New York: Cambridge University Press.
Morrell, Michael E. 2005. "Deliberation, democratic decision-making and internal political efficacy." *Political Behavior* 27(1):49–69.
Mueller, Claudia M. and Carol S. Dweck. 1998. "Praise for intelligence can undermine children's motivation and performance." *Journal of Personality and Social Psychology* 75(1):33–52.
Mvukiyehe, Eric and Cyrus Dara Samii. 2015. Promoting democracy in fragile states: insights from a field experiment in Liberia. Technical report The World Bank.
Mycoff, Jason D., Michael W. Wagner, and David C. Wilson. 2009. "The empirical effects of voter-ID laws: Present or absent?" *PS: Political Science & Politics* 42(01):121–126.
Nadeau, Richard, Richard G. Niemi, and Timothy Amato. 1995. "Emotions, issue importance, and political learning." *American Journal of Political Science* 39(3):558–574.
Neiheisel, Jacob R. and Barry C. Burden. 2012. "The impact of election day registration on voter turnout and election outcomes." *American Politics Research* 40(4):636–664.
Neisser, Ulric, Gwyneth Boodoo, Thomas J. Bouchard Jr., A. Wade Boykin, Nathan Brody, Stephen J. Ceci, Diane F. Halpern, John C. Loehlin, Robert Perloff, and Robert J. Sternberg. 1996. "Intelligence: knowns and unknowns." *American Psychologist* 51(2):77–101.
Netemeyer, Richard G. and Scot Burton. 1990. "Examining the relationships between voting behavior, intention, perceived behavioral control, and expectation." *Journal of Applied Social Psychology* 20(8):661–680.
Neuman, W. Russell. 1986. *The Paradox of Mass Politics*. Cambridge, MA: Harvard University Press.
Nickerson, David W. 2007. "Does email boost turnout." *Quarterly Journal of Political Science* 2(4):369–379.
2008. "Is voting contagious? Evidence from two field experiments." *American Political Science Review* 102(1):49–57.
Nickerson, David W., Ryan D. Friedrichs, and David C. King. 2006. "Partisan mobilization campaigns in the field: Results from a statewide turnout experiment in Michigan." *Political Research Quarterly* 59(1):85–97.
Nickerson, David W. and Todd Rogers. 2010. "Do you have a voting plan? Implementation intentions, voter turnout, and organic plan making." *Psychological Science* 21(2):194–199.
Nie, Norman H., Jane Junn, and Kenneth Stehlik-Barry. 1996. *Education and Democratic Citizenship in America*. Chicago, IL: University of Chicago Press.
Niemi, Richard G. and Jane Junn. 2005. *Civic Education: What Makes Students Learn*. Yale University Press.
Niemi, Richard G. and Mary A. Hepburn. 1995. "The rebirth of political socialization." *Perspectives on Political Science* 24(1):7–16.

Niemi, Richard G., Michael J. Hanmer, Benjamin B. Bederson, Frederick G. Conrad, and Michael W. Traugott. 2009. *Voting Technology: The Not-so-simple Act of Casting a Ballot*. Washingtong, DC: Brookings Institution Press.

Nores, Milagros and W. Steven Barnett. 2010. "Benefits of early childhood interventions across the world: (Under) Investing in the very young." *Economics of Education Review* 29(2):271–282.

Nyhan, Brendan, Christopher Skovron, and Rocio Titiunik. 2017. "Differential registration bias in voter file data: A sensitivity analysis approach." *American Journal of Political Science* 61(3):744–760.

Olds, David L., John Eckenrode, Charles R. Henderson, Harriet Kitzman, Jane Powers, Robert Cole, Kimberly Sidora, Pamela Morris, Lisa M. Pettitt, and Dennis Luckey. 1997. "Long-term effects of home visitation on maternal life course and child abuse and neglect: Fifteen-year follow-up of a randomized trial." *Jama* 278(8):637–643.

Oliver, J. Eric. 1996. "The effects of eligibility restrictions and party activity on absentee voting and overall turnout." *American Journal of Political Science* pp. 498–513.

Oros, Andrew L. 2007. "Let's debate: Active learning encourages student participation and critical thinking." *Journal of Political Science Education* 3(3):293–311.

Pacheco, Julianna Sandell and Eric Plutzer. 2007. "Stay in school, do not become a parent: Teen life transitions and cumulative disadvantages for voter turnout." *American Politics Research* 35(1):32–56.

Park, Daeun, Eli Tsukayama, Geoffrey P. Goodwin, Sarah Patrick, and Angela L. Duckworth. 2017. "A tripartite taxonomy of character: Evidence for intrapersonal, interpersonal, and intellectual competencies in children." *Contemporary Educational Psychology* 48:16–27.

Pasek, Josh, Lauren Feldman, Daniel Romer, and Kathleen Hall Jamieson. 2008. "Schools as incubators of democratic participation: Building long-term political efficacy with civic education." *Applied Development Science* 12(1): 26–37.

Paternoster, Ray and Greg Pogarsky. 2009. "Rational choice, agency and thoughtfully reflective decision making: The short and long-term consequences of making good choices." *Journal of Quantitative Criminology* 25(2):103–127.

Persson, Mikael and Henrik Oscarsson. 2010. "Did the egalitarian reforms of the Swedish educational system equalise levels of democratic citizenship?" *Scandinavian Political Studies* 33(2):135–163.

Pettigrew, Stephen. 2016. "The downstream effects of long lines: How long waits at the precinct depress future turnout." *Working Paper, Presented at the 2016 Annual Meeting of the Midwest Political Science Association; Chicago IL.*

Pitcairn, T. K. and Jennifer G. Wishart. 1994. "Reactions of young children with Down's syndrome to an impossible task." *British Journal of Developmental Psychology* 12(4):485–489.

Plutzer, Eric. 2002. "Becoming a habitual voter: Inertia, resources, and growth in young adulthood." *American Political Science Review* 96(01):41–56.

Plutzer, Eric and Nancy Wiefek. 2006. "Family transitions, economic status, and voter turnout among African-American inner-city women." *Social Science Quarterly* 87(3):658–678.

Ponoroff, Christopher and Wendy R. Weiser. 2010. *Voter Registration in a Digital Age*. Brennan Center for Justice.

Popkin, Samuel L. 1994. *The Reasoning Voter: Communication and Persuasion in Presidential Campaigns*. University of Chicago Press.

Prior, Markus. 2005. "News vs. entertainment: How increasing media choice widens gaps in political knowledge and turnout." *American Journal of Political Science* 49(3):577–592.

2010. "You've either got it or you don't? The stability of political interest over the life cycle." *The Journal of Politics* 72(03):747–766.

2018. *Hooked: How Political Interest Fuels Our Democracy*. Cambridge University Press.

Putnam, Robert D. 2000. *Bowling Alone: America's Declining Social Capital*. New York, NY: Simon and Schuster.

Quintelier, Ellen and André Blais. 2015. "Intended and reported political participation." *International Journal of Public Opinion Research* 28(1): 117–128.

Ravitch, Diane and Joseph P. Viteritti. 2003. *Making Good Citizens: Education and Civil Society*. New Haven, CT: Yale University Press.

Reed, Justy, Brian L. Pritschet and David M. Cutton. 2013. "Grit, conscientiousness, and the transtheoretical model of change for exercise behavior." *Journal of Health Psychology* 18(5):612–619.

Riker, William H. and Peter C. Ordeshook. 1968. "A theory of the calculus of voting." *American Political Science Review* 62(01):25–42.

Rimfeld, Kaili, Yulia Kovas, Philip S. Dale, and Robert Plomin. 2016. "True grit and genetics: Predicting academic achievement from personality." *Journal of Personality and Social Psychology*.

Ritchie, Stuart J. and Elliot M. Tucker-Drob. 2018. "How much does education improve intelligence? A meta-analysis." *Psychological Science*.

Rogers, Todd and Masa Aida. 2011. "Why bother asking? The limited value of self-reported vote intention." *Working Paper*.

Rosenberg, Morris. 1965. "Rosenberg self-esteem scale (RSE)." *Acceptance and Commitment Therapy. Measures Package* 61:52.

Rosenstone, Steven and John M. Hansen. 1993. "Mobilization, participation and democracy in America."

Rotter, Julian B. 1966. "Generalized expectancies for internal versus external control of reinforcement." *Psychological Monographs: General and Applied* 80(1):1.

Rubenson, Daniel, André Blais, Patrick Fournier, Elisabeth Gidengil, and Neil Nevitte. 2004. "Accounting for the age gap in turnout." *Acta Politica* 39(4):407–421.

Ryff, Carol D. 1989. "Happiness is everything, or is it? Explorations on the meaning of psychological well-being." *Journal of Personality and Social Psychology* 57(6):1069.

Sandell, Julianna and Eric Plutzer. 2005. "Families, divorce and voter turnout in the US." *Political Behavior* 27(2):133–162.

Sapiro, Virginia. 2004. "Not your parents' political socialization: Introduction for a new generation." *Annual Review of Political Science* 7:1–23.

Schafer, Jerome P. and John B. Holbein. Forthcoming. "When time is of the essence: A natural experiment on how time constraints influence elections." *Journal of Politics*.

Schafer, Jerome Pablo. 2016. "Time Discounting in Political Behavior: Delayed Gratification Predicts Turnout and Donations." *Working Paper Available at SSRN* (2756566). http://papers.ssrn.com/sol3/papers.cfm?abstract_id=2756566

Schilbach, Frank. 2016. "Alcohol and self-control: A field experiment in India." *Working Paper*.

Schudson, Michael. 1998. *The Good Citizen: A History of American Civic Life*. Free Press.

Sexton, Renard. 2017. "The perverse effects of civic education: Evidence from a field experiment in Peru." *Working Paper*.

Shadish, William R., Thomas D. Cook, and Donald Thomas Campbell. 2002. *Experimental and Quasi-Experimental Designs for Generalized Causal Inference/William R. Shedish, Thomas D. Cook, Donald T. Campbell.* Boston: Houghton Mifflin.

Shechtman, Nicole, Angela H. DeBarger, Carolyn Dornsife, Soren Rosier, and L. Yarnall. 2013. "Promoting grit, tenacity, and perseverance: Critical factors for success in the 21st century." *Washington, DC: US Department of Education, Department of Educational Technology* pp. 1–107.

Shineman, Victoria Anne. 2018. "If you mobilize them, they will become informed: Experimental evidence that information acquisition is endogenous to costs and incentives to participate." *British Journal of Political Science* 48(1):189–211.

Sigel, Roberta S. and Marilyn B. Hoskin. 1981. *The Political Involvement of Adolescents*. Rutgers University Press.

Silver, Brian D., Barbara A. Anderson, and Paul R. Abramson. 1986. "Who overreports voting?" *American Political Science Review* 80(02):613–624.

Singh, Kulwant, Siew Meng Leong, Chin Tiong Tan, and Kwei Cheong Wong. 1995. "A theory of reasoned action perspective of voting behavior: Model and empirical test." *Psychology & Marketing* 12(1):37–51.

Sirin, Selcuk R. 2005. "Socioeconomic status and academic achievement: A meta-analytic review of research." *Review of Educational Research* 75(3): 417–453.

Smith, Rogers M. 1997. *Civic Ideals: Conflicting Visions of Citizenship in US History*. Yale University Press.

Sniderman, Paul M. 1975. *Personality and Democratic Politics*. University of California Press.

Sniehotta, F. F., J. Presseau, and V. Araújo-Soares. 2014. "Time to retire the theory of planned behaviour." *Health Psychology Review* 8(1):1.

Söderlund, Peter, Hanna Wass, and André Blais. 2011. "The impact of motivational and contextual factors on turnout in first-and second-order elections." *Electoral Studies* 30(4):689–699.

Soldz, Stephen and George E. Vaillant. 1999. "The Big Five personality traits and the life course: A 45-year longitudinal study." *Journal of Research in Personality* 33(2):208–232.

Sondheimer, Rachel M. and Donald P. Green. 2010. "Using experiments to estimate the effects of education on voter turnout." *American Journal of Political Science* 54(1):174–189.

Sorensen, Lucy C. and Ken A. Dodge. 2016. "How do childhood interventions prevent crime?" *Child Development* 87(2):429–445.

Stoker, Laura. 1992. "Interests and ethics in politics." *American Political Science Review* 86(2):369–380.

Strayhorn, Terrell L. 2014. "What role does grit play in the academic success of black male collegians at predominantly white institutions?" *Journal of African American Studies* 18(1):1–10.

Syvertsen, Amy K., Michael D. Stout, Constance A. Flanagan, Dana L. Mitra, Mary Beth Oliver, and S. Shyam Sundar. 2009. "Using elections as teachable moments: A randomized evaluation of the student voices civic education program." *American Journal of Education* 116(1):33–67.

Taylor, Rebecca D., Eva Oberle, Joseph A. Durlak, and Roger P. Weissberg. 2017. "Promoting positive youth development through school-based social and emotional learning interventions: A meta-analysis of follow-up effects." *Child Development* 88(4):1156–1171.

Theiss-Morse, Elizabeth and John R. Hibbing. 2005. "Citizenship and civic engagement." *Annual Review Political Science* 8:227–249.

Timpone, Richard J. 1998. "Structure, behavior, and voter turnout in the United States." *The American Political Science Review* 92(1):145.

Torney-Purta, Judith and Jo-Ann Amadeo. 2004. *Strengthening Democracy in the Americas through Civic Education: An Empirical Analysis Highlighting the Views of Students and Teachers: Executive Summary*. Organization of American States, Social Development and Education Unit.

Tucker-Drob, Elliot M., Daniel A. Briley, Laura E. Engelhardt, Frank D. Mann, and K. Paige Harden. 2016. "Genetically-mediated associations between measures of childhood character and academic achievement." *Journal of Personality and Social Psychology* 111(5):790–815.

Uhlaner, Carole Jean. 1989. "Relational goods and participation: Incorporating sociability into a theory of rational action." *Public Choice* 62(3):253–285.

Valentino, Nicholas A., Ted Brader, Eric W. Groenendyk, Krysha Gregorowicz, and Vincent L. Hutchings. 2011. "Election night's alright for fighting: The role of emotions in political participation." *Journal of Politics* 73(01): 156–170.

Vavreck, Lynn and Donald P. Green. 2004. Do public service announcements increase voter turnout? Results from a randomized field experiment. In *Annual Meeting of the American Political Science Association, Chicago, September*.

Vazsonyi, Alexander T., Albert J. Ksinan, Gabriela Ksinan Jiskrova, Jakub Mikuska, Magda Javakhishvili, and Guangyi Cui. 2019. "To grit or not to grit, that is the question!" *Journal of Research in Personality*.

Verba, Sidney, Kay Lehman Schlozman, and Henry E. Brady. 1995. *Voice and Equality: Civic Voluntarism in American Politics. Cambridge, MA*: Harvard University Press.

Vercellotti, Timothy and David Anderson. 2006. "Protecting the franchise, or restricting it." In *American Political Science Association Annual Meeting, Philadelphia.*

Wechsler, David. 1943. "Non-intellective factors in general intelligence." *The Journal of Abnormal and Social Psychology* 38(1):101.

West, Martin R., Matthew A. Kraft, Amy S. Finn, Rebecca E. Martin, Angela L. Duckworth, Christopher F. O. Gabrieli, and John D. E. Gabrieli. 2016. "Promise and paradox: Measuring students? Non-cognitive skills and the impact of schooling." *Educational Evaluation and Policy Analysis* 38(1):148–170.

White, Clarissa, Sara Bruce, and Jane Ritchie. 2000. *Young People's Politics*. York: Joseph Rowntree Foundation.

White, Karl R. 1982. "The relation between socioeconomic status and academic achievement." *Psychological Bulletin* 91(3):461.

Willoughby, Michael T., Clancy B. Blair, R. J. Wirth, and Mark Greenberg. 2012. "The measurement of executive function at age 5: Psychometric properties and relationship to academic achievement." *Psychological assessment* 24(1):226.

Winne, Philip H., John C. Nesbit, Vive Kumar, Allyson F. Hadwin, Susanne P. Lajoie, Roger Azevedo, and Nancy E. Perry. 2006. "Supporting self-regulated learning with gStudy software: The Learning Kit Project." *Technology Instruction Cognition and Learning* 3(1/2):105.

Wolfinger, Raymond E. and Steven J. Rosenstone. 1980. *Who Votes?* New Haven, CT: Yale University Press.

Woodcock, Richard W., Kevin S. McGrew, Nancy Mather, and Fredrick A. Schrank. 2003. "Woodcock-Johnson III diagnostic supplement to the tests of cognitive abilities." *Itasca, IL: Riverside* 10.

Woodcock, Richard W., M. Bonner Johnson, and Nancy Mather. 1989. *Woodcock-Johnson Tests of Achievement: Form B.* Riverside Publishing Company.

1990. *Woodcock-Johnson Psycho-Educational Battery–Revised.* DLM Teaching Resources.

Yang, Yaling and Adrian Raine. 2009. "Prefrontal structural and functional brain imaging findings in antisocial, violent, and psychopathic individuals: A meta-analysis." *Psychiatry Research: Neuroimaging* 174(2):81–88.

Youniss, James and Peter Levine. 2009. *Engaging Young People in Civic Life.* Vanderbilt University Press.

Zaller, John R. 1992. *The Nature and Origins of Mass Opinion.* Cambridge University Press.

Zukin, Cliff, Scott Keeter, Molly Andolina, Krista Jenkins, and Michael X. Delli Carpini. 2006. *A New Engagement?: Political Participation, Civic Life, and the Changing American Citizen.* New York: Oxford University Press.

Index

CPSIA information can be obtained
at www.ICGtesting.com
Printed in the USA
LVHW021711150320
650088LV00003BA/461

9 781108 726337